Garden
Herbs

the GARDENERS HANDBOOKS

Garden Herbs

CONSULTANT EDITOR
Frances Hutchison

FOG CITY PRESS

Published by Fog City Press
814 Montgomery Street
San Francisco, CA 94133 USA
Copyright © 2003 Weldon Owen Pty Ltd

FOG CITY PRESS
CHIEF EXECUTIVE OFFICER John Owen
PRESIDENT Terry Newell
PUBLISHER Lynn Humphries
MANAGING EDITOR Janine Flew
ART DIRECTOR Kylie Mulquin
DESIGN COORDINATOR Helen Perks
COVER DESIGN John Bull
PICTURE EDITOR Tracey Gibson
EDITORIAL COORDINATORS Tracey Gibson and Paul McNally
EDITORIAL ASSISTANT Kiren Thandi
PRODUCTION MANAGER Caroline Webber
PRODUCTION COORDINATOR James Blackman
SALES MANAGER Emily Jahn
VICE PRESIDENT INTERNATIONAL SALES Stuart Laurence
EUROPEAN SALES DIRECTOR Vanessa Mori

PROJECT EDITOR Rosemary McDonald
PROJECT DESIGNER Lena Lowe
CONSULTANT EDITOR Frances Hutchison

A catalog record for this book is available from the
Library of Congress, Washington, DC.
ISBN 1 876778 95 4

Color reproduction by Bright Arts Graphics (S) Pty Ltd
Printed by LeeFung-Asco Printers
Printed in China

A Weldon Owen Production

DISCLAIMER

This book is intended as a reference volume only, not as a medical manual or
a guide to self-treatment. The information that it contains is general, not specific
to individuals and their particular circumstances, and is not intended to substitute
for any treatment that may have been prescribed by your physician. Any plant
substance, whether ingested or used medicinally or cosmetically, externally or
internally, can cause an allergic reaction in some people. The publishers cannot
be held responsible for any injury, damage or otherwise resulting from the use
of herbal preparations. We strongly caution you not try self-diagnosis or attempt
self-treatment for serious or long-term problems without consulting a qualified
medical practitioner. Always seek medical advice promptly if symptoms persist.
Never commence any self-treatment while you are undergoing a prescribed
course of medical treatment without first seeking professional advice.

CONTENTS

HOW TO USE THIS BOOK

This book is divided into two parts. The first part is the general section (sample page below) and the second part is a plant directory (sample page on page 9). These combine to provide a comprehensive guide to herbs.

Clear and simple step-by-step photographs demonstrate various techniques.

Illustrations show various herbs. There are many other helpful illustrations in the book.

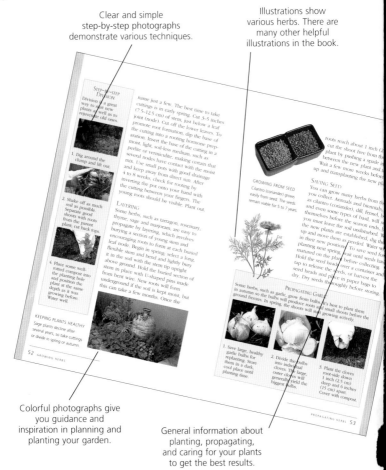

STEP-BY-STEP DIVISION

Division is a great way to start new plants as well as to rejuvenate old ones.

1. Dig around the clump and lift out.

2. Shake off as much soil as possible. Separate good shoots with roots from the parent plant, cut back tops.

4. Place some well-rotted compost into the planting hole and position the plant at the same depth as it was growing before. Water well.

KEEPING PLANTS HEALTHY
Sage plants decline after several years, so take cuttings or divide in spring or autumn.

name just a few. The best time to take cuttings is in early spring. Cut 3–5 inches (7.5–12.5 cm) of stem, just below a leaf joint (node). Cut off the lower leaves. To promote root formation, dip the base of the cutting into a rooting hormone preparation. Insert the base of the cutting in a moist, light, soil-less medium, such as perlite or vermiculite, making certain that several nodes have contact with the moist mix. Use small pots with good drainage and keep away from direct sun. After 4 to 8 weeks, check for rooting by inverting the pot onto your hand with the cutting between your fingers. The young roots should be visible. Plant out

LAYERING
Some herbs, such as tarragon, rosemary, thyme, sage and marjoram, are easy to propagate by layering, which involves burying a section of young stem and leaf node. Begin in spring, select a long, flexible stem and bend and lightly bury it in the soil with the stem tip upright above ground. Hold the buried section of stem in place with U-shaped pins made from bent wire. New roots will form underground if the soil is kept moist, but this can take a few months. Once the

GROWING FROM SEED
Cilantro (coriander) grows easily from seed. The seeds remain viable for 5 to 7 years.

Some herbs, such as garlic, grow from bulbs. In autumn so the bulbs will produce roots and small shoots before the ground freezes. In spring, the shoots will start growing actively.

roots reach about 1 inch (2 cut the shoot free from th plant by pushing a spade in between the new plant and Wait a few more weeks befor up and transplanting the new pla

SAVING SEED
You can grow many herbs from you collect. Annuals and biennials, as cilantro (coriander), dill, fennel, b and even some types of basil, se themselves before the season ends. I you must leave the soil undisturbed. Wi the new plants are established, dig the up and move them as needed. Water w in their new position. To save seed fo planting next spring, wait until seeds hav matured on the plant before collecting. Hold the seed heads over a container and tap to release the seeds, or harvest the seed heads and place in paper bags to dry. Dry seeds thoroughly before storing.

PROPAGATING GARL
It's best to plant then

1. Save large, healthy garlic bulbs for replanting. Store them in a dark, cool place until planting time.

2. Divide the bulbs into individual cloves. The large, outer cloves will generally yield the biggest bulbs.

3. Plant the cloves root-side down 1 inch (2.5 cm) deep and 6 inches (15 cm) apart. Cover with compost.

Colorful photographs give you guidance and inspiration in planning and planting your garden.

General information about planting, propagating, and caring for your plants to get the best results.

Photograph of individual plants, showing what they look like when grown in the right conditions.

Quick-reference information on best climate and site, ideal soil, growing habit and parts used.

Family name

Botanical name

Common name

Hamamelis virginiana

HAMAMELIDACEAE

CLIMATE AND SITE
Zones 5–9. Full sun to partial shade.

IDEAL SOIL
Moist, humus-rich garden soil; pH 6.0–7.0.

GROWING HABIT
Deciduous shrub or small tree with smooth, gray to brown bark; height 8–15 feet (2.4–4.5 m).

PARTS USED
Leaves, branches, twigs, bark.

Helianthus annuus

ASTERACEAE

CLIMATE AND SITE
Zones 5 and warmer. Full sun.

IDEAL SOIL
Rich, well-drained soil; pH 6.0–7.5.

GROWING HABIT
Giant tender annual with erect stems and large, drooping flower heads; height 3–10 feet (90–300 cm).

PARTS USED
Whole plant, seeds, oil.

WITCH HAZEL

THE FORKED BRANCHES OF WITCH HAZEL ARE USED AS WATER DIVINING RODS, AND AN EXTRACT FROM ITS BARK HAS BEEN A POPULAR ASTRINGENT FOR CENTURIES.

Growing guidelines Propagate by seed planted outdoors in autumn. Germination is slow and erratic and can take 2 years. Or take cuttings or layerings from established plants.

Flowering time Autumn; yellow threadlike petals followed by black seed capsules.

Pest and disease prevention Usually free from pests and diseases.

Harvesting and storing Leaves are collected in summer; branches, twigs and bark in spring.

Precautions Can cause skin allergies.

Medicinal uses For dysentery, diarrhea, burns, sore throats and eye and skin inflammations. An infusion of the young, flower-bearing twigs can be used on a compress for bruises, sprains, muscle aches and insect bites.

Other uses In commercial eye drops, skin tonics and skin creams. Also used as an astringent.

Other common names American or Virginian witch hazel.

Gardener's trivia The twigs of witch hazel are often used for water divining.

SUNFLOWER

ALL PARTS OF THE SUNFLOWER ARE USABLE. EACH FLOWER CONTAINS MORE THAN 1,000 SEEDS WHICH HAVE BEEN USED MEDICINALLY FOR MORE THAN 3,000 YEARS.

Growing guidelines Propagate by seed sown in spring. Sow ½ inch (12 mm) deep and 6 inches (15 cm) apart. Thin to stand 1½–2 feet (45–60 cm) apart. Cultivate or mulch. Drought-tolerant, but regular watering will produce larger seed heads. Avoid planting near potatoes as growth may become stunted.

Flowering time Yellow-petaled flowers in summer with heads up to 1 foot (30 cm) across; disc flowers are red or purple, or possibly brown, but cultivars vary

Pest and disease prevention Provide good air circulation to avoid mildew. Stems may collapse through *Sclerotinia* rot. Flowers attract beneficial insects, such as lacewings and parasitic wasps, which eat such pests as aphids.

Harvesting and storing Whole plants are cut as flowering begins. Seeds are collected in autumn. Rub the seed heads to dislodge the seeds and store them in airtight containers in a cool place. Keep well watered and cut and dry the heads when they start to droop.

Special tips Sunflowers bloom relatively quickly but take a long time to ripen their seeds. Very

Detailed information about the plant.

Each section is color-coded for easy reference.

Part One

Growing Herbs

INTRODUCTION TO HERBS

VERSATILE BLOOMERS
Echinacea are pretty plants for the herb garden but their roots and rhizomes are also used medicinally.

People have been growing herbs for thousands of years. Herbs were once an essential part of life—used to flavor and preserve food and make it more nourishing, for medicinal purposes and for religious ceremonies.

Botanically, a herb is a plant, usually succulent and soft, that does not develop woody tissue at any stage of its life. However, there are many plants which today we think of and use as herbs but that do not strictly fall into this category. Rosemary is a perfect example. The stems are quite woody, resulting in its classification as a shrub. However, the upper sprigs of the plant are soft and are used in cooking, so there's a blurring between the scientific and culinary terms of herbs.

You don't need a degree in botany to be a successful gardener, but understanding a little about how plants are named, plant groups, the life cycles of plants and what their needs are, can help you be a successful herb gardener.

BOUNTIFUL HERB GARDEN
Marjoram, borage, purple sage and thyme are planted together with vegetables and flowers in this garden.

UNDERSTANDING NAMES

At first, the scientific names of plants can seem confusing, but becoming familiar with the names of the plants you want to grow helps you buy exactly what you want. Most botanical names are based on Latin and have two parts. The first name is the genus to

WHAT'S IN A NAME?

A botanical name can tell you about the plant it identifies, such as its flower color or growing habit. Listed below are some of the most common words.

Albus: white
Argenteus: silver
Contorta: twisted, contorted
Edulis: edible
Grandiflora: large flowers
Grandifolia: large leaves
Montana: of the mountains
Nigra: dark
Odorata: scented flowers
Orientalis: from the East, Asia
Pendula: hanging
Perennis: perennial
Prostratus: trailing
Pubescens: hairy
Purpurea: purple
Reptans: creeping
Roseus: rosy
Ruber: red
Variegatus: variegated
Vulgaris: common

Sweet cicely
Myrrhis odorata

which the plant belongs; this refers to a group of closely related plants. The second word indicates the species, a particular kind of plant in that genus. Horticulturists and botanists recognize two other classifications of plants: varieties and cultivars. Although the names are sometimes used interchangeably, plants that develop a natural variation in the wild are called varieties, and the varietal name is included as part of the botanical name after the abbreviation "var."

Cultivars, the names of which are set in single quotes after the botanical names, are plants that horticulturists have propagated as part of a breeding program or that have resulted from a chance mutation. You may also come across hybrids, which are blends of two species. The "x" indicates the plant is a hybrid. When the term "spp." is used, this denotes several related species in the same genus.

CHARACTERISTICS OF HERBS

You can grow herbs in your garden for a variety of reasons: for medicinal or culinary uses, or simply because they are attractive plants. No matter what your reasons are, knowing about the functions and characteristics of the various plant parts will help you identify, select and maintain your herbs most effectively.

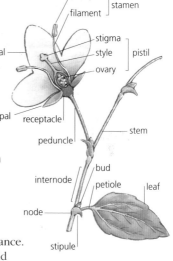

anther
filament] stamen
stigma
style] pistil
ovary
petal
sepal
receptacle
peduncle
stem
bud
internode
petiole
leaf
node
stipule

COMMON PLANT PARTS

This diagram identifies some of the most common plant parts. Knowing these will help you understand the plant descriptions you read in books and catalogs.

ROOT SYSTEMS

As a gardener, you probably select plants for their aboveground appearance. But when selecting herbs, you should also consider their root system. In certain plants, such as iris and ginger, the root may be the part that is used herbally. Roots help to hold the plant firmly in the soil and provide it with a system for absorbing water and nutrients. They may also act as storage organs, as in the carrot family, holding nutrients for use during times of vigorous growth or flowering. Most herbs have a fibrous root system, made up of many fine and branching roots. Annual herbs tend to have shallow root systems. As fibrous roots do not penetrate particularly deeply, you'll need to pay special attention to the water requirements of such plants when rain is scarce.

Some herbs have strong central roots, called taproots, that travel straight down in search of water and nutrients.

ROOT TYPES

The two basic types of root system: the taproot (left) and fibrous roots (right).

Taprooted plants can more easily withstand fluctuating soil moisture conditions, but many plants, such as parsley and lovage, are more difficult to transplant because their roots are so sensitive.

bulk

rhizome

PLANT STEMS

The stems of your herbs not only support the leaves, but also serve as pathways for movement of nutrients and water between roots and leaves. Like roots, stems are storage organs, too. Some herbs have stems that travel horizontally along the soil surface. These are called stolons (also called rhizomes or runners). At certain intervals along the stolon, new shoots and roots will form, giving rise to new plants. Mint, woodruff and violet are herbs that form new plants this way.

Many herbs can be propagated by stem cuttings. Swollen buds, or nodes, along the stems are the sites for new growth. When you take stem cuttings from your herbs to make new plants, the new root systems form underground at active nodes on the cutting.

FOLIAGE

One of the main reasons to grow herbs is for their flavorful and aromatic leaves. Among herbs you will find every shape, texture and color of leaf imaginable. Leaves that are

simple

whole and undivided, such as bee balm, are simple. Leaves that are divided into two or more parts, such as dill, caraway and parsley, are called compound. Along

UNDERGROUND STEMS

Although it grows in the ground, a bulb is not a root, but a type of stem, compressed and covered with scalelike leaves. A rhizome is also not a true root—it is an underground runner or stem that spreads just below the surface.

entire

toothed

LEAF VARIETY

Leaf edges are a good clue to help you identify unknown herbs. By incorporating herbs with different leaf shapes into your garden, you will help to give it added interest.

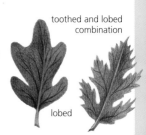

toothed and lobed combination

lobed

with size, the shapes of herb leaves can vary tremendously. Compare the feathery sprays of dill to the grasslike straps of lemongrass foliage.

Herb leaves vary in their edges as well as their shapes. A leaf, such as sweet bay, with its smooth edge, is called entire; those with jagged edges, such as lemon balm, are called toothed; and the wavy-edged leaf of parsley is called lobed. Once you become familiar with herbs, you will depend on all these leaf differences for their identification.

COLORFUL LEAVES
When planning your herb garden, don't forget to consider colorful leaves, such as those of the decorative coleus.

COLOR

Herb leaves offer a tremendous variety of color. It's true that most leaves are green, but there are many shades of green. Leaves that are striped or blotched with different colors, such as those of some types of geranium, are called variegated. Sage also has several variegated cultivars. Variegated herbs taste just as good as their green counterparts and add color and interest to any planting.

TEXTURE

Texture is a quality you have to feel before you fully appreciate it. Some herbs, such as borage, have leaves covered in hairy bristles that can become quite coarse as they age. This is why it's best to pick the younger leaves for salads. Other herbs, such as mint, have crinkled leaves

WHAT ARE HERBS?

The terms "herb" and "herbaceous" are often confused, but generally a herb is a plant valued for its flavor, scent or medicinal properties.
"Herbaceous" refers to perennial plants which have a long-lived root system that sustains recurring annual aboveground foliage and flowers.

Sage

MIXED PLANTINGS

In a cottage garden, herbs and flowers intermingle freely. If you don't have space for a separate herb garden, grow herbs among the flowers.

while parsley has the wonderful texture of its tightly curled leaves. Keep texture in mind when thinking of combining plants in your herb garden.

SCENT

Perhaps the most distinguishing attribute of herbs is the wonderful aroma or perfume that most of them exude. Crush the leaves of rosemary, mint or thyme in your hand and relish the scent. So why banish herbs to the vegetable garden out in the yard? Plant a pot of these perfumed wonders where they can be brushed against, or better still, grabbed by the handful on the way to the front door to add to a tasty meal.

FLOWERS AND FRUITS

Tasty leaves aren't the only reason to grow herbs—many produce beautiful flowers as well. Most herb flowers are either single or clustered. A common clustered floral arrangement is the umbel, which is like an upside-down umbrella. Flowers arranged along a tall stem, like those of lavender, are called spikes.

You can also grow herbs for their seeds or fruit. Some herbs, such as dill and anise, produce an abundance of seeds that are easy to see and to collect. And don't forget to use the fruit of plants. Compare the taste of a vanilla pod to a few drops from a bottle. The reward is a taste sensation that will keep you returning to the real thing.

Potted basil and parsley

CONTAINER GARDENING
If you live in an area with a cold climate, you can still grow your favorite herbs in pots on a sunny window sill or in a sheltered site.

LOCAL CONDITIONS
The key to having a beautiful and productive herb garden that will thrive, is using herbs that are adapted to your local climate.

CLIMATE

Climate is the way temperature, moisture and wind interact in a particular region to produce local weather. It is most important for gardeners to understand their local climate, as this will influence their choice of plants.

Before making your garden plans and selecting herbs to grow, you should consider the normal weather patterns of your area. Since "normal" weather includes the unexpected, enthusiastic gardeners need to become avid weather watchers. You will have to monitor the weather over a period of time in order to provide your plants with three basic requirements: a suitable temperature range, a favorable frost-free period and an adequate supply of moisture.

TEMPERATURE RANGE

Most plants have upper and lower air temperature preferences and are therefore classified as cool-season, warm-season or adaptable to both. Cool-season herbs, such as mustard and chives, continue growing even when the temperature drops as low as 40°F (4°C), but they stop growing or die during the heat of summer. Warm-season herbs, such as basil, are heat lovers, and won't grow unless the temperature is 50°F (10°C) or above. Basil is very sensitive to the cold and usually dies with the first cold snap in autumn.

Hardy perennial herbs (those that live for more than 2 years) are cold-

Catnip

tolerant and will survive the extremes of winter by becoming dormant. Dormancy means that the chemical processes normally occurring inside a plant slow down and the plant is in a resting stage. Likewise, any plant that is sensitive to heat will often become dormant in response to any high-temperature conditions.

Find out what hardiness zone you live in so you can choose the right plants for your area. Refer to the zone maps on pages 308–311 to find your zone, and try to limit your selections to plants recommended for your area.

It's important to remember that herbs are basically wild plants that have been adapted to grow in backyard gardens, so it makes sense to grow them in conditions that compare with their original habitat. If you want to grow herbs that thrive in dry, hot summers and you live in a cold area, grow them on a sunny window sill.

Soil temperature also has an effect on plant growth. Roots tend to grow more slowly in cool soil, so your herbs may have trouble getting the nutrients they need for their flush of spring growth. An early spring application of compost will supply your herbs with nutrients until their roots start spreading again. Mulches help control soil temperature. In summer, a good layer of mulch around your plants helps reduce the amount of sunlight and wind that reaches the soil, so water evaporates from the soil more slowly, keeping it cooler. In autumn, mulch can help hold in soil warmth, encouraging good root growth.

Chives do best in areas where winters are mild, but can be successfully grown in areas where winter temperatures drop well below freezing. Their adaptability makes chives a useful herb for all conditions.

Moderate-climate Herbs

These herbs prefer climates where winter temperatures do not fall below 10°F (-5°C) and that have warm, dry summers with cool nights.

Agrimony, basil, bay, calendula, cilantro (coriander), fennel, fenugreek, feverfew, geranium (scented), germander, horehound, lavender (English), lemon verbena, madder, marjoram, mint, oregano, orris, parsley (curled), passionflower, pennyroyal, rosemary, rue, safflower, sage, santolina, southernwood, thyme, violet, witch hazel.

Fennel

Sage

Frost-free Period

In most climates, the growing season begins after the last frost of the cold season and ends when frosts begin again in autumn. Most plants need to sprout, flower and set seed within this period. Plants vary in the amount of time they require to do this. If you are growing herbs for their foliage, they don't need to flower and set seed so the frost-free period is less important. Plants vary in their susceptibility to frost so keep this in mind when choosing plants. You can extend the growing season by selecting plants suited to the conditions, planting them at the right time and shielding them from the cold spring or autumn temperatures. Look for cultivars that are suited to cold conditions.

TOPOGRAPHY, EXPOSURE AND MOISTURE

Topography, exposure and moisture will affect the types of plants you choose for your garden. Topography refers to the lie of the land, exposure refers to the amount of sunlight your garden receives and moisture to the amount of rainfall.

TOPOGRAPHY

If your garden is in a valley, on a hill or on a slope, you will face different conditions from the average climate in your region. Valleys tend to be cooler and wetter than the higher land around them and can suffer from frosts. On a hill, the air temperature tends to be lower than on flat land but you'll have greater protection from frost compared with a valley, because cold air rolls downhill. Excessive winds, however, can damage plants, increase soil erosion and speed the loss of moisture from the soil. Soil is generally thinner and nutrients will be lost more easily through runoff.

Gardening on slopes has advantages as warm air tends to rise over them keeping frosts at bay. They are, however, subject to erosion from water drainage and wind and

TERRACED GARDEN
Slopes and rolling terrain can add interest to your garden. If you can, save flat spots for your entertaining and play areas, and build terraces for your garden beds above.

plants may suffer from lack of soil moisture and nutrients.

EXPOSURE

Exposure refers to the amount of sun and shade that your garden receives in the course of the day. While most herbs prefer full sun, there are some that will grow in partial to full shade. Quantity and duration of light are critical factors in your garden and affect the growth of your herbs, especially their germination, flowering and reproduction.

To make sure your plants get the right amount of light, identify the direction your property faces. Consider shade from trees, buildings, fences, hedges and hills when planning your garden. Plants that need full sun are able to stand uninterrupted, unfiltered sunlight from sunrise to sunset. Plants

PREVENTING EROSION
A retaining wall helps to prevent water cascading downhill and taking with it valuable topsoil.

HILLTOP GARDENING
Clary prefers sun and well-drained soil, so it is an ideal herb for planting in a garden on a hilltop.

Moisture-loving Herbs

Most herbs need well-drained conditions, but some grow best in moist soils. Some are tough and tolerant, such as horseradish, which will grow in most conditions except badly drained clay. Other herbs are more particular. Watercress, which grows wild at the edge of flowing streams, must be flooded with clean water every day or so. If your garden has moist, well-drained conditions, try growing the following:

Angelica, basil, bee balm (bergamot), catmint, chamomile, chervil, chives, comfrey, elder, feverfew, horseradish, lemon balm, lovage, marjoram, mint, parsley, rose, sweet cicely and woodruff.

Angelica

that prefer partial sun will usually be able to stand about five to six hours of direct, cool sunlight, with shade or filtered sun the rest of the day.

Where your garden is located will play a big part in your plant selection. Locating a garden on the south side of your house provides the maximum amount of light in the Northern hemisphere, while planting your garden on the north side provides the most light in the Southern hemisphere. No matter which direction your garden faces, space your plants correctly and weed regularly to reduce competition for sunlight.

Moisture

A garden that is actively growing and flowering will need a source of moisture at all times. The amount you water will depend on several factors, including the type of soil you have, the amount of natural rainfall, the plants you grow and the stage of growth the plants are in.

As a general rule, your herb plants will require the equivalent of 1 inch (25 mm) of rainfall each week. Rain is the best source of moisture during the growing season, but you will need to supplement this by irrigation if rains fail or are inadequate.

Group plants with similar water needs together. Drought-tolerant plants, such as lavender and echinacea, will need about ½ inch (12 mm) of water per week. However, for other herbs, such as comfrey, elder and horseradish, which thrive in moist conditions, you will need to water regularly between periods of rain.

You have to expect to coddle new plants until their roots establish and spread far enough to support themselves. If the weather is warm and dry, you may have to water daily until drenching rain comes. If the season is cool and rainy, you can let nature handle the irrigation.

Wind is another factor you will need to consider when watering your garden. Your herbs will require more water under windy conditions, as wind draws away moisture lost through transpiration by the plant faster than normal.

Shady side Northern hemisphere, Sunny side Southern hemisphere

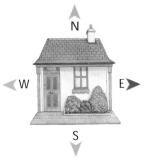

Shady side Southern hemisphere, Sunny side Northern hemisphere

HOUSE ASPECT
By identifying the direction your house faces, you can make sure your plants get the right amount of light, sun and shade, depending on the aspect.

THE RIGHT CONDITIONS
Plants need sun or shade according to how they grow in the wild, although some can adapt. They will always do best given the right growing conditions.

Soil

Good soil is the herb gardener's key to success. Besides providing physical support for plant roots, soil contains the water and nutrients plants need to survive. A good soil is loose and well drained, but it also holds enough water and air for healthy root growth.

Soil Composition

Soil is a mixture of mineral and organic matter, water and air. Soil contains about 45 percent mineral matter, 5 percent organic matter, 25 percent water and 25 percent air. Organic matter is an essential part of soil makeup because it supplies nutrients to the plants and can help to improve drainage. Soils with lots of organic matter are usually dark in color.

Soil Texture

Soil texture is determined by different-sized mineral particles in the soil. Soil texture can have a great effect on the growth of your plants. Roots will spread easily in open sandy soil, but water will drain away quickly, so your plants may need more frequent watering. In clay soil, roots cannot penetrate so readily or widely and the soil will tend to become water-logged. To check the texture of your soil, take a handful of damp garden soil and squeeze it. If it crumbles slightly when you release your grip, its texture is satisfactory; if it runs through your fingers, it is too

UNDERSTANDING SOIL
Healthy soil builds healthy plants. You need to understand your soil so your garden will thrive.

Sand   Silt

sandy; if it forms a sticky lump, it is too clayey. In general, loamy soils, which contain moderate amounts of clay, silt and sand, often suit most plants best.

SOIL STRUCTURE

The structure of soil depends on the way the various particles—sand, silt and clay—come together to form clumps or aggregates. Most plants prefer a soil with a loose, granular structure. This type of structure has lots of open space (called pore space) that can hold air or water. The water forms a thin film around the granules and holds dissolved nutrients, such as calcium and potassium. Plants can take up these nutrients when tiny

Dark gray clay

HEALING HYDRANGEAS

Hydrangeas prefer moist, well-drained, humus-rich soil. *Hydrangea arborescens* is a traditional American herb used medicinally to treat kidney stones.

THE NITROGEN CYCLE

One of the most important plant nutrients is nitrogen. The nitrogen cycle is where animals feed on plants, animal manures add nitrogen to the soil, plants take up nitrogen, plants decompose and put nitrogen back into the soil. Some nitrogen is lost to the air, but is returned with thunderstorms.

hairs on the tips of their roots enter the water film between the soil particles. Adding plenty of organic matter, especially compost, is an effective way to promote a good soil structure.

AIR AND WATER

Your plants will require a good deal of water but they must also be able to take in air (for oxygen) through their roots. Most garden plants grow best in well-drained garden soil. They don't like to have wet feet, since flooding cuts off the supply of oxygen to the roots. Plants obtain their oxygen from air-filled pores in the soil and, during the daytime, take in carbon dioxide from the air. Oxygen they can't use is given off from their leaves during the daytime.

SOIL NUTRIENTS

The availability of soil nutrients depends on the texture and structure of the soil, the amount of moisture and organic matter, and the pH. A fine texture, a loose structure, ample moisture, high organic matter content and near-neutral pH are all conditions that make the most nutrients available to your plants. One of the most important plant nutrients is nitrogen, which is found in soil in various chemical combinations that plants

can absorb. Keeping an adequate supply of nitrogen in the soil can be a challenge, since nitrogen is used up very quickly by plants. It dissolves in water and leaches out of the soil. For plants to thrive, nitrogen must be continually replenished.

SOIL TYPE

Checking up on the type of soil in your garden and its depth, is a useful first step in establishing any garden. Loamy, moist soil with plenty of organic material suits most plants best.

To check the nutrient content of your soil, it may be worthwhile to have a laboratory test your soil. Even soils known to be highly fertile often lack specific nutrients or essential minerals your herbs will need. Private soil-testing agencies will indicate any specific needs. You can test it again in a few years time to monitor the results of your gardening practices and make adjustments if necessary.

Soil pH

It is helpful to know how acid or alkaline your soil is. If you have the soil tested, the results will include pH, which is the measure of acidity or alkalinity. Soil pH is important because it influences soil chemistry. Many herbs prefer a soil on the slightly acid side, with a pH around 6. Heavy, dense, clay soils are often more acid than is desirable. Lime or dolomite will make them less acid and improve their structure. If your soil is too

SOIL TESTING

To check the texture of your soil, take a handful of damp garden soil and squeeze it. The soil should crumble slightly when squeezed (top). Clay soil forms a sticky lump when it is squeezed (bottom).

Puzzling Out pH

Herbs can absorb most nutrients from the soil when the soil pH is in the neutral range (around 7.0). A home test kit, which you can buy at your garden center, or a laboratory test will give you very specific information on your soil's acidity or alkalinity. The pH scale is as follows:

1–5	=	strongly acidic
5–6	=	moderately acidic
6–7	=	slightly acidic
7	=	neutral
7–8	=	slightly alkaline
8–9	=	moderately alkaline
9–14	=	strongly alkaline

acid for the plants you plan to grow, the laboratory will be able to tell you how much lime to add. If your soil pH is high, you can lower it by adding a sphagnum peat substitute or sulfur. It's important not to add lime or sulfur unless it has been advised.

SOIL DEPTH

The actual depth of your soil has an impact on root growth and this in turn affects what plants—either deep- or shallow-rooting—will thrive in your garden. It's easy to tell which conditions you have—just dig down into the soil in your garden with a shovel. If you can go 2 feet (60 cm) without hitting rock or a band of compacted soil, you'll be able to grow a wide range of herbs without any trouble. If your soil is shallow, you may decide to build raised beds.

SUBSTITUTE TEA

Bee balm (bergamot) prefers soil slightly on the acid side. The dried red flowers and leaves are infused to make a soothing tea that became popular after the Boston Tea Party in 1773.

GARDEN PLANNING

For an herb garden to be effective, it has to match your site conditions, your style, the amount of time you can set aside for gardening, your resources and the results that you want to achieve.

ROOM TO MOVE

In your planning, don't forget to make paths wide enough to give you proper access. You many only need room for a wheelbarrow, or you may need to provide access for a truck to deliver soil.

PRODUCTIVE CONTAINERS

Where your garden space is limited, a decorative and practical solution is to use pots and hanging containers brimming with herbs.

If you're planning a new herb garden, you will need to consider your garden's size, location and design. Do you want a formal or informal garden? Do you want a garden full of culinary herbs, a medicinal herb garden, a scented garden or simply a wild garden with a variety of different herbs?

THE GARDEN SITE

First decide where to locate your herb garden. You could reassign a section of your existing vegetable or flower garden, or create a whole new garden devoted to herbs. Or you may choose to place herbs in several different sites around your garden. If you're starting from scratch, put as much thought as you can into site selection. You can avoid many problems by choosing a good location.

Your garden site has to suit the plants you plan to grow. If your site is shady, choose herbs that will tolerate shade. If your site has wet conditions part of the year, choose plants that can tolerate this. If you have a range of sites, choose the one that provides as closely as possible the specific requirements of the plants you want to grow.

When planning your garden, take into consideration its space and size and the look you want to achieve. Ideally, a well-organized garden will place culinary herbs as close as possible to the kitchen.

SITE CONSIDERATIONS

To choose a site, walk around your garden, keeping in mind the following:

- Choose a level site with good drainage.
- Avoid hills; they lose moisture quickly.
- Avoid low-lying land; there may be poor drainage and little air circulation, which could encourage pests and diseases.
- Plan to garden across slopes to prevent erosion.
- Avoid areas where soil is compacted.
- Be sure you have access to a good water supply.
- Choose a site where your plants will get adequate light.
- Avoid planting in the root zone of trees, as they will compete with your herbs for moisture and nutrients.

GARDEN SIZE

The size of your herb garden will be determined by how much you want to grow and harvest, the suitable space available to you, the amount of time you want to devote to gardening and the availability of resources. If you're a beginner, it may be best to start with a small garden until you gain experience.

The time a garden needs varies with climate and season, but you will need to allow time to perform regular maintenance tasks, such as weeding, watering, pest control and harvesting. A large garden will require more resources than a smaller one, so factor this in. Also work out how much you want your garden to produce. One or two plants of an herb may be enough for occasional use, but if you want to grow enough basil for a batch of pesto sauce each week, you have to allow for more plants.

GARDEN STYLE

Regardless of your garden's size, shape or location, its style is a reflection of your own tastes. The number of possible herb-garden styles is limited only by your imagination, creativity and the effect you want to create.

GARDEN SHAPES

The simplest gardens to set out and manage are square or rectangular in shape. Land is most often sold in boxlike shapes, so it makes sense to follow the general outline of your property. You may, however, choose to follow the curve of a hill, stream, fence or wall, or plan garden beds to accentuate the shape of a building. If you choose to garden in several small areas, position plants that need daily attention or frequent picking close to the house. If space is limited, take advantage of borders along paths or fences and use containers and window boxes.

MIXED PLANTINGS
This charming cottage garden combines annuals, perennials and shrubs, as well as a focal point.

FORMAL GARDENS

Formal landscapes use straight lines, sharp angles and symmetrical plantings with a limited number of plants. They are usually laid out in squares or rectangles with low hedges of clipped evergreens or brick walls to define different areas of the garden. The key to success with a formal garden is uniformity—you want the plants to be evenly spaced and evenly developed. Often plants are repeated to form a mirror image.

GARDEN FEATURES

Keep in mind the following points when planning your garden.

- Paths are important in your overall garden design for the effect they can bring as well as for defining shapes.

- Plan to include a focal feature, such as a sundial or bird bath.

- Enclosures are an important aspect of traditional herb gardens. When building a wall, choose materials that will match your house. For hedges, choose a species that will survive the winter conditions in your area. Plant lavender or rosemary for low hedges and box or yew for higher hedges.

- Fences can either be solid, which offers privacy but blocks out light, or open, which allows better ventilation and light for your plants.

INFORMAL GARDENS

Informal landscapes use curving lines to create a more natural feeling. They tend to have few permanent features such as walls or hedges, and generally include different kinds of plants—trees, annuals, perennials, herbs and vines. Informal designs are relaxed and lively and are better suited to the ordinary small backyards of many houses today. Herbs can be planted in any part of the garden—beds, borders, raised beds or containers.

COTTAGE GARDENS

The ultimate in informality, cottage gardens defy many gardening "rules:" Plants are packed closely together, colors aren't organized into different groupings, tall plants pop up in front of shorter ones and flowers are allowed to grow through each other to create a delightful, casual mixture. While cottage gardens may appear effortless and unorganized, they need to be planned, planted and maintained just like any other garden.

GARDEN DESIGN

Once you have chosen a style, go to your chosen site and outline the shape of the planting area with a flexible hose or rope. Step back and walk around to see how it looks from several different viewpoints, including from inside.

PUT YOUR IDEAS ON PAPER

Whatever garden style you have chosen, try it out on paper first. Measure the length and width of the area you have targeted for the garden and draw it to scale on graph paper. Choose the largest scale that allows your design to fit on one sheet: 1 inch (2.5 cm) on paper to 1 foot (30 cm) of planting area works well. Draw in the major existing features, including buildings, fences, paths and trees. Jot down other features, such as soil conditions, poor drainage, the amount of sunlight the area receives and if neighbors' houses cast shadows over the garden. Make several photocopies of your base plan or lay sheets of tracing paper over the original sketch. This way you'll always have a fresh base plan to

DESIGN RULES

Keep the garden in balance. Include plants of mixed heights and sizes. In formal gardens, make a mirror image by planting the same design on each side of the garden. In informal gardens, match bright perennials of one color with shrubs of another to balance brighter color with larger size.

Create a sense of rhythm. Repeat groupings of the same plant or use other plants with similar colours. Let plants drift from the foreground to the background, giving a sense of movement.

Establish a dominant feature, such as a tree, as a focal point.

CONSERVING RESOURCES

Tansy, parsley and bee balm (bergamot) are plants that have similar growing requirements. Grouping together plants with similar needs helps you conserve resources in your garden.

TRANQUIL FEATURE
Water features give a sense of coolness and tranquillity to your garden. Plant moisture-loving herbs such as mint, chervil and angelica nearby.

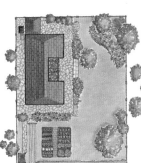

PLANNING THE DESIGN
It is worth the effort to work out an initial plan for your garden. Factors to take into consideration include the size of your garden, sunlight, moisture, soil and topography.

GARDEN LAYOUT
Check your garden layout using a hose for the outline, and buckets and other items to represent the various plants you wish to grow.

work with. Start sketching your ideas until you have come up with a design you are happy with.

PLANNING YOUR PLANTS
To visualize color combinations, cut circles representing each group of flowers out of colored paper, matching the paper color to the flower color. Juggle these around until you find combinations that you like. If you are planning different herb groupings, such as culinary, medicinal or fragrant herbs, cut out pieces of cardboard to represent each group.

CONTAINER HERB DESIGNING
If you live in an apartment, you can still design a functional herb garden using the space you have. More herbs are grown in containers than anywhere else, so if you have a balcony, stairway or window sill with plenty of light, design your own productive garden using hanging baskets, window boxes and beautiful containers.

CONTAINER GARDENING

If you don't have room for garden beds, create a lush green oasis with container-grown plants on a balcony or in a courtyard or window box.

Containers are great receptacles for growing herbs, especially if space is tight. Many of the most popular culinary herbs will thrive in containers. You can plant sun-lovers, such as basil, sage, rosemary and thyme, in the same container. If you have a partly shady area, plant lemon balm, tansy, oregano and parsley. They will tolerate as little as 4 hours of sun per day. Mint is ideal for containers, because it spreads rapidly in a garden bed. Mint likes moist soil, so add water-saving granules to the container mix and keep it well watered.

TYPE OF CONTAINER

The first step to successful container gardening is choosing the right pot. Large pots provide the best conditions for growth, because they hold more soil, nutrients and water, but they are heavy to move around. For herbs, pots that hold about 2–4 gallons (9–18 l) of growing medium work best. Small trees or shrubs can start out in pots of this size, but you will need to move them to larger containers after their first season.

The material that a container is made from can be just as important as its size. Clay and terracotta pots look attractive

BALCONY GARDENING

You can grow a productive garden of shrubs and herbs in the confined space of a balcony. Make sure you check the conditions of your balcony so you know if your plants will be exposed to high winds.

CHOOSING CONTAINERS

The natural beauty of terracotta lends itself to containers and window boxes. But you'll need to keep your plants well watered.

and are generally heavier than other materials, meaning that plants won't blow over in the wind. However, these pots are porous and lose moisture quickly. They can also crack and break in cold weather if the soil freezes, so they may need to be moved inside during winter or emptied and stored until the next growing season.

Plastic and fiberglass pots are much lighter than clay and terracotta pots, so can be moved more easily. They don't dry out as fast and are usually less expensive. However, as they are much lighter, they tend to blow over more often in the wind. They also require good drainage and soil aeration.

Wood is a good alternative for some containers, as it insulates the plant roots from overheating in summer and freezing in winter, but it rots over time. To reduce the risk of decay, use plastic liners inside wooden planters.

HEALTHY PLANTS

Herbs will thrive in containers if placed in a sunny position and given a little attention. Always use a soil mix that is designed especially for container plants; garden soil alone is unsuitable for plants in containers.

POTTED CITRUS

Citrus trees grow well in pots. They need full sun and feeding in summer.

Whatever kind of container material you choose, look for pots that are light in color, especially if you live in a hot climate. They help to reflect the heat and keep the roots cool. Black pots are the worst choice in hot climates, since they can absorb enough heat to damage tender roots.

DRAINAGE

When choosing a container, make sure it has adequate drainage holes. This is critical for healthy root growth and top growth. Medium-sized containers need at least six holes ½ inch (12 mm) in diameter. More are needed in larger pots. If you are using a pot without drainage holes, place a few blocks of wood in the base and place your potted plant on top.

STRAWBERRY BARREL
Strawberries are an excellent choice for containers. They both taste delicious and look attractive.

Don't overwater your herb plants, as they prefer to be slightly on the dry side rather than being continually moist. If the container mix is of good quality and has adequate drainage, water will not collect

WITHIN REACH

Just because you live in an apartment doesn't mean you have to be deprived of a garden. A decorative hanging basket filled with your favorite herbs, such as parsley and oregano, can be hung just outside your kitchen window ready for you to reach out and snip off foliage as you need it.

in the container and the roots will not become waterlogged. How often to water depends on the size of the pot and the requirements of the particular plant. Because unglazed clay pots are very porous and tend to dry out rapidly, they will require more frequent watering.

CONTAINER MIXES

Once you have picked your container, fill it with the best possible growing medium. While soil is fine in the garden, it is a bad choice for plants in pots when used alone. The frequent watering will cause most real soil to compact into a bricklike mass, or if your garden soil is very sandy, it will dry out too quickly in a container. You can buy commercial container mixes, but the most economical way is to make your own. A good mix is 2 parts good garden loam or well-rotted compost, 1 part leaf mold, 1 part well-rotted manure and 2 parts coarse sand.

HERBS FOR BALCONIES AND COURTYARDS

A wide variety of herbs can be grown on your balcony or courtyard. Try planting these herbs:

Aloe, anise hyssop, basil, bay, bee balm, chamomile, chervil, chives, citrus, cilantro (coriander), dill, echinacea, gardenia, geranium, jasmine, lavender, lemon balm, lemongrass, marjoram, mint, oregano, parsley, rosemary, roses, sage, sweet cicely, thyme.

Lemon grass

Choosing Your Plants

Before you start buying plants for your herb garden, work out the type of garden that you want and the types of plants that will grow in it. These factors will affect the plants you choose.

Herbs can be grown for a variety of reasons—their fruits, foliage or perhaps fragrant flowers. If it is your first herb garden, you may want to choose annual herbs with a bias towards culinary use.

Annuals

Annuals germinate, flower, set seed and die all within 1 year. They are easy to grow and will require full sun and plenty of water, because they are shallow rooted. Many annual seedlings can be planted directly outdoors in garden soil, but others will require a warm start indoors. Some annuals, such as basil, need plenty of space, while others, such as dill and chives, form clumps.

Biennials

Biennial herbs have a life span of 2 years. During their first year, they produce plenty of foliage and strong root systems.

Easy Annuals and Biennials

Annual and biennial herbs are among the easiest herbs to grow. Both grow quickly from seed.

Annuals: Anise, basil (sweet), borage, calendula, cayenne pepper, chervil, cilantro (coriander), dill, fennel, fenugreek, mustard, nasturtium, plantain, safflower, vervain.

Biennials: Burdock, caraway, clary, parsley.

Nasturtium

HERB VARIETY

Herbs vary enormously in their characteristics and size. Keep these factors in mind when choosing your plants, so that you don't pick ones that are unsuitable for your needs.

In the second year, they flower and produce seeds before they die. How you grow a biennial herb depends on what you want to harvest from it. Most people grow parsley for its first-year foliage and not for its second-year flowers and seeds, so you can grow it as an annual.

PERENNIALS

Perennial herbs live for more than 2 years. These make up the vast bulk of edible herbs. Some, such as lavender, will reach their prime growth within 3–5 years, while others, such as tansy and mint, thrive and continue growing, unless their growth is checked with thinning.

There are two types of perennials, herbaceous and woody. Some herbaceous perennials have stems that usually die back to the ground in winter and grow again in spring from a persistent root-

CAREFUL CHOICES

If you consider what you want from your plants and what growing conditions you have available, your herbs will fulfill your needs and provide years of enjoyment. Here, a walled garden shelters roses on a pergola and in beds, sweet Williams, lavender, campanula and lamb's ears.

POPULAR PERENNIAL HERBS

Herbaceous or non-woody perennials: Agrimony, aloe, angelica, anise hyssop, arnica, bee balm (bergamot), betony, burdock, catnip, chamomile, chicory, chives, comfrey, costmary, dock, garlic, ginger, goldenrod, horseradish, hyssop, lady's bedstraw, lavender, lemon balm, lemongrass, lovage, marjoram, marsh mallow, mint, oregano, orris, pennyroyal, saffron, sage, santolina, savory, soapwort, sorrel, southernwood, sweet cicely, sweet woodruff, tansy, tarragon, thyme, valerian, violet, wormwood, yarrow.

Woody perennials: Barberry, bay, bearberry, birch, cascara sagrada, coffee, eucalyptus, geranium, lemon verbena, New Jersey tea, passionflower, rosemary, roses, witch hazel.

Lemon verbena

stock. Woody perennials have stems that expand each year as the plants build up layers of woody growth.

BUYING HERBS

The easiest way to buy plants is in pots. Some herbs, however, such as dill and parsley, don't transplant well, so look for seedlings growing in peat pots. This way you can plant both the seedling and pot straight into the ground and avoid disturbing the root system.

Look for healthy, vigorous plants with bright, new growth. Healthy seedlings are usually deep green, although you can expect color to vary among plants and cultivars. An overall pale, washed-out appearance often indicates that a nutrient is lacking. Seedlings should be free of insects and diseases. Check the undersides of leaves for insect pests and see that the stems are strong, with no signs of injury or rot.

Check the roots as well—strong, healthy roots are a vital part of determining plant health. Gently remove the plant. The roots

VIGOROUS PLANTS

Plants that look strong and healthy at the nursery are likely to grow well when you get them home.

SICKLY SPECIMENS

Sickly plants may be cheaper to buy, but they can bring pests and diseases into your garden and will fail to thrive.

COTTAGE CHARM

This cottage-garden style border features an exuberant yet harmonious mix of herbs and flowers, including white and pink roses, catmint, irises, alliums, foxgloves, artemisia and peonies.

should be uniformly white and moist. Avoid plants with matted roots or plants that are tightly rooted to their neighbors.

WHERE TO BUY

Most nurseries and garden-supply stores offer a wide variety of container-grown plants. The advantage of buying this way is that you can inspect the plants before buying; however, some nurseries have a more limited selection and the plants can be more expensive. You can also buy plants through specialist nursery catalogs; these offer you a wider choice of plants, but the plants may be stressed by postage and handling. If you would prefer to start your own seedlings, see "Planting Seeds" on pages 46–49.

Planting Seeds

Starting herbs from seed is a good choice when planning your herb garden. They are cheap—a single packet of seeds can produce dozens of plants—and you have a greater variety of plants to choose from.

Sowing Seed Indoors

If you have the space, starting seed indoors will enable you to begin the new season earlier than if you wait and plant outdoors. Sow your annual herb seeds indoors about 6–8 weeks before you plan to transplant them to the garden. Raising new perennials may require an additional 6 weeks if germination is slow.

Getting Started

New seedlings need a light, moist growing medium for a quick start. Fill seed trays with a seed-raising mix, moisten with warm water and sow the seed onto the surface. If the seeds need to be covered, sprinkle seed-raising mix over them. Set

SIMPLE TOOLS

Transplanting requires a minimum of tools—just a simple trowel or hand fork will do the job. You'll also need a watering can with a fine spray for watering your seedlings.

Sowing Seeds in Trays

1. Fill container with a moist seed-raising mix.

2. Scatter the seeds across the surface.

3. Gently water seeds with a fine spray, taking care not to dislodge them.

4. Cover with plastic or glass to maintain moisture.

1.

2.

3.

4.

INDIVIDUAL POTS

There are advantages to sowing seed in individual pots. They have good drainage, are easy to clean and can be used over again.

the containers in a well-lit spot out of direct sunlight. Most annual seeds will sprout at an average indoor temperature of between 60° and 75°F (16° and 24°C). Once your seeds have germinated, they will need between 10 and 16 hours of light each day, so keep them on or near a window sill and make sure the air can circulate freely—poor ventilation may encourage fungal diseases. Water regularly with a fine mist to keep the seedlings moist but not soggy.

THINNING AND POTTING UP

Once seedlings have developed their first set of leaves, thin them out to give them adequate space to grow. The best way to do this with least disturbance is by cutting some off at soil level with scissors. If you plan to wait before transplanting them outdoors, or if your seedlings are crowded together, you'll need to transfer them to their own small pots. About 6–12 hours

THINNING OUT

Thin seedlings by clipping them off at soil level with a sharp pair of scissors.

HEALTHY START

Seedlings need plenty of light for compact, sturdy growth. Near a window is a good spot. Use high-quality seed, packed for the current year.

before potting them up, give the seedlings a thorough soaking to ensure the stems are turgid (filled with fluid). Using a pencil, make a hole in the medium in the new pot, then use the pencil to carefully dig one seedling at a time from the original container. Lift each seedling by one of its leaves (not the fragile stem), and move it to its new container. Firm the soil around the roots of the seedling and water gently. Place the new containers away from direct sun and wind in a sheltered position, until the shock of transplanting is over. Feed the young plants lightly with compost tea or liquid seaweed.

TRANSPLANTING

Two weeks before transplanting, gradually reduce watering and withhold fertilizer. This encourages plants to develop more roots in proportion to the rest of the plant, making transplanting easier. One week before you transplant, move the plants outdoors for short periods of time to a spot protected from strong light and wind. Day by day, gradually increase the time spent outdoors. Within a week, they should

If you live in a warm climate, you can sow seed directly outdoors. Before the season begins, check your seed packets for the best time to plant. If you are planting seeds of frost-sensitive plants, wait until the frost season has ended.

be outdoors permanently. They'll need more water at this time, because sun and wind quickly dry the soil. Once your seedlings have adjusted to the outdoors, plant them out. Make a hole with your trowel, remove the small plant from its container and insert it into the hole. Firm the soil around the roots and water gently.

Sowing Seed Outdoors

Some herbs, such as angelica, anise, basil and caraway, can be sown directly outdoors in early spring. Planting seed directly outdoors is not a good idea for seeds that are hard to germinate, or, in cool areas, for plants that need a long, warm growing season.

Get ready for planting by clearing weeds from your planting site. Prepare the soil and rake it smooth to create a fine-textured surface. Sow the seed in shallow trenches. A good rule of thumb is to plant the seed to a depth of three times its thickness. Completely cover the seeds by gently raking soil over them and firming it down well. Keep the soil moist to encourage the best germination. Avoid watering with a strong spray that may wash the seeds out. Don't overwater.

COLORFUL BLOOMER
Echinacea, or purple coneflowers, can be sown direct in spring or summer when the temperature reaches 70°–75°F (21°–24°C). They tolerate dry soil and wind.

Propagating Herbs

Tarragon

Propagating is a great way to increase your herb crops. Depending on which propagation method you choose, you can end up with dozens of new plants, taken from a single plant. Annuals are quick and easy to grow from seed but perennial herbs and shrubs are best grown from a vegetative method of propagation.

Division

Most perennial herbs spread underground as well as aboveground and increase in size each growing season. If they are taking up more space than you want them to, divide them every few years in spring or autumn. The many herbs easily propagated by division include chives, germander, horehound, marjoram, mint, sorrel, tansy, tarragon and woodruff.

Dig around the perimeter of the plant's root system with a spade then lift the plant up soil, roots and all. Set the clump on the ground and divide it into smaller clumps by hand or with a trowel. Pry apart larger clumps using garden forks. Separate sections with young shoots from the outer sides of the clump and replant immediately. Plants that send

PROPAGATING GINGER

Ginger can be propagated by placing a rhizome in good-quality potting mix in spring. Growth will be rapid and shoots will appear in a matter of days. Leave in pots or plant out into garden beds in well-drained, humus-rich soil for optimum growth.

PRODUCTIVE PRUNING

Some herbs, such as scented geraniums and wormwood, become straggly after a few years and new plants should be started. Use the spring prunings for propagation.

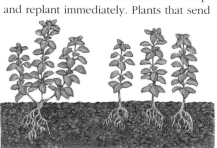

Sorrel

out underground rhizomes, such as mint, can be divided without digging up the whole plant. Follow the underground stems that sprout new plants and lift out each plant with a spade. Reduce the clump to several smaller plants and replant them in holes lined with fresh compost.

CUTTINGS

Cuttings of small pieces of plant stem or root are a great way to propagate perennial herbs, such as scented geranium, bay, lavender, oregano and wormwood, to

STOOL LAYERING
Stool layering is a simple method of propagating herbs that have sprawling stems. Mound soil up over the base of the parent plant. After 4–6 weeks, remove and replant any new plants that have grown.

Division is a great
way to start new
plants as well as to
rejuvenate old ones.

1. Dig around the
   clump and lift out.

2. Shake off as much
   soil as possible.
   Separate good
   shoots with roots
   from the parent
   plant; cut back tops.

4. Place some well-
   rotted compost into
   the planting hole
   and position the
   plant at the same
   depth as it was
   growing before.
   Water well.

KEEPING PLANTS HEALTHY
Sage plants decline after
several years, so take cuttings
or divide in spring or autumn.

name just a few. The best time to take
cuttings is in early spring. Cut 3–5 inches
(7.5–12.5 cm) of stem, just below a leaf
joint (node). Cut off the lower leaves. To
promote root formation, dip the base of
the cutting into a rooting hormone preparation. Insert the base of the cutting in a
moist, light, soil-less medium, such as
perlite or vermiculite, making certain that
several nodes have contact with the moist
mix. Use small pots with good drainage
and keep away from direct sun. After
4–8 weeks, check for rooting by inverting
the pot onto your hand with the cutting
between your fingers. The young roots
should be visible. Plant out.

LAYERING

Some herbs, such as tarragon, rosemary,
thyme, sage and marjoram, are easy to
propagate by layering, which involves
burying a section of young stem and
encouraging roots to form at each buried
leaf node. Begin in spring; select a long,
flexible stem and bend and lightly bury
it in the soil with the stem tip upright
above ground. Hold the buried section of
stem in place with U-shaped pins made
from bent wire. New roots will form
underground if the soil is kept moist, but
this can take a few months. Once the

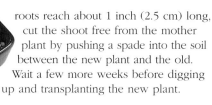

roots reach about 1 inch (2.5 cm) long, cut the shoot free from the mother plant by pushing a spade into the soil between the new plant and the old. Wait a few more weeks before digging up and transplanting the new plant.

GROWING FROM SEED
Cilantro (coriander) grows easily from seed. The seeds remain viable for 5–7 years.

Dill

SAVING SEED

You can grow many herbs from the seed you collect. Annuals and biennials, such as cilantro (coriander), dill, fennel, borage and even some types of basil, will seed themselves before the season ends, but you must leave the soil undisturbed. When the new plants are established, dig them up and move them as needed. Water well in their new positions. To save seed for planting next spring, wait until seeds have matured on the plant before collecting. Hold the seed heads over a container and tap to release the seeds, or harvest the seed heads and place in paper bags to dry. Dry seeds thoroughly before storing.

PROPAGATING GARLIC

Some herbs, such as garlic, grow from bulbs. It's best to plant them in autumn so the bulbs will produce roots and small shoots before the ground freezes. In spring, the shoots will start growing actively.

1. Save large, healthy garlic bulbs for replanting. Store them in a dark, cool place until planting time.

2. Divide the bulbs into individual cloves. The large, outer cloves will generally yield the biggest bulbs.

3. Plant the cloves root-side down 1 inch (2.5 cm) deep and 6 inches (15 cm) apart. Cover with compost.

Part Two

Maintaining Your Herb Garden

WATERING

Water makes up 85 to 95 percent of the weight of living plants. It's not surprising that when water is lacking, a plant stops growing and wilts. Garden plants require about 1 inch (25 mm) of rainfall each week under average soil and climate conditions.

Gardens in hot, dry climates will lose moisture faster and will need more water than those in cool, wet climates. To monitor rainfall, place a rain gauge in your garden. Check it immediately after rain. If natural rainfall is inadequate, you should plan to water regularly to maintain plant health and growth. You should water sufficiently to keep your plants growing, but be careful not to overwater. Excess water in the soil fills the pore spaces that would normally contain air. In most soils, one good soaking is better than several shallow waterings because it encourages roots to spread over a larger area and go deeper in search of water.

SPRINKLERS

Sprinklers have two main disadvantages. They assume a plentiful water supply and encourage fungal diseases that thrive in moist conditions. The advantage, however, is that this type of watering

DRIP SYSTEMS

Drip irrigation systems with individual emitters deliver a supply of water directly to the plant. Less water runs off and more water sinks in. Plant foliage remains dry, discouraging fungal diseases.

HAND WATERING

If you have plenty of time, hand watering with a watering can is often a more realistic option for irrigating small gardens, potted plants and for spot watering thirsty plants. But make sure you don't stress your plants by overwatering.

GARDEN HOSES

Hand watering with a hose is fine for small gardens as you know how much water you are applying and where it is going. For larger gardens, however, you will probably need to use sprinklers or install soaker hoses or a drip irrigation system.

system is inexpensive and suits most backyard gardens.

Drip Irrigation and Soaker Hoses

Drip irrigation is the most economical system in terms of water used as it applies water directly to the soil where plants need it. And since foliage remains dry, fungal diseases are not encouraged. The disadvantage is that drip systems require more time and expense to install them. Once installed, however, you need only turn on the water and your herbs are irrigated most efficiently.

You can design your own simpler drip system by using soaker hoses. These are much less expensive but provide many of the same benefits. Some soaker hoses release water over their entire length, while others spurt water through tiny holes. A soaker hose system needs no assembly; lay the hoses between plants and conceal them with mulch.

Drought-tolerant Herbs

The herbs listed below can tolerate slightly drier soil.

Arnica, burdock, catnip, chicory, costmary, germander, goldenrod, hyssop, marjoram, New Jersey tea, oregano, pennyroyal (American), rosemary, rue, safflower, sage, santolina, savory (winter), southernwood, thyme, wormwood.

Thyme

Weeding

Like pests and diseases, weeds can pop up in even the most carefully tended gardens. The trick is to take care of the problem early, before the weeds get large enough to compete with your plants for space, light, water and nutrients.

Weeds are simply plants growing in the wrong place at the wrong time. They do, however, have their importance in the plant world. Many of the plants we call weeds have culinary or medicinal uses that were discovered long ago.

Weeds hold the soil in place, break up compacted soil with their vigorous root systems and help to conserve nutrients that leach away when the soil is left bare. Some plants that are considered to be weeds, such as clover and vetch, are also legumes and can be grown to fix nitrogen in the soil.

On the negative side, weeds are major garden pests when they compete with your garden herbs for nutrients, moisture and light. They often harbor diseases or insect pests that can easily find their way to your herb plants and some, such as poison ivy and nightshade, are poisonous.

Controlling Weeds

Your first step in the battle against weeds is to identify the ones you need to control. Annual weeds live only one season, but this is long enough for them to produce lots of seeds that can sprout next spring.

HEALTHY PLANTS

Healthy plants are better able to compete with weeds. Planting your herbs in the right conditions will ensure that they thrive, not the weeds.

WEED CONTROL

Once your herbs are established, you can control most weeds if you apply mulch and compost regularly.

HAND-WEEDING
Thorough hand-weeding of the garden bed before planting will help you get new herbs off to a weed-free start.

Pulling and hoeing are often sufficient to control annual weeds.

Biennial weeds have a cycle that spreads over 2 years. You can either dig them out, roots and all, the first year or wait until the second year and cut the plant down to the ground. If you wait until the weed is just about to flower, the plant will have used up its stored energy and will likely not return.

Perennial weeds can live for more than 2 years and are the most difficult weeds to control. They shouldn't be dug in, as this distributes their hardy root pieces. You need to either dig up all of the underground structures or force them to use up their food reserves by repeatedly removing their aboveground growth.

Weed control should start while you are preparing the bed for your new herbs. Digging and composting can remove many of the existing weeds. If you keep your plants healthy, they will be better able to compete with weeds.

HOEING YOUR GARDEN
Hoeing once or twice early in the season can control most weeds until your plants fill in to cover the soil.

ADDING ORGANIC MATTER

Organic matter is the decayed remains of once-living plants, animals and soil organisms. A layer of decomposed organic matter on the soil surface has enough bulk to smother weeds and keep moisture from evaporating from the soil. Organic matter is also food for soil microorganisms.

Decayed organic matter can do great things for your garden. Not only does it help loosen soil and improve soil structure, but it also prevents weeds, regulates soil temperature and holds nutrients on its surface, releasing them slowly into the soil water for plants to absorb.

Organic matter breaks down at different rates. On the surface of the ground you can recognize leaves and decaying plant parts, such as stems and fruits. As you dig deeper, the material becomes less identifiable as it decays into humus. Humus is well-decayed organic matter which is dark brown and crumbly with an earthy smell and is very valuable in the soil.

You can add organic nutrients to your soil in several ways.

COMPOST

Compost is decayed plant waste, such as kitchen scraps and grass clippings, and is a balanced source of organic matter. See "Compost" on pages 62–65.

SOIL DECOMPOSERS
Millipedes, bacteria and other soil organisms play an important role in breaking down dead plant material in the soil.

MULCHING BENEFITS
Mulching not only helps to control weeds, regulate soil temperature and prevent moisture from evaporating from the soil, but it also adds organic nutrients.

SOIL IMPROVER

Scatter organic matter around the bases of plants. The nutrients will be released slowly, promoting healthy

USEFUL CLIPPINGS

Clippings and prunings add valuable organic matter when used as mulch, added to the compost pile, or worked into the soil.

Manures

Manures are an excellent source of organic matter and the amount of nutrients will vary depending on the type of animal and its diet. See "Manure" on pages 66–67.

Mulches

Mulching smothers weeds and prevents moisture from evaporating quickly from the soil. If you use the right mulch, it can also add organic matter to the soil. See "Mulch" on page 67.

Dried Animal Parts

The dried blood and ground bones of animals that have become human food are used as fertilizers and are high in organic matter.

Rock Powders

Rock powders are rocks pulverized to a fine powder. Microorganisms can then take up the minerals and release them very slowly for plants to absorb.

COMPOST

RECYCLED SCRAPS
Keep a container in your kitchen to collect compostable food scraps.

HOME-MADE BINS
ABOVE: A wood-and-wire bin is a good way to keep your compost contained and easily accessible.

BELOW: Circular mesh bins are easy to make and use. The large stick helps direct water to the center of the pile, keeping it evenly moist.

Compost is the key to success in any kind of gardening. It is a balanced blend of recycled garden, yard and household wastes that break down to dark, crumbly organic matter. Worked into the soil or used as a mulch, compost can add nutrients, loosen up clay soils and increase the water-holding capacity of dry, sandy soils.

How to Start
Save any organic wastes that you would normally discard, such as vegetable scraps from the kitchen, grass clippings, fallen leaves and soft plant clippings. Don't use waste products containing fats, bones or meat scraps, as they may attract scavenging animals and slow down the process of decomposition. If you have access to manure from animals such as chickens, cows or horses, you can add this as well but avoid human, dog or cat feces. Also avoid pesticides and pesticide-treated plant material, such as clippings from treated lawns. Don't add weeds or insect-infested or diseased plants unless you have a hot compost pile (see pages 64–65). It's also not a good idea to add roots of perennial weeds in case they survive the composting process and are distributed throughout your garden as you spread around the finished compost.

Compost can be in an open pile, but bins look neater and keep animals out of the compost. You can choose from

a variety of commercially sold timber or plastic containers, or you can make your own from timber, bricks or even chicken wire nailed to garden stakes. If you have the space, a multi-bin system is ideal, so when one bin is full, you can start filling up the other bin. Whatever design you choose, position it in a sunny, level, well-drained spot. A coarse material, such as straw, is best as the bottom layer of the heap so that air can circulate freely.

If all the green material added to your compost is relatively moist, it will not be necessary to add extra water. If materials have been allowed to dry out, you may need to moisten them for effective decomposition. By adding a few shovelfuls of good garden soil or finished compost to the pile, you will add to the microorganisms that help carry out the composting process.

Don't make your compost pile too large. It should be around 3 feet

VERSATILE COMPOST
Compost can be worked into the soil, used as a mulch and made into a liquid nutrient boost for your plants.

COMPOST TEA

Compost tea is a liquid fertilizer made by soaking compost in water. Put a shovelful of compost into a hessian bag and suspend it in a watering can filled with water. Keep it covered for a few days. Nutrients from the compost diffuse into the water from the bag. Dilute the liquid before using it on young plants, as strong water can burn seedlings.

(90 cm) on each side and no higher than 6 feet (1.8 m) to break down properly.

Hot Compost

Hot composting takes some work, but it will provide you with high-quality compost in a matter of weeks. Blend both soft and green (high-nitrogen) plant scraps, such as lawn clippings and lettuce scraps, with tough and brown (high-carbon) scraps, such as fallen leaves, straw and woody flower stalks. Pile up in layers and add some finished compost in between each layer and enough water to keep the pile moist. Turn the pile with a pitchfork every few days to add oxygen. The ideal temperature is below 160°F (71°C), since higher temperatures will kill important decomposer organisms. The turning process helps maintain a constant temperature. If odor is a problem, the pile needs to be turned and aerated

COMPOST TROUBLESHOOTING

- Pile doesn't heat up. Add more high-nitrogen material. If the pile is dry, add water. Or turn pile.

- Pile smells bad. Add more high-carbon material. If the pile is too wet, turning will add more air.

- Finished compost is covered with seedlings. Avoid adding materials with seeds or make sure they're in the center of a hot compost pile.

- Material doesn't break down. Chop them into smaller pieces before adding them. Add more high-nitrogen ingredients to help balance these high-carbon materials.

READY COMPOST

If you have the space, an ideal way to make compost is a multi-bin system. When one bin is full but still needs more time to break down completely, you can start on the next. Eventually you will have compost ready for instant application whenever your garden needs it.

more; if it is too wet, mix in more dry materials and turn. If the breakdown is too slow, try adding more green or nitrogenous material.

COLD COMPOST

Making cold compost is easier than making hot compost because it requires no turning over with a garden fork, but it is a much slower process of decomposition. Cold compost will not heat up enough to kill seeds or disease organisms so don't add materials contaminated with pests. Choose a shady, well-drained site in your garden and over time, add your waste material, building up a pile no larger than 3 feet (90 cm) wide by 3 feet (90 cm) high and simply wait around 6–12 months. When your compost is fully decomposed, you can use it as it is or screen out the lumps.

SOIL BOOST
Dig fresh compost into a new garden bed or spread it over the surface to instantly enrich the soil.

USING COMPOST

There are many different ways to add compost to your garden. You can work it in as you dig or spread it over the surface of your beds each year. As a general rule, cover the bed with 2 inches (5 cm) a year to maintain fertile soil. Or you can use compost as a mulch. Use more if you are growing moisture-loving perennial herbs, such as elder, or less around perennials such as yarrow that prefer drier, less-fertile soil. Compost breaks down gradually over the growing season, so add more as needed. Use compost indoors as potting medium or for starting seeds.

COMPOST MULCH
Compost is an ideal soil-building mulch for both herb and flower gardens. It adds valuable nutrients to the soil.

Manure and Mulch

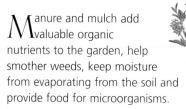

Alfalfa

Manure and mulch add valuable organic nutrients to the garden, help smother weeds, keep moisture from evaporating from the soil and provide food for microorganisms.

BENEFICIAL MANURES
Like mulches and compost, green manures can do great things for your garden, such as protecting the soil from erosion and, in the case of legumes, adding nitrogen.

RYE GRASS
Rye grass can survive cold winters and is a good green manure to grow between your annual herb crops.

Manure

There are many different types of manure, including animal manure and green manure. Both are valuable sources of organic material for your garden and if applied regularly, will ensure your herb garden thrives.

The amount of nutrients in animal manure varies, depending on the type of animal and what it has been eating. All can be valuable, as long as you know what you are applying and what effect it's likely to have on your plants. Some fresh animal manure, such as horse manure, is so high in nitrogen that it will burn plants if added directly to them. You need to compost first before applying.

Green manures are crops, including legumes, that are grown to improve the soil. You turn the crop under before it matures and it adds valuable organic matter and nutrients to the soil as it breaks down. Most green manure crops grow best in well-drained soil, but some, such as clover, can take wetter conditions. You can plant a grass or legume as a green manure, or a mix of both. About 5 weeks before you are ready to plant your next crop of herbs, work the green manure crop into the ground.

MULCH

Mulching simply means covering the surface of your garden soil with a layer of organic or inorganic material. Mulching keeps your soil warmer in winter and cooler in summer. It also helps retain soil moisture and protects soil from erosion.

If you are planting in early spring, wait until the soil warms up before mulching. If you are planting in autumn, apply the mulch right after planting. Mulch earlier in dry climates to trap the moisture from spring rains. In wet climates, mulch a bit later to give the soil a chance to dry out.

Take your time in choosing a mulch. Organic mulches, such as compost, add valuable organic matter to the soil but will decompose and need replacing every season. Inorganic mulches, such as black plastic and landscaping fabrics, don't decompose but they also don't improve soil as organic mulches do.

DIFFERENT TYPES OF ANIMAL MANURE

Fresh horse manure is high in nitrogen; compost it first before applying to your plants or it will burn them.

Cow manure contains more moisture than horse manure and less nitrogen.

Poultry manure is high in nitrogen. Use it dehydrated to add nitrogen, phosphorus, potassium and organic matter to the soil.

Worm castings are the manure of earthworms. This is a rich source of organic nutrients and a good all-round soil improver.

ORGANIC MULCHES

Organic mulches, such as compost, bark chips, grass clippings and straw, improve your soil and add valuable nutrients as they decompose, enhancing soil productivity.

CARING FOR CONTAINER HERBS

POTTING AND REPOTTING HERBS

- Water the herb. If repotting, choose a pot that is larger than the old one.
- Place small stones in the base of the new container.
- Remove the herb, place in its new pot and fill with fresh container mix.
- Keep the plant out of direct sunlight for several days.
- Water the container thoroughly.
- Compost regularly.

HEALTHY BASKETS

One of the keys to lush-looking container plants is regular fertilizing. Give them a boost by watering them with a liquid fertilizer.

In many ways, caring for container plants is the same as caring for other plants in that they all need good soil, periodic fertilizing and regular watering. However, container plants will need more watering and feeding to remain healthy.

REGULAR WATERING

Unlike regular garden plants, which can search for moisture and nutrients in the soil with their roots, container plants require regular watering and feeding to remain healthy. Herbs in containers dry out quickly, so you may need to water every day during hot weather. Terracotta containers and hanging baskets dry out especially quickly and you may have to water these as often as twice a day. If you find they are drying out too quickly, consider using water-retaining granules or adding extra vermiculite to the container mix.

If a pot or basket dries out completely, place in a larger container of water and leave until air bubbles stop rising, then place in a shady spot until the plants perk up again. Move the pot or basket back to its original spot, but be extra careful to keep it well watered from then on.

REGULAR FERTILIZING

Container plants need regular fertilizing. Give them a boost by watering them with diluted fish

emulsion or compost tea (see page 63). Start in late spring by feeding once every 2 weeks. If plants look lush but aren't flowering well, change to fertilizing once every 3 weeks. If the plants look a little spindly, start fertilizing every week. If the plants seem to be growing and flowering well, stick with the 2-week schedule.

Repotting Herbs

Your herbs will eventually need to be repotted, either because they have grown too big for their pots or because they need to be moved into fresh container mix. You should repot your plants every year in the spring or summer, when plants are actively growing. If they get too big for their pot, they can become root-bound, which means they have grown so many roots there isn't enough container mix left to support further growth.

MIXED HERBS

It's a good idea to group herbs that have similar needs, but perennial herbs need a little more care than annuals because they don't get pulled out at the end of the growing season. In cold winters, move them inside to protect against freezing.

PREVENTING PESTS

Gardening offers many pleasures and also a few challenges, such as pests and diseases. Herbs are more likely to be resistant to problems when they are grown in an appropriate site with good soil and proper care.

BENEFICIAL INSECTS

Most of the insects you will discover among your herbs won't be doing any damage at all—in fact, there are more friends in the insect world than enemies. Some insects directly benefit plants, so it's worth attracting them to your garden. Ladybugs (ladybirds), for example, can eat 50 to 60 aphids a day, while the larvae of hover flies prey on aphids, caterpillars, thrips and sawflies. Many of the small-flowered herbs, such as fennel, dill and thyme, attract beneficial insects. You can entice these insects to visit by providing them with food, water and shelter.

POLLINATORS
Bees are a vital part of a healthy garden. Without their pollination efforts, many plants could not set fruit or seed, so they are worth attracting to the garden.

VORACIOUS EATERS
Praying mantids aren't picky—they'll eat any insects that cross their path, pest and beneficial species alike.

BENEFICIAL WASPS
Most wasps are valuable beneficial insects. They may prey on aphids or be important pollinators.

IDENTIFYING SOME COMMON PESTS

Unfortunately, not all insects in your garden will be beneficial—occasionally, insect pests will attack your herbs. Try to identify the culprit so you can choose an effective control measure.

Fortunately, there are clues you can look for to help pin down problems. Give plants a thorough inspection once a week. Look at both sides of the leaves, around buds and flowers and along the stem. Check the undersides of plant leaves and scratch the soil or mulch looking for likely culprits. Also search for clusters of eggs, webs or pellet-like insect droppings. Use the following list to help identify them.

Aphids

Aphids are tiny, sap-sucking, soft-bodied insects that feed on a variety of plants. They tend to cluster near the growing tips and on the undersides of leaves and leave a trail of sugary excrement.

Japanese Beetles

These shiny, metallic blue-green beetles with bronze wing covers feed on many different annuals, perennials and shrubs. They eat the green part of leaves, so that only the leaf veins remain.

MULCH TO DETER PESTS

Mulching is effective in controlling some pests and diseases. Materials such as newspaper and black plastic mulch help to control thrips, leaf-miners and other pests that must reach the soil to complete their life cycle. Mulches also prevent raindrops from splashing soil-borne disease spores onto plant leaves.

Leafminers

Leafminers are the tiny larvae of small flies that tunnel inside leaves, leaving light-colored trails on the surface of the leaf.

Spider Mites

These spider-like pests attack plants, especially in hot, dry weather. The brown, pinkish red or green mites make webs on plants and suck the sap from the underside of a leaf, causing it to curl and become speckled.

Slugs and Snails

These are a problem in damp, shady gardens. They chew holes in leaves, stems and flowers and are easy to spot because they are large and leave slimy trails behind them.

Thrips

Thrips are minute, quick-moving insects that feed on flowers and leaves. They give the affected plant tissue a pale, silvery look in damaged areas.

Other Pests

You also may find mealybugs (soft-bodied insects) under leaves and along stems; leafhoppers (which look like tiny grasshoppers) on stems and leaves; borers (fat pink caterpillars), which tunnel through leaves and make cavities in rhizomes; plant bugs, which are green or brown with triangles on their forewings and leave holes in leaves and distort plant growth; and cutworms (fat, brown or green caterpillars), which chew through the stems of many seedlings.

ROTATING PLANTS

Crop rotation is a good idea to help avoid pest problems. If you have a mixed garden, simply rotate your herbs and vegetables to avoid planting them in the same position 2 years running.

LARVAL PREDATORS

Adult lacewings feed mostly on pollen and nectar, but their larvae are voracious predators of aphids and other pest insects.

Managing Insect Pests

Once you know what pests you are dealing with, you can target their weaknesses. There are many simple solutions you can use that don't involve toxic sprays; see "Simple Solutions" on pages 78–81.

An effective way to correct most pest and disease problems is to change your gardening habits. Plant herbs in the conditions they prefer. Build up the soil with plenty of organic matter and give well-drained soil to plants that are prone to rot. Don't nick plants with your rake, as wounds are an open invitation for pest and disease attack. Stay out of a planting when the foliage is wet, so you don't spread diseases as you brush past. Plant all your herbs with the recommended spacing to let air circulate freely through the foliage. Check your plants for pests once a week. Don't worry if you find a few. In most gardens, as in nature, the life cycles of beneficial predators and parasites are usually closely synchronized with those of the pests. When the pests increase, so do the predators, so leave pests to become food for insect predators and parasites.

If you must spray, choose a product that is formulated specifically for the pests you have identified. To control aphids and mites, the most common pests found on herbs, use insecticidal soap products, whose active ingredients are of organic origin and break down quickly once applied. If you are growing culinary herbs, it's preferable never to spray any toxic insecticides on herbs you plan to use in the kitchen.

REPELLENT PLANTS

Some herbs, such as pennyroyal, can be planted in the garden to repel insect pests. They deter insects from settling on neighboring plants.

PREVENTING DISEASES

Downy mildew attacks leaves and causes yellow spots.

The dusty spots of powdery mildew are easy to identify.

Rusts show as light-colored spots. Destroy infected leaves.

SPACING PLANTS
Good air circulation helps eliminate the moist, humid conditions that encourage many fungal diseases.

Plant diseases are frustrating to deal with. Symptoms such as stunted growth or wilted, yellowed or misshapen leaves are often the only clues you'll have when trying to diagnose the problem. Diseases are usually caused by organisms such as fungi, bacteria, viruses or nematodes.

PREVENTING DISEASES

Your best defense against disease is prevention. If you keep your plants healthy, with good soil management and watering techniques, they are more likely to be able to resist disease. When purchasing new herbs, inspect them carefully for signs of disease and reject any that look unhealthy. Symptoms such as discolored leaves or stunted growth could be due to poor growing conditions, but they could also indicate disease. Good sanitation practices are essential. If you have been handling infected plants or soil, clean your boots and hands with a 5-percent solution of bleach. If wet weather prevails, stay away from the garden until the weather is fine again.

If the leaves of your roses have dark, circular spots, you can be fairly sure that black spot fungi are at work.

Many disease organisms require moisture for reproduction and are easily spread on water that you carry from plant to plant.

Inspect your plants regularly for any signs of disease and remove unhealthy specimens. It's best to burn them, since a few pathogens can survive even the hottest compost pile. If burning of rubbish is prohibited in your area, put the diseased plant materials in sealed bags for disposal with the household trash. Mulch herbs regularly with compost. Beneficial microbes in the compost suppress the development of some disease organisms.

Careful watering can help reduce disease outbreak. Avoid wetting plant leaves where possible. If foliage stays wet overnight, fungal spores have time to germinate and attack leaves. Use a ground-level irrigation system such as drip irrigation or a trickle system.

Fungal wilts stop leaves and stems from getting water.

Mosaic virus produces yellow or white streaks or mottling.

WHEN PROBLEMS STRIKE

Despite the best garden practice, there will be times when plant diseases will strike. It is impossible to see organisms that cause disease, so you have to rely on symptoms. If the leaves are deformed

This leaf has signs of iron deficiency, not disease.

CLEAN GARDENS

Keeping your garden neat, well-maintained and free of debris helps remove sites where pests and diseases can survive.

and discolored, it could be leaf curl. Cut off and destroy the infected parts. If the leaves or stems are speckled or silvery, the problem could be thrips. Spray the plant with a soap solution. If the leaves are black and sticky or shiny, it may be sooty mold fungus. Wipe the leaves with a damp cloth. If the leaves and stems have small, hard scales, gently scrap the bumps off with your fingernail. If the leaves or shoots have white spots, it could be powdery mildew. Pick off infected leaves and spray the rest with fungicidal soap.

DISEASE LOOK-ALIKES

Changes in gardening techniques or the environment can produce disease-like symptoms. If your herbs lack vigor and wilt and the leaves become yellow, you may be overwatering. Raised beds and improved drainage can help. If your plants are stunted and the leaves are pale, wilted or scorched, you may not be watering enough. Regular deep

irrigation will help. If tender growing tips and buds die, leaves turn yellow or drop, and the stems and bark crack, your plants may be stressed due to cold weather. Row covers and other frost shields can help. If plants become spindly and leaves become unevenly colored, then there may be insufficient light. Move your plants to a sunnier spot. If your plants become less vigorous and yield poorly, and leaves curl, are stunted, or die at the growing tips, your plants may be suffering from nutrient deficiencies. Adding organic matter and compost can help.

WHEN ALL ELSE FAILS

If your herbs do occasionally fall prey to plant diseases, you can choose from several environmentally friendly control options. Organically acceptable fungicides, such as sulfur and copper sprays or dusting powders, will protect your plants from fungal diseases, but only if they are in place before infection and before wet weather, when plants are more likely to be infected and before the organisms penetrate the leaf. For safe, homemade fungicides, see "Simple Solutions" on pages 78–81.

PREVENTING PROBLEMS

If your plants are healthy, they are more likely to resist disease. Regular applications of compost and good watering techniques will help.

Simple Solutions

There are many ways you can treat and control pests and diseases in your garden without resorting to harmful poisonous sprays. Picking off or trapping pests, planting insect-repelling herbs nearby or using a homemade pest control remedy are all safe options.

Helpful Herbs

Many varieties of herbs are natural insect repellents. Plant these herbs among your other plants, such as vegetables, to keep pests at bay.

Tansy deters flying insects, so it is useful not only in the garden but also in a pot on a window sill or planted near an open door to keep flies out of the house. Tansy, rue, wormwood, lavender and elder are all good insect repellents for the garden.

BENEFICIAL INSECTS
Provide a water source in your garden to attract beneficial insects and insect-eating birds that will prey on pests. Change the water regularly to prevent mosquitoes from breeding.

WASH AWAY PROBLEMS
If your plants are invaded by aphids, don't despair. Spray them off with a jet of water from the hose or with a tea made from basil, rhubarb or elder leaves.

Hyssop helps plants suffering from bacterial invasion and chamomile helps sick plants to recover from a variety of ailments. You can either plant these herbs in individual pots and move them around the garden to act as nursemaids to your ailing plants, or you can make a spray using their essential oils. Use 5 drops to every 8 cups (2 l) of water and spray on troubled plants.

You can also use teas made from herbs to combat pests and diseases. Elderflower tea discourages molds on most plants. Chive tea is especially useful against gray mold (botrytis) on roses. Nettle tea combats mildew and horsetail tea helps to protect against all kinds of fungi. Use 1 cup of fresh herbs to 2 cups (500 ml) of boiling water. Mix and leave to stand for 6 hours. Then strain the liquid and store. Mix 2 tablespoons of this tea into 8 cups (2 l) of water in a watering can and water on ailing plants. A strong tea made from wormwood will deter pests such as moth and butterfly caterpillars, flea beetles, slugs and snails. Brew the

HOME REMEDIES

- Use baking soda to treat fungal problems such as black spot and powdery mildew. Mix 2 tea-spoons of baking soda in 8 cups (2 l) of water. Drench plants at the first sign of disease.

- Snails and slugs can't resist beer. Sink containers into the soil and fill with beer to lure them.

- Snails and slugs won't crawl over sand or sawdust, so sprinkle some around your herbs.

- Protect seedlings from root maggots by sprinkling chili powder, pepper, ginger or paprika around the plants.

- For insect pests, mix 1 cup (250 ml) of each of soapy water and cooking oil. Combine 2 teaspoons of the solution with 1 cup (250 ml) water and spray on plants.

Hyssop

Handpicking large, slow-moving pests, such as snails, is an easy way to stop them damaging your plants.

SLUG TRAPS

Lure slugs with shallow dishes of beer. Sink the dish so the top is level with the soil.

leaves in water, cool, then use at half strength on mature plants.

If plants are troubled by aphids, use the leaves of basil, rhubarb or elder. Take 8 oz (250 g) of leaves and simmer in 4 cups (1 liter) of water for 30 minutes. Cool, then strain. Mix 1 teaspoon of dish-washing liquid or soapflakes in 2½ cups (625 ml) of cold water. Mix both solutions together and spray on plants. Don't use food utensils when making sprays.

HANDY HOME REMEDIES

Despite your best efforts, pests and diseases can occasionally get out of hand. When things get to this stage you have several choices: Try a natural home remedy, resort to an organically acceptable chemical, or remove and dispose of the infected plant. Many gardeners have reported success with natural remedies, so why not try these first.

NEW PLANTS

Whenever you buy or are given new herbs, check to make sure no pests are lurking under the leaves or in the leaf axils. A good prevention is to invert the plant and swish the foliage in a bucket of water with a couple of drops of mild dishwashing liquid added.

NATURAL PEST CONTROLS

Snails
- Remove all debris from the garden.
- Pick them off by hand.
- Trap in a shallow container of beer set into the soil.
- Surround plants with sand or sawdust.
- Spray with wormwood tea.

Slugs
- Surround plants with sand or sawdust.
- Pick them off plants at night.

Ants
- Destroy ant nests by pouring boiling water over them.
- Encourage beneficial insects and small lizards into your garden.

Caterpillars
- Pick them off by hand.
- Spray with wormwood tea.

Aphids
- Spray with a hard jet of water from the hose.
- Encourage beneficial insects into your garden.
- Spray with a diluted solution of water and soap or dishwashing liquid. Rinse off later.
- Spray with a tea made from basil, rhubarb or elder leaves.

Black spot, powdery mildew
- Spray with a baking soda mixture or nettle tea.

Mold
- Spray with elderflower tea or chive tea.

EARTHWORMS

Start a compost bin with your kitchen vegetable and fruit scraps to encourage earthworms. Earthworms are invaluable in gardens as they not only burrow and create tiny tunnels that transport water to the plants' roots, but they aerate the soil as well. Worms also eat fungi and harmful insect eggs. A healthy compost will encourage earthworms to your garden.

EASY TARGETS

It's easy to handpick sawfly larvae off foliage, as they rear up when disturbed.

DETERRING PESTS

Garlic is a useful herb in deterring many flying pests. It has fungicidal and insecticidal properties. Mix 3 oz (90 g) of minced garlic with 2 teaspoons of mineral oil. Add 2 cups (500 ml) of water and two drops of dishwashing liquid and spray on affected plants.

CITRUS CONTROL

Oils extracted from orange and lemon peel will control many pests, including aphids and spider mites.

COMPANION PLANTING

EFFECTIVE LURE

Marigolds are popular companion plants. They have been proven to repel nematodes, and will also attract beneficial insects.

FRAGRANT REPELLERS

Interplant fragrant herbs, such as thyme and lemon balm, in your flower garden to repel insect and animal pests.

Companion planting is the technique of growing together plants that will benefit each other. If your vegetables are regularly attacked by insects, you can use herb companion plants to lure, repel or trap pests. Other herbs provide food and shelter to attract beneficial insects.

REPELLING WITH SMELLS

Many insects use their sense of smell to find their way to favored crops. One way to protect your plants is to mask their odors with other powerful smells. Garlic, for example, releases deterrent aromas into the air that may chase away insects, such as bean beetles and potato pests. Onions can prevent pests from attacking strawberries or tomatoes, while mint may keep cabbage loopers off cabbage plants. Plant pungent herbs as an edging around garden beds or mix them in among your vegetable crops. If you can't grow the repellent herbs close enough to your crops, you can spread clippings of these strong-smelling plants over garden beds for the same effect.

LURING PESTS

Some plants have an almost irresistible appeal for certain pests. Nasturtiums, for instance, are an excellent attractant plant because they're a favorite of aphids. Attractant plants can protect your crops in two ways. First, they act as decoys to lure pests away from your desirable crops. Second, they make it easier to control the pests because the insects are concentrated on a few plants.

BENEFICIAL INSECTS

Not all insects are garden enemies. Many will help your garden by eating plant pests. You can encourage these beneficial creatures to your garden by planting various herbs. Growing dill, for example, can attract pest-eating spiders, lacewings and parasitic wasps, which will help to control caterpillars on cabbages, beetles on cucumbers and aphids on lettuces.

EFFECTIVE LURE
Besides producing pretty (and edible) flowers, nasturtiums will help lure aphids from your crops.

GOOD COMPANION GROUPINGS

Heavy Feeders
- Asparagus, celery, corn, parsley, rhubarb, sunflowers.

Light Feeders
- Basil, dill, fennel, garlic, leeks, onions, sage, thyme.

Height Groupings
- Cabbage (short, bushy) with thyme (sprawling).
- Corn (tall, upright) with squash (sprawling).
- Tomatoes (tall, bushy) with basil (short).

Herbs to Repel Insects
- Rue or garlic with roses to repel aphids.
- Tansy with roses to repel insects.
- Chives with carrots to deter carrot rust fly.

Herbs for Beneficial Insects
- Hyssop flowers attract pollinating insects.
- Marjoram attracts bees.
- Dill attracts many beneficial insects.
- Lemon balm attracts bees.

COMPLEMENTARY CROPS
Some herbs make ideal vegetable companions because they don't compete, even when planted close together. Lettuces act as a living mulch, keeping the soil moist, while sunflowers provide shade for the lettuces.

Part Three

Preserving, Storing and Using Herbs

Harvesting Herbs

The intended use of your herbs, the plant's maturity and the climate all affect the time of harvesting. Herbs that are to be used fresh can be picked anytime; those for preserving require more care.

The best time to pick herbs is just after the morning dew has dried, but before the sun has had a chance to warm them, because essential oils lose their quality when exposed to heat.

RARE HARVEST
Saffron stigmas are harvested for their rich color and flavor. The difficulty of collecting the threads is the reason saffron is so expensive.

Perennials

Avoid harvesting perennial herbs during the first year of growth, to allow them to establish themselves. Trim lightly to promote bushiness. Once they're established, you can harvest up to two-thirds of the foliage at one time in the spring and again in autumn, but stop 40–60 days before you expect the first frost. During winter, perennials will subsist mainly on foods they have stored in their roots. Plenty of foliage and lots of autumn sun will let perennials manufacture and store adequate food for winter. If food reserves are low, they are less likely to make it through a stressful winter.

Annuals

Since annuals are limited to one season of growth, your only concern in cold climates is harvesting as much as you can before the killing autumn frosts. The same is true if you are growing biennial herbs, such as parsley and clary, for their foliage. During the growing season, harvest annuals and biennials for foliage so that at least 4–5 inches (10–12.5 cm) of growth remains. A good rule is to harvest no more than the top half of the plant at one cutting. Most annuals and biennials may be harvested several times each season. If you are growing biennial plants such as caraway for their seeds, avoid harvesting the foliage the first year. The more energy the plants can make and store, the more seeds they can set the following year.

How to Harvest

Use sharp scissors or a garden knife when harvesting your herbs. If you're collecting leaves, cut the whole stem before stripping away the foliage. With small-leaved perennials, such as rosemary and thyme, save only the leaves and discard the stems—or use them for potpourris. When harvesting herbs that

Harvesting for the Kitchen

Rosemary

For the best flavor, harvest herbs just before the buds open, when the concentration of essential oils is at its greatest. Herbs grown for their seeds should be harvested after the seeds have turned from green to brown and before they begin to fall from the plant. For garnish or flavor, harvest fresh blossoms such as chives or borage at full bloom. If you're picking flowers such as chamomile for tea, pinch them off when they are fully open.

Harvest herbs grown for their roots when the roots are fully developed in autumn. Use a sharp knife to harvest the largest roots, but make sure that you leave enough roots on the plant so it can re-establish itself. Scrub the roots well before using or drying.

Chives

HANDLE WITH CARE

Nettles can be used to make a soothing tea, but wear gloves when harvesting them because they sting. However, they lose the sting if boiled.

spread from a central growing point, such as parsley and sorrel, harvest the outer stems or leaves first. If you're collecting leaves or flowers from bushy plants, do so from the top of the plant; new growth will come from below.

Herbs retain their best qualities if they're left unwashed until it's time to use them. Some growers advise sprinkling the plants the day before harvesting, to wash away the dirt and dust. If your plants are surrounded by a mulch that limits their contact with soil, you may not have to wash them. If they are gritty with soil, swish them through cold water and pat dry, or hang them in the shade to drip.

If you plan to dry your herbs, bunching them as you collect them saves handling time later. Collect enough stems to make a 1-inch (2.5-cm) thick bundle, then wrap a rubber band over the cut ends. When harvesting annuals in autumn, pull and hang the whole plant, after first cutting away the roots and soil. Expose all herbs to minimum sun and light after harvesting.

FULL BLOOM

If you are picking chamomile flowers for tea, pinch them off when they are open.

DECORATIVE BUNCHES

Dried bunches of herbs can add a decorative look to a kitchen, but remember to harvest them with enough stems for tying and hanging.

DRYING HERBS

Some growers claim that dried, summer-grown herbs have better flavor than herbs grown indoors in winter. Most herbs dry easily and under the proper conditions, they will retain their aroma and flavor.

The best place for drying herbs is somewhere dry and dark, with good ventilation. Options include an attic, around the hot-water heater, on top of the refrigerator, or in a gas oven with a pilot light.

DRYING IN BUNCHES

Long-stemmed herbs, such as lavender, mint and yarrow, are easy to dry in bunches. Select the highest-quality foliage and blossoms, removing any dead or wilted leaves. Make bunches about 1 inch (2.5 cm) in diameter and tie with string or a rubber band. Hang your herbs until they're dry, or if dust is a problem, place the bunches inside paper bags. Herb bunches can take up to 2 weeks to dry. When the bunches are crispy dry, remove the leaves from the stems.

DRYING ON SCREENS

Herbs with short stems and small leaves, such as thyme, are difficult to bunch. The best drying method is to snip off the foliage and spread it on a screen. You can construct your own with scrap lumber and window screening, then set it on bricks so that air circulates freely. If the herbs

COLORFUL BUNCHES
Dried herbs store best in cool, dark places. If you like the look of herb bunches, hang them around your home for decoration. But store the herbs you plan to use for cooking in airtight containers.

DETERRING DUST
If dust is a problem for your drying herbs, place the bunches inside paper bags. Punch a hole in the base of the bag, pull the stems through and fasten with string. To increase air circulation, cut flaps in the side of the bag.

are fine, spread paper on the screen first. Your herbs should be dry in 7–10 days.

DRYING IN THE OVEN

The best method for drying herbs is oven-drying, since the herbs dry quickly and retain their aromatic oils. Spread the herbs on paper towels on baking sheets and place in the oven with the temperature set at about 80–100°F (25–38°C). Drying should be complete in 3–6 hours depending on the herb. Remove when they are crispy dry and before they turn brown.

You can also dry herbs in a microwave oven. Place between sheets of paper towels and place in the microwave with a cup of water for about 1 minute on a low setting. If your herbs turn brown or black, try heating for shorter periods.

DRYING ON SCREENS

Screens can be used to dry short-stemmed herbs as well as seeds. Make your own out of wood and wire screening, but make sure that air can circulate underneath or the herbs won't dry completely and will become moldy.

DRYING HERB SEEDS

Many of the herbs you'll grow are used for their seeds. If you're collecting cilantro (coriander), dill, caraway or other herb seeds for the kitchen, snip off the seed heads when they have turned brown. Place the seeds in a sieve and pour boiling water over them to kill any insect eggs. Shake well. Spread the seeds on paper or a fine mesh screen to dry in the sun. If you plan to sow the seeds, don't blanch them first.

PRESERVING AND STORING HERBS

If your herbs are grown, harvested, dried and stored properly, they will remain green and fragrant for a long time. Herbs can be dried, frozen, salted or stored in oil to preserve them for the winter months.

VERSATILE LAVENDER

Dried lavender retains its aroma for several months. Dried petals can be used in a tea, sprinkled into potpourri, or used as an insect repellent or a long-lasting fragrance.

When your herbs have dried thoroughly, strip the leaves from their stems. Store dried herb foliage, blossoms, roots or seeds in airtight containers in a cool, dry place away from bright light. You can also place dried herbs in plastic bags, squeezing out the air before you seal them.

FREEZING HERBS

If you have more freezer space than cupboard space, you may want to freeze your herbs instead of drying them. Chervil, dill, fennel, marjoram, mint, parsley and tarragon freeze very well. Harvest the herbs at their peak and wash and dry thoroughly. Chop the herbs and place in freezer bags, squeezing out the air, and seal. Be sure to label the bags, because most frozen herbs tend to look alike. When you're ready to use them, simply break off a corner and return

Chilies

CHOOSING CONTAINERS

Store herbs that you plan to use in the kitchen in glass containers. Plastic and metal containers are not suitable because they can affect the chemistry of some herbs.

WINTER BOUNTY

In winter, grow herbs on a sunny window sill, or use herbs you have dried and preserved during the bountiful growing season.

the bag to the freezer. Or make herb cubes by puréeing the herbs with water or oil and pouring into ice-cube trays.

SALTING HERBS

Salting is an old method of herb preservation and it works well with basil, chives, garlic, marjoram, oregano, rosemary, savory, thyme and tarragon. Harvest the herbs at their peak and wash and dry thoroughly. Pack alternate layers of fresh leaves and salt in a jar and seal. Use the salted herbs in stews and sauces.

STORING HERBS IN OIL

Herbs keep well when stored in oil. Use only the very best olive oil. Place fresh, dry herb leaves in a glass jar and cover with oil. Seal and store in a dark place and use in cooking as needed.

FREEZING HERBS

1. Blanch herbs by holding the stems and dipping them in boiling water.
2. When the color brightens, remove from water and drain herbs on clean paper towel.
3. When dry and cool, lay the herbs in single layers on wax paper, then roll up and label.
4. Store in the freezer for enjoyment through winter. Break off and use as needed.

1.

2.

3.

4.

HERBS IN THE KITCHEN

FLAVORSOME OIL
Herb-flavored oils can be as varied and distinct in taste as wine. Try combinations of herbs to add flavor to salads, sauces and marinades.

TASTY INGREDIENTS
Bay, thyme, parsley, chives, mint and sage are all useful herbs in the kitchen.

Herbs are a welcome addition to any kitchen. Your own herb garden brimming with herbs lets you add a special touch to all your dishes. Make your own herbal vinegars, oils and butters or add herbs to your cooking to transform a routine meal into a culinary delight.

COOKING WITH HERBS

Culinary herbs should be used sparingly, to enhance the natural flavors of other ingredients in your recipes. Most herbs should be added at the end of the recipe. Their flavors are released with gentle heat, but are lost if cooked for longer than 30 minutes. An exception is bay leaf, which stands up to a long stewing time.

It's very important to wash and dry herbs thoroughly before using them in the kitchen. Snip the leaves with kitchen shears, or if you need larger quantities, bunch the leaves on a cutting board and mince the pile with a sharp knife. Food processors are useful for chopping large batches of herbs for recipes such as tabbouleh.

If your recipe calls for a fine powder, grind herbs with a pestle and mortar, or purchase a special spice grinder. Ground herbs should be used immediately.

You can substitute fresh for dried herbs in most recipes. Since fresh herbs contain more water than dried ones, use 2 or 3 times more fresh herbs than dried to get the same amount of essential oil.

Herb–Flavored Oils

Herb-flavored oils can be used in marinades or vinaigrettes, brushed over meat prior to cooking or drizzled over Italian bread for a tasty snack. Flavored oils go well with herbal vinegars in salads. Extra-virgin olive oil (made from the first pressing of the olives) or sesame oil are best to use, but other oils such as safflower, macadamia or walnut work well, too. Use any single herb or try the following combinations:

> 6 tablespoons of either:
> basil, lemon thyme and rosemary;
> bay, thyme, rosemary and oregano;
> basil, lemon thyme, chives and garlic;
> dill seeds, burnet and garlic;
> 1 pint (600 ml) extra-virgin olive oil
> or an oil of your choice

Place the herbs in the bottom of a hot, sterilized jar. Heat the oil in a

GOURMET COOKING
Using herbs such as rosemary, bay, garlic, lemon and chili fresh from your garden brings an added excitement to cooking.

PESTO SAUCE
Basil is the key ingredient of pesto sauce. Use a food processor to chop large quantities of herbs.

HERBAL VINEGAR

Ingredients

2 sprigs of fresh
sage, thyme,
rosemary or other
pungent herb
2 long spirals of
lemon zest
4 teaspoons
white peppercorns
4 cups (1 l) white
wine vinegar

1. Place the herbs,
   lemon zest and
   peppercorns in
   a sterilized
   bottle. Add the
   vinegar.
2. Place on a sunny
   window sill for
   2 weeks.
3. For long-term use,
   strain and discard
   the herbs,
   peppercorns and
   lemon zest.
4. Rebottle into a
   hot sterilized jar,
   adding a few
   sprigs of
   fresh
   herbs.

saucepan until just warm, then pour it
into the jar. Let the oil cool, then cover
tightly and store in the refrigerator.

HERBAL VINEGARS

You can use herbal vinegars in most
recipes that call for vinegar. Some herb
growers simply pack the jar with
fresh herbs, then fill with vinegar,
or you can heat the vinegar almost
to boiling—warm vinegar releases
the essential oils faster. Wine-based
vinegars are ideal as a base for
herbal vinegars, since their flavor
is mild and blends well with that
of herbs. Use white-wine vinegar
with chive blossoms, lavender,
marjoram, nasturtium flowers and
leaves, basil, tarragon and thyme.
Use red-wine vinegar with bay
leaves, dill, fennel, garlic, lovage,
mint, sweet basil and thyme.

SALAD DRESSINGS

Homemade salad dressings are far superior
to the commercial versions. Shake together
herbs, oil and vinegar 30 minutes before
serving. Use any single herb or a
combination that suits your menu.

HERB BUTTER

Herb butters are fragrant
spreads for bread, vegetables
and meat. Parsley and garlic
are popular choices, but also
try basil, mint or tarragon.

Herbal Honey

Use herb-flavored
honey instead of sugar
in drinks or cooking.
Try anise, cilantro,
fennel seed, lavender,
sage, thyme, mint and
rosemary. You will
need:
1 tablespoon fresh
herbs, washed and
dried well, or
1½ teaspoons dried
herbs, or ½ teaspoon
herb seeds
2 cups (500 ml)
honey

Place the herbs in a
saucepan. Add the
honey and heat until
warm. Pour into hot,
sterilized glass jars
and seal tightly.

Dried Herb Dressing

1 cup dried parsley
½ cup each dried basil, thyme,
summer savory and marjoram
¾ cup (180 ml) olive oil
¼ cup (60 ml) vinegar

Mix together the dry ingredients and
store in an airtight container. Each time
you need a dressing, shake together
1 tablespoon of the dry herb mixture
with the oil and vinegar.

Herbal Teas

Tea made from aromatic leaves, flowers
or roots steeped in boiling water is one
of the most ancient drinks. Herbal teas
don't have to be medicinal for you to
enjoy them. Start with herbs that have
familiar flavors, such as mint, sage and
chamomile. Use 1 teaspoon fresh herb
leaves or flowers for each 1 cup (250 ml)
boiling water. Pour the boiling water over
the herbs and steep for 5–10 minutes for
the best flavor. A strong tea will be bitter
and might cause unexpected side effects.

MEDICINAL HERBS

Compared with the precision of modern medicine, herbal remedies can seem out of place today. But herbal preparations were once the only medications available. In many countries, herbal remedies remain the only readily available treatment. And, of course, many of today's medicines are derived from naturally occurring plants.

THE HISTORY OF MEDICINAL HERBS

Examples abound of the importance herbs played in the health and well-being of ancient peoples. In 300 BC, a medical school was set up in Alexandria, where research was conducted into the uses of herbs in treating illnesses. This led to the creation of a document listing more than 600 herbs with a prescription for how to prepare each of them as a treatment for specific diseases.

Native Americans used many different herbal medicines. From willow bark they extracted a pain-relieving ingredient, used in today's aspirin. Iris roots ground with suet, lard and beeswax made an ointment for cuts. Coca leaves were used as a local anesthetic and lady's slipper roots relieved colds.

Chinese people have been using natural herbs to treat a wide variety of diseases and ailments for over 3,000 years. Herbal medicines are composed of roots, bark, flowers, seeds, fruits, leaves and branches. In China today, there are up to 5,000 different herbs that can be used in traditional medicine.

GINSENG ROOT

Ginseng is the most famous of all Chinese medicines and has been used for centuries as a cure-all and aphrodisiac. It stimulates the appetite, eases stomach aches, relieves constipation, helps nervous strain and lowers cholesterol.

POWDERED HERBS

Fresh and dry herbs are both important in herbal medicine. If you need to grind herbs, use a mortar and pestle.

HEALING HERBS

Herbs are the oldest medicines in the world and have been used since prehistoric times to improve health. Many herbs, however, have poisonous properties and should be used with caution.

STAR ANISE

Star anise promotes digestion and relieves flatulence, rheumatism and bronchitis.

Herbal Remedies

You can prepare your own herbal remedies, such as infusions, decoctions, compresses, poultices and tinctures, from herbs you have harvested to treat a number of common ailments.

Herbal Infusions

Infusions are made by pouring boiling water over herb leaves or flowers and steeping them for 15 minutes to release the aromatic oils. Strain before drinking.

   1 teaspoons dried herbs or
   2 teaspoons of fresh herb leaves or
   flowers, washed and dried well
   1 cup (250 ml) boiling water

Herbal Teas

An herbal tea is an infusion that is steeped for a short period of time. Use a teaspoon of fresh herb leaves to 1 cup (250 ml) of boiling water. Use a china pot because metal can change the flavor of herbs.

HERBAL TEAS

Herbal teas are made by infusing aromatic leaves, flowers or roots of herbs in boiling water.

Herbal Decoctions

Decoctions are made from the roots, bark, berries or seeds of herbs and need to be boiled gently to extract their ingredients.

2 tablespoons dried herbs, or 1$^1/_2$ cups fresh bark, roots or stems

2 cups (500 ml) boiling water

Wash the herbs, add to the boiling water and simmer for 30 minutes. Strain. Decoctions are drunk fresh.

Herbal Compress

Make an infusion or decoction, then soak a towel in the warm liquid. Wring it out and lay it upon the affected area, covering it with a dry towel. Continue treatment until the skin is flushed or tingly. A hot compress made with mustard, cayenne, garlic or ginger will

Yarrow

improve circulation and is good for treating chest congestion. Compresses prepared with herbs such as comfrey or aloe are good for sprains and bruises.

Herbal Poultice

A poultice is similar to a compress, except that plant parts are used. Use them to draw impurities out of the skin.

Aloe

¹/₄ cup dried herbs or 3 cups fresh herbs, washed, dried and minced

4 cups oatmeal

Mix the herbs and oatmeal with hot water to form a paste, place directly on the skin and cover with a towel. As the poultice cools, replace it with a warm one. Continue treatment for 30 minutes. Don't use hot, spicy herbs, such as mustard, that may burn the skin.

Herbal Tincture

Tinctures are made from alcohol and powdered herbs.

¹/₂ cup powdered dried herbs

2 cups (500 ml) brandy, vodka or gin

Mix the ingredients together in a bottle and allow to steep for several weeks, shaking occasionally. Strain, then store in a cool, dark place. Use 10 drops straight or mixed in 1 cup (250 ml) of water.

Licorice

HEALING HERBS

Aloe: Apply the fresh gel to scalds and cuts.

Burdock: Prepare a poultice from the roots to soothe skin sores and ulcers.

Calendula: Make a compress from the flowers for stings, cuts and bruises.

Chamomile: Make an infusion from the flowers to relieve stress and insomnia.

Echinacea: Make a tea from the root to relieve respiratory infections.

Garlic

Fennel: Make an infusion from the seeds to relieve upset stomachs and flatulence.

Garlic: Use cloves for an antibiotic and antiseptic infusion.

Ginger: Make an infusion from the root for travel sickness, nausea and morning sickness.

Licorice: Chew the root to relieve constipation.

Sage: Make a gargle from the leaves to relieve sore throats and ulcers.

Yarrow: Make an infusion from the flowers and leaves for indigestion and menstrual cramps.

AROMATHERAPY

Aromatherapy is a way of healing the body through massage, inhalation or bathing, and uses essential oils extracted from certain plants. Aromatherapy literally means "therapy by smell." The fragrant natural essential oils of herbs and flowers have a beneficial effect on the body.

HEATING OILS

Diffusers are especially made to heat essential oils in order to release their aroma. A few drops of the oil are added to water in a bowl; the bowl is then heated from below.

MASSAGE THERAPY

Essential oils need to be diluted before applying them to the skin, because they are highly concentrated. Choose a base oil that is pure, has no scent and is cold-pressed, so that the properties of the essential oil remain.

Essential oils are found in small glands in various parts of aromatic plants. They can be extracted from leaves, flowers, fruits, berries, seeds, wood, resin, roots and bark. Each herb releases different scent molecules, which are detected by the olfactory nerves in the nose. These nerves are directly linked with areas of the brain that deal with emotions, memory and creativity. Messages picked up by these nerves travel quickly to the brain and can have an immediate effect on particular chemicals being injected into the body; in turn this can affect the workings of bodily functions.

MASSAGE

In massage it's important not to apply essential oil directly to the skin. Dilute it first with a lubricating oil to allow the hands to glide over the skin. Mix together 15 drops of your favorite essential oil with 2 fl oz (50 ml) of a base oil such as almond, apricot kernel or evening primrose oil. Only use vegetable oils, as they do not evaporate when warmed.

When buying products containing essential oils, shop at health-food stores rather than stores that sell cosmetics. Essential oils are expensive, but cheaper synthetic oils don't have the same healing power as the natural ones.

ESSENTIAL OILS

These popular essential oils will alleviate the following conditions.

Basil: anxiety, stress, respiratory problems

Black pepper: stimulates circulation, muscular aches, colds

Chamomile: skin problems, insomnia

Clary: menstrual problems, insect bites

Clove: toothache, infections, fatigue

Coriander: rheumatic pain, indigestion

Eucalyptus: colds, cuts, insect bites

Juniper: eczema, water retention, fatigue

Lavender: insomnia, infections, indigestion

Lemon: stomach ache, water retention, acne

Rosemary: bronchitis, memory problems

Sage: menopause problems, fatigue

Thyme: depression, muscular pain

Clary

ADDING OILS TO THE BATH

Fill a bath, and add 8 drops of oil and swish around so that the oil rises and mixes with the steam. It's important not to add the oil to a running bath or it will evaporate. Soak in the bath for 10–15 minutes, lightly splashing the oil over your body and inhaling the steam.

INHALATION

Vaporization is the easiest method of releasing the aroma of essential oils; the aroma is then absorbed by the body through inhalation. Add 6 drops of oil to 4 cups (1 l) of steaming water in a bowl. Cover your head with a towel and lean over the bowl, keeping your eyes closed. Breathe deeply through your nose for about 1 minute. Or use a small burner that heats the oil to release its aroma, but make sure that the bowl isn't porous, so it can be used for different oils.

Part Four

Plant
Directory

Acacia farnesiana

CLIMATE AND SITE
Zones 7–9. Full sun. Occurs throughout dry tropical to warmer temperate regions.

IDEAL SOIL
Well-drained soil; pH 4.5–7.0.

GROWING HABIT
Straggly, many-branched tree with sparse, feathery leaves divided into leaflets; height to 23 feet (7 m).

PARTS USED
Bark, flowers, pods, seeds.

WATTLE (MIMOSA)

WATTLE TREES ARE POPULAR AS ORNAMENTALS FOR GARDENS IN WARMER REGIONS AND ARE FAST GROWING AND QUICK TO FLOWER WHEN YOUNG.

Growing guidelines Propagate by scarifying seed (soaking in boiling water until seed swells or rubbing the coat of the seed with sandpaper until coating is thin enough to let water in). Also by semiripe cuttings of lateral shoots in late summer.

Flowering time Masses of golden, strongly perfumed ball flowers are produced in summer.

Pest and disease prevention Prone to leaf miner, borer, acacia scale and galls.

Harvesting and storing Flowers are picked as they open and dried for infusions and baths, or distilled for oil. Seeds and pods are collected when ripe and pressed for oil.

Culinary uses Ripe seeds are pressed for cooking oil and also used in cakes and cookies.

Medicinal uses For skin complaints and gastric disorders. Used in baths to relieve dry skin (flowers).

Other uses Oil is distilled from the flowers and used in insecticides and perfumes. The bark and pods are used for a black dye. Also used in some countries as a fence to keep out animals.

Achillea millefolium

CLIMATE AND SITE
Zones 2–9. Full sun but shade tolerated.

IDEAL SOIL
Fertile, well-drained soil; pH 6.0–6.7.

GROWING HABIT
Perennial with fernlike, finely divided, aromatic leaves that are rich in vitamins and minerals; height to 3 feet (90 cm).

PARTS USED
Whole plant.

YARROW

YARROW DISPLAYS LIGHT, DELICATE FERNY FOLIAGE AND ATTRACTIVE, LONG-LASTING FLOWERS. IT IS FROST HARDY AND VERY EASY TO GROW FROM SEED AND DIVISION.

Growing guidelines Sow seed shallowly indoors in early spring, or outdoors in late spring. Divide large clumps in spring and autumn to extend the planting. To prolong flowering, pick blossoms often.

Flowering time Summer to autumn; numerous tiny white, pink or red florets in dense, flat clusters; has a pungent scent.

Pest and disease prevention Flowers attract beneficial insects that prey on aphids. Prone to powdery mildew.

Harvesting and storing Pick flowers with plenty of stem and strip foliage before hanging in bunches to dry; holds color well.

Special tips Add a finely chopped leaf to a wheelbarrow load of compost to speed the process of decomposition. Cut flowers last well in water.

Precautions May cause allergic skin reactions when taken internally.

Medicinal uses For colds, influenza, diarrhea, arthritis, measles and to protect against blood clotting after a stroke or heart attack.

Other uses In dried arrangements and to make a yellow or olive dye.

Aconitum carmichaelii

MONKSHOOD

NAMED AFTER THE CHARACTERISTIC HOOD
SHAPE OF ITS FLOWERS, MONKSHOOD IS
EXTREMELY TOXIC AND WAS USED IN THE
PAST TO MAKE ARROW POISONS.

Growing guidelines Propagate by
seed sown in spring or by division
in autumn and winter. Dislikes
disturbance once established, so
plant or sow seed where plant is
to grow.

Flowering time Spikes or racemes of
deep blue, hoodlike flowers appear
in summer and autumn. Removal of
dead flower heads will encourage a
second crop of flowers.

Pest and disease prevention Usually
free from pests and diseases.

Harvesting and storing Young roots
are removed from the mother plant
in autumn or winter.

Precautions Monkshood contains
the chemical aconitine, which is
one of the most toxic plant
compounds known. Should only
be used by qualified practitioners
as all parts are extremely toxic.

Medicinal uses For sedation,
painkilling, arthritis and stimulation
of the heart and kidneys. Recent
research has found it to be effective
in congestive heart failure. Also as
an anesthetic.

Other names Azure monkshood.

Aesculus hippocastanum

CLIMATE AND SITE
Zones 3–8. Full sun to partial shade.

IDEAL SOIL
Tolerates different soils but prefers deep, moist, well-drained, rich soil; pH 6.0–7.5.

GROWING HABIT
Large, deciduous tree; height to 83 feet (25 m). Bright green, palm-shaped leaves that turn a rich brown in autumn.

PARTS USED
Seeds, bark.

HORSE CHESTNUT

HORSE CHESTNUT HAS FOLIAGE THAT TURNS RICH BROWN IN AUTUMN AND EDIBLE SEEDS THAT RESEMBLE CHESTNUTS. IT HAS LONG BEEN USED AS A FODDER.

Growing guidelines Propagate by seed sown in summer, or cuttings taken in winter. Keep well watered until established. Growth is rapid. Pruning is not necessary.

Flowering time Upright, pyramidal clusters of small, white flowers occur in spring, followed by round, spiny fruits containing large shiny seeds sometimes called "conkers."

Pest and disease prevention Prone to Japanese beetles, fungal leaf blotch and canker.

Harvesting and storing Bark and seeds are collected in autumn and treated for medicinal use. Seeds are roasted before use.

Precautions Harmful if eaten.

Medicinal uses For hardening of the arteries, stroke, heart attack, varicose veins, chilblains and fever. Contains a chemical which has a potent anti-inflammatory effect. Used for swollen joints and fractures.

Other uses In cosmetics and hair products. Used as a fodder and medicinal plant for cattle and horses.

Other common names Buckeye, due to the resemblance of the seeds to the eyes of deer.

Agastache foeniculum

CLIMATE AND SITE
Zones 6–10.
Prefers full sun
but tolerates
partial shade.

IDEAL SOIL
Rich, well-
drained garden
soil; pH 6.0–7.0.

GROWING HABIT
Perennial; height to
3 feet (90 cm); tall
and branched at
the top.

PARTS USED
Leaves, flowers.

ANISE HYSSOP

SIMILAR IN APPEARANCE TO MINT WITH
SQUARE STEMS AND ATTRACTIVE LAVENDER
BLOSSOMS, THE LEAVES HAVE A DISTINCTIVE
LICORICE SCENT.

Growing guidelines Sow seed
shallowly in spring indoors or
outdoors, thinning to 1 foot (30 cm);
transplants very well. The tall plants
occasionally require staking.

Flowering time Late summer to
autumn; topped with spikes of
lavender flowers.

Pest and disease prevention Usually
free from pests and diseases.

Harvesting and storing Harvest fresh
leaves as necessary throughout the
summer. The best time to collect
foliage for drying is just before
blooming; hang in bunches to dry.
Or cut whole plants after blooming,
and hang them to dry for both
foliage and dried flowers.

Culinary uses Used fresh in salads;
use dried leaves as a seasoning and
as a flavoring of meat, and as a tea.

Medicinal uses For coughs, nausea
and colds. Also helps to improve
appetite and can lower a fever by
increasing perspiration.

Other common names Licorice mint,
anise mint, giant hyssop, fennel
giant hyssop.

Gardener's trivia The flowers attract
bees and other beneficial insects.

Agave americana

CLIMATE AND SITE
Zones 9–10.
Requires full sun.
Drought-resistant.

IDEAL SOIL
Well-drained soil;
pH 4.6–7.9.

GROWING HABIT
Long-living
perennial with a
spread of 6 feet
(1.8 m) or more.
Leaves are gray,
smooth and linear
with spiny, serrated
edges.

PARTS USED
Whole plant,
leaves, roots, sap.

AGAVE (CENTURY PLANT)

ITS GIGANTIC LEAF ROSETTES MAKE AGAVE,
ESPECIALLY THE VARIEGATED FORMS, AMONG
THE MOST STRIKING FEATURE PLANTS. AGAVE
IS USED IN STEROID DRUGS.

Growing guidelines Propagate with
offshoots taken from the parent
plant in spring and left to dry for
some days before potting. Seed
slow to germinate. Apply manure
regularly. Water only in summer.

Flowering time Can take up to
10 years before sending up a 20-foot
(6-m) flower spike of greenish
yellow petals.

Pest and disease prevention Prone
to attack by mealybugs and to rot
if watered in winter.

Harvesting and storing Parts are
harvested as required and used
fresh or dried.

Precautions Fresh sap has been
known to cause skin irritation
and dermatitis.

Culinary uses Tender plant core is
cooked as a vegetable. Sap is used
to make alcoholic drinks.

Medicinal uses For indigestion,
constipation, jaundice, flatulence
and dysentery.

Other uses Roots are used in the
manufacture of soap.

Other names Foxtail plant,
spiked aloe.

CLIMATE AND SITE
Zones 5–9. Full sun to partial shade.

IDEAL SOIL
Light garden soil with good drainage; pH 6.0–7.0.

GROWING HABIT
Perennial with upright, hairy stems and downy leaves; height 2–3 feet (60–90 cm).

PARTS USED
Whole plant.

AGRIMONY

THIS EASY-TO-GROW, AROMATIC HERB HAS DARK GREEN, HAIRY FOLIAGE AND YELLOW BLOSSOMS. IT IS MOST COMMONLY USED AS A TEA AND GARGLE FOR SORE THROATS.

Growing guidelines Sow seed outdoors in early spring and thin to 6 inches (15 cm) apart. Agrimony can self-sow each year. Or divide older plants in spring. Thrives with little attention.

Flowering time Summer; tall spikes with small, lightly scented yellow flowers followed by bristly fruits.

Pest and disease prevention Keep foliage dry to stop powdery mildew.

Harvesting and storing Collect foliage just before blooming. Avoid flower spikes with burs. Strip the leaves and spread them to dry or hang in bunches for use in infusions, tinctures, pills and liquid extracts. Store in airtight containers.

Culinary uses As a tea.

Medicinal uses For food allergies, diarrhea, cystitis, rheumatism, sore throats, hemorrhoids and skin conditions. Also used to help control bleeding. Has anti-inflammatory properties.

Other common names Sticklewort, cocklebur, church steeples.

Gardener's trivia The flowers attract bees and other beneficial insects.

Allium cepa

CLIMATE AND SITE
Zones 4 and
warmer for bulb
onions. Full sun.

IDEAL SOIL
Rich, well-drained
and humusy soil;
pH 6.0–7.5.

GROWING HABIT
Robust biennial
with a large bulb
up to 4 inches
(10 cm) across;
height 4 feet
(1.2 m); hollow
green leaves.

PARTS USED
Bulb.

ONION

A STAPLE SINCE BEFORE THE PHARAOHS, THE
BULB OF THE ONION PROVIDES PLENTY OF
GOOD EATING IN LITTLE GARDEN SPACE. ITS
SMELL IS CAUSED BY SULFUR COMPOUNDS.

Growing guidelines Sow seed in
autumn or spring, or by "sets"
(small bulbs). Plant 3–4 inches
(7.5–10 cm) apart a month before
last frost. Keep well weeded; young
onions have slender, grasslike
leaves and are easily shaded out.
Fertilize with fish emulsion or
compost tea to encourage good
early growth, which will determine
eventual bulb size.

Flowering time Star-shaped, green-
white flowers in summer.

Pest and disease prevention Onion
fly and maggots can cause
problems. Downy mildew is
prevalent in wet conditions and
will rot growing bulbs.

Harvesting and storing Pull onions
for fresh use as needed. Dry in the
sun before storing.

Culinary uses Onions are an
indispensable vegetable and add
flavor to most meat and vegetable
dishes. Also eaten raw in salads
or pickled.

Medicinal uses For bronchitis,
gastric infections, boils and acne.

Other species Red (Spanish) onion
A. cepa 'Noordhollandse Bloedrode'.

Allium cepa Aggregatum Group

CLIMATE AND SITE
Zones 4 and warmer; may be planted in autumn in Zones 6 and warmer. Full sun.

IDEAL SOIL
Deep, humus-rich, well-drained soil; pH 6.0–7.5.

GROWING HABIT
Small, firm bulbs produced in sets; height 8 inches (20 cm).

PARTS USED
Bulbs, young leaves.

SHALLOT

SHALLOTS PRODUCE SMALL, FIRM BULBS IN CLUSTERS THAT KEEP LIKE GARLIC BUT ARE MILDER IN FLAVOR. THEY ARE USED MEDICINALLY AS A DIURETIC.

Growing guidelines Shallots do not grow from seed but from bulblets, or "sets." In cold climates, plant 2–4 weeks before last spring frost, 1 inch (2.5 cm) deep and 4–6 inches (10–15 cm) apart. Mulch and water regularly to encourage strong early growth. Each set will divide and produce 8–10 shallots. Where climate permits, autumn planting will produce larger shallots the following summer.

Pest and disease prevention To avoid root maggots, do not plant where shallots or their relatives, such as onions or leeks, have grown the previous year.

Harvesting and storing Harvest in spring, summer or late autumn. When the tops are nearly dry, pull plants and dry the bulbs in a well-ventilated, sunny area by hanging in a cool, dry place, or clip the stems and store the bulbs in mesh bags.

Culinary uses As a vegetable to flavor meat, chicken and vegetable dishes. Can be eaten raw in salads.

Medicinal uses For coughs, colds, bronchitis and as a diuretic and antibiotic. Can reduce blood pressure and blood sugar levels.

Allium porrum

CLIMATE AND SITE
Zones 6 and warmer; grow as a winter vegetable in mild areas. Full sun.

IDEAL SOIL
Loose, very rich, well-drained soil; pH 6.0–7.5.

GROWING HABIT
Perennial with cylindrical bulb; height 3 feet (90 cm).

PARTS USED
Bulb, stems.

LEEK

LEEKS ARE GROWN FOR THEIR STOUT, FLAVORFUL BULB AND STEM. THESE ONION RELATIVES HOLD WELL IN THE GROUND FOR LATE HARVEST.

Growing guidelines By seed planted in spring or autumn, or by division. Transplant to small, individual pots when large enough to handle. This produces better leeks. Set out after frost, in a 6-inch (15-cm) deep trench covering all but 1 inch (2.5 cm) of leaves. Keep well weeded. As they grow, fill in the trench gradually or, if planted on level soil, "hill" them by drawing soil up around the stems. This produces a longer white stem, which is the edible part. Keep soil moist.

Pest and disease prevention To avoid root maggot damage, do not plant where other onion family members have grown the previous year.

Harvesting and storing Dig or pull when large enough for use. Harvest wintered leeks before the spring growth begins.

Culinary uses Cooked in soups, stir-fries, stews and meat dishes. They are popular ingredients in French cooking.

Medicinal uses For coughs, colds, respiratory tract infections, earaches, infections and bronchitis.

Gardener's trivia The leek is the national emblem of Wales.

Allium sativum

CLIMATE AND SITE
Zones 7–10.
Ideally in full sun.

IDEAL SOIL
Deep, well-drained
soil, rich in humus;
pH 4.5–8.3.

GROWING HABIT
Perennial bulb;
height to 2 feet
(60 cm); foliage
resembles that of
onions, iris or
tulips, depending
on variety.

PARTS USED
Bulbs.

GARLIC

GARLIC IS ONE OF THE MOST FAMILIAR
HERBS, USED TO FLAVOR DISHES FROM
ALMOST EVERY ETHNIC GROUP. IT IS ALSO
AN INSECT-REPELLING PLANT.

Growing guidelines Separate
individual cloves from the bulb
immediately before planting, then
plant in late autumn. Space 6 inches
(15 cm) apart and 2 inches (5 cm)
deep. For largest bulbs, prune away
flowering stems that shoot up in
early summer; side-dress with
compost in early spring. In severe
winter areas, plant in early spring.

Flowering time Early summer; small,
white to pinkish blooms atop a tall,
central stalk.

Pest and disease prevention Avoid
overwatering the soil to prevent
bulb diseases.

Harvesting and storing Dig bulbs
after tops begin to fall over, and
before bulb skins begin to decay
underground. Place in a single layer
in a shaded spot to dry. Cut away
tops or plait together and hang.

Culinary uses Adds flavor to most
meats, seafood and vegetables. Raw
garlic is used in sauces and added
as a condiment to butter, vinegar
and salt.

Medicinal uses Prevents infection
and treats colds, whooping cough,
skin problems and dysentery.

Allium schoenoprasum   ALLIACEAE

CLIMATE AND SITE
Zones 5–10.
Full sun.

IDEAL SOIL
Rich, well-drained,
moist soil;
pH 6.0–7.0.

GROWING HABIT
Perennial bulb with
green, tubular
leaves; height
6–12 inches
(15–30 cm).

PARTS USED
Leaves, flowers,
bulbs.

CHIVES

THE GRACEFUL LEAVES AND BLOSSOMS
OF CHIVES HAVE A MILD ONION FLAVOR,
ESPECIALLY WHEN USED FRESH. USE IN
COOKING AND AS A GARNISH.

Growing guidelines Sow seed
indoors in late winter, covering seed
lightly and keeping the soil moist;
transplant in clumps in early spring;
space 5–8 inches (12.5–20 cm)
apart. Sow outside in spring. Or
grow by division in autumn or
spring. Every 3 years, divide older
clumps in early spring to prevent
overcrowding and freshen with
compost or rotted manure. Chives
are hardier than some other
members of the allium family, and
can tolerate wetter conditions.

Flowering time Summer; pink or
lavender to purple globular flowers.

Pest and disease prevention Avoid
wet areas that encourage stem and
bulb diseases.

Harvesting and storing Use fresh
leaf tips all summer once plants are
6 inches (15 cm) tall; leave at least
2 inches (5 cm) remaining. Flowers
should be picked soon after they
have opened for use in garnishes.
Chives are best used fresh; they are
not suited for drying as the delicate
flavor is soon lost. Leaves and
flowers can be frozen.

Special tips Chives are good
companion plants for carrots,

Chives continued

Chives are native to Europe and have been cultivated since the 16th century. They are the only onion species that grows wild in North America and are one of the most popular herbs.

grapes, roses and tomatoes as they ward off pests and diseases. Infuse as a spray for aphids, apple scab and mildew.

Culinary uses Chives are one of the most commonly used herbs in the kitchen for flavoring and as a garnish. Leaves and bulbs are added to soups, salads, omelets, sauces and soft cheeses. Also used in egg and potato dishes. Flowers have a mild onion flavor and are added to salads.

Medicinal uses All alliums contain some iron and vitamins and are a mild antibiotic. Sprinkle on food to stimulate the appetite and to promote digestion.

Other species Garlic chives *A. tuberosum* are somewhat similar in appearance but flowers are white and starlike and leaves are flat and broader. They have a garlicky aroma and flavor, and are eaten as a vegetable in China. They are also known as Chinese chives.
A. schoenoprasum 'Forescate' are larger chives with cylindrical leaves and pink flowers.
Siberian chives *A. schoenoprasum* var. *sibiricum.*

Gardener's trivia Chives are one of the easiest herbs to grow. They were recorded over 4,000 years ago in China and were enjoyed by the explorer Marco Polo.

Aloe vera syn. A. barbadensis

ALOEACEAE

CLIMATE AND SITE
Zones 9–10. Full sun to partial shade. Suitable to be grown indoors.

IDEAL SOIL
Gritty, well-drained soil low in organic matter; pH 6.7–7.3.

GROWING HABIT
Clump-forming perennial with rosettes of spiny, tapered leaves; height 2–3 feet (60–90 cm).

PARTS USED
Sap, leaves from 2-year-old plants.

ALOE

THE LONG, TAPERING LEAVES OF ALOE CONTAIN A MEDICINAL AS WELL AS COSMETIC GEL WHICH IS USED TO CONTROL FUNGAL INFECTIONS AND SKIN PROBLEMS.

Growing guidelines Sow in spring by separating new shoots from established plants then drying for 2 days before planting. In cool climates, plant in pots and move indoors in winter. Aloes thrive with little attention. Indoors, avoid overwatering and mix coarse sand with the potting soil to facilitate good drainage.

Flowering time Rarely flowers in cool climates; in warmer climates, produces drooping, tubular, yellow to red flowers in summer on top of a tall stalk up to 3 feet (90 cm) high. *A. vera* rarely forms seed.

Pest and disease prevention Spray with insecticidal soap to control mealybugs or purchase biological controls. Control insect pests before bringing pots indoors.

Harvesting and storing Inside each leaf is clear, gelatinous sap. Cut leaves for gel as needed from plants at least 2 years old; remove outer leaves first. Sap can be used fresh or evaporated to be made into creams, pills and tinctures.

Special tips Grow indoors on light, sunny window sills in the kitchen and bathroom.

Aloe continued

This clump-forming herb has a stemless rosette of spiny, tapered leaves. The yellow to red flowers are drooping and tubular and appear on top of a tall, leafless stalk.

Precautions Aloe is not given to pregnant women or to people with hemorrhoids. It is also not recommended for people with irritable bowel syndrome. This herb is subject to legal restrictions in some countries.

Medicinal uses For burns, sunburn, cuts, constipation, poor appetite, dermatitis, eczema and digestive problems. Has anti-inflammatory properties and aids healing. Also used to prevent nail biting.

Other uses In pharmaceutical preparations, facial creams and in cosmetics. Also as a violet dye from some species.

Other common names First-aid herb, healing herb, medicine plant.

Other species Zanzibar aloe *A. perryi* gives a rich violet-blue dye. *A. variegata* used as a popular ornamental pot plant.

Gardener's trivia This plant is important historically. It was used for embalming and Christian records show that the body of Jesus was wrapped in a cloth that had been impregnated with aloe and myrrh. It has also been identified in ancient Egyptian wall paintings, and it was reputed to be one of Cleopatra's secret beauty ingredients.

Aloysia triphylla

CLIMATE AND SITE
Zones 9–10 or
greenhouse in
cooler areas.
Full sun.

IDEAL SOIL
Fertile, light,
well-drained soil;
tolerates most soils;
pH 6.0–6.7.

GROWING HABIT
Large perennial,
deciduous, woody
shrub with green,
lancelike leaves
in whorls; height
5–10 feet (1.5–3 m).

PARTS USED
Leaves, oil.

LEMON VERBENA

GROWN FOR ITS STRONG LEMON AROMA
AND FLAVOR, LEMON VERBENA IS WELL
WORTH THE EXTRA CARE REQUIRED. IT IS
USED IN TEAS AND COSMETICS.

Growing guidelines In cold climates,
grow in pots placed outdoors in
summer and indoors in winter.
Outdoors, thin or transplant to
3 feet (90 cm) apart. Keep the soil
moist but never soggy; feed with
compost tea regularly. Pinch tips
to encourage bushy growth. In
autumn, prune away long branches
before bringing pots indoors.

Flowering time Late summer to
autumn; tiny white to lavender
blossoms on spikes from leaf axils.

Pest and disease prevention Wash
mites from foliage with a spray of
water directed at the undersides
of leaves. For stubborn infestations,
wipe with cotton soaked in alcohol
or spray with a botanical insecticide.

Harvesting and storing Snip sprigs of
leaves or cut foliage back halfway
in midsummer and again in autumn.
Dry foliage in a shady spot.

Special tips Will train as a standard.

Culinary uses Fresh leaves are used
in salads, herbal teas and stuffing.

Medicinal uses For colds, flatulence,
stomach cramps and indigestion.

Other uses In potpourri.

Alpinia galanga

CLIMATE AND SITE
Zone 10. Partial shade; drought and frost tender.

IDEAL SOIL
Well-drained, moist soil; pH 4.5–6.8.

GROWING HABIT
Perennial, upright plant with long, narrow leaves; height 6 feet (1.8 m). Creeping rhizome with a reddish exterior and a grayish white interior.

PARTS USED
Rhizomes, oil.

GALANGAL

TROPICAL GALANGAL IS A MEMBER OF THE SAME FAMILY AS GINGER, AND HAS MUCH IN COMMON BOTH IN FORM AND FLAVOR. IT IS POPULAR IN ASIAN COOKING.

Growing guidelines Propagate by rhizome division as new growth becomes apparent.

Flowering time Small, pale green flowers with white lip that resemble orchids are produced all year.

Pest and disease prevention Prone to attack by red spider mite.

Harvesting and storing Roots of plants 3–6 years old are lifted and used raw, dried or distilled for oil. Store fresh root galangal in an airtight container.

Culinary uses Rhizomes used in cooking for their ginger-like flavor. Oil is used in liqueurs, soft drinks and bitters.

Medicinal uses Lesser galangal *A. officinarum* is used for digestive disorders, rheumatic pain, catarrh and respiratory problems. A drink made from grated galangal and lime juice is taken as a tonic in Southeast Asia. Also for skin infections and gum disease.

Other common names Greater galangal, Siamese ginger.

Gardener's trivia In some countries, galangal is worn as a charm to protect children from evil spirits.

Althaea officinalis

CLIMATE AND SITE
Zones 6–9.
Requires full sun.

IDEAL SOIL
Light, moist,
moderately fertile
soil that stays
damp; pH 6.0–8.0.

GROWING HABIT
Robust perennial
with soft, gray,
velvety foliage that
dies down in
autumn; height to
4 feet (1.2 m).

PARTS USED
Leaves, roots.

MARSH MALLOW

THE ROOTS OF THIS HERB WERE ORIGINALLY USED TO PRODUCE THE CONFECTIONERY OF ITS NAME. USE THE LEAVES TO ADD FLAVOR TO SALADS OR COOK ROOTS LIKE POTATOES.

Growing guidelines Sow seed shallowly outdoors in spring, thinning to 2 feet (60 cm). Divide clumps or take basal cuttings from foliage or roots in autumn.

Flowering time Summer; pink or bluish white mallow-like blossoms in clumps with five petals that grow up the stem; followed by circular downy seedpods called "cheeses." Each holds one seed.

Pest and disease prevention Usually free from pests and diseases.

Harvesting and storing Harvest leaves in autumn, just before flowering. Collect and dry flowers at their peak. If you plan to use the tap roots, dig them in autumn from plants at least 2 years old; scrub them then slice before drying.

Culinary uses Use the leaves to add fresh flavor to salads. Cook the roots and eat like potatoes.

Medicinal uses For bronchitis, asthma, cystitis and insect bites.

Other common names Mortification root, white mallow, sweet weed.

Gardener's trivia There are over 1,000 species in the *Malvaceae* family with healing properties.

Anethum graveolens

CLIMATE AND SITE
Zones 6–10. Full sun with wind protection.

IDEAL SOIL
Rich, well-drained soil; pH 5.0–7.0.

GROWING HABIT
Hardy annual resembling fennel with one upright, hollow stem and feathery aromatic leaves; height 2–3 feet (60–90 cm).

PARTS USED
Leaves, seeds, oil.

DILL

DILL IS AN AROMATIC ANNUAL AND HAS BEEN AN IMPORTANT MEDICINAL HERB SINCE BIBLICAL TIMES. SELECT VARIETIES FOR EITHER SEED OR FOLIAGE AND USE IN COOKING.

Growing guidelines In spring, sow seed shallowly outdoors about 10 inches (25 cm) apart in prepared beds. Firm down the soil. Keep seedlings moist and weed diligently. The soft, delicate seedlings do not transplant well and are easily blown over by strong winds. Dill bolts if planted in poor, dry soil, or if overcrowded. The plants do best in a sunny, moist, sheltered position.

Flowering time Tiny, highly aromatic, yellow flowers arranged in umbels appear in summer.

Pest and disease prevention Usually free from pests and diseases.

Harvesting and storing Clip fresh leaves at the stem as needed. Freeze whole leaves, or chop first; or dry foliage on nonmetallic screens. Collect flower heads before the seeds mature and fall; hang in paper bags or dry on paper in the sun. Store dried foliage and seeds in an airtight container. Fresh leaves can be refrigerated for 1 week. Seeds will retain their flavor for at least a year.

Special tips Sow seed every 2–3 weeks for a continuous leaf harvest through to autumn. Do not plant near fennel as they cross-

Dill continued

Dill is an attractive plant with fine, feathery leaves and flat flower heads made up of small, bright yellow flowers. Use the seed as a salt substitute as it contains mineral salts.

pollinate and the flavors mix. The seeds remain viable for 3–10 years.

Culinary uses Both seeds and leaves are used in Scandinavian cooking where they are pickled and added to fish dishes, especially gravadlax. Dill also used with potatoes, seafood and eggs. Seeds used in cakes and bread. Also added to vinegar.

Medicinal uses For flatulence, colic, indigestion and to control infection. Used traditionally to prevent nausea and to cure excessive wind and to treat hiccups.

Other uses Oil is used in soaps, detergents, commercial medicines and as a food flavoring.

Other cultivars *A. graveolens* 'Bouquet' is considered the best cultivar for seed production. It is a compact plant with prolific seed heads; height 2–3 feet (60–90 cm). *A. graveolens* 'Fernleaf' is a dwarf cultivar with luxuriant, dark blue-green foliage; height 1½–2 feet (45–60 cm).

Gardener's trivia There is only one species in the genus. Dill was traditionally given to babies who were suffering from colic and as described by the English herbalist Nicholas Culpepper in the 17th century, dill was "a gallant expeller of wind and provoker of terms."

Angelica archangelica

CLIMATE AND SITE
Zones 6–9. Full sun to partial shade.

IDEAL SOIL
Rich, cool, moist garden soil; pH 6.0–6.7.

GROWING HABIT
Herbaceous or monocarpic perennial often grown as a biennial; height to 8 feet (2.4 m); hollow stems with broad, lobed leaves.

PARTS USED
Leaves, stems, seeds, roots.

ANGELICA, EUROPEAN

THIS TALL, SWEET-SCENTED HERB RESEMBLES ITS CLOSE RELATIVES PARSLEY AND CORIANDER. THE LEAF STEMS ARE USED IN CAKE DECORATIONS AND THE ROOTS AS A TEA.

Growing guidelines Angelica seed needs light to germinate, so sow uncovered and not too deeply. When sowing, press lightly into the soil surface and leave uncovered. Indoors, sow seed in early spring in peat pots and place in plastic bags in the refrigerator; in 6–8 weeks, place in bright, indirect light. Or sow seed outdoors in spring or summer, preferably where it will grow, as angelica transplants poorly. Will self-seed. Can also be grown in pots. Water regularly and apply a liquid manure at 10–14-day intervals as soon as roots begin to show at the drainage holes.

Flowering time Angelica blooms the second or third year in summer, then dies; has tiny, honey-scented, yellow-green flowers in clumps held out on long stalks.

Pest and disease prevention Wash aphids from seed heads with a spray of water.

Harvesting and storing Collect small stems the first summer, then harvest roots in autumn. Pick stems and leaves in spring of the second year. Harvest the ripe seeds before they fall, dry them and store.

Angelica, European continued

The name comes from Latin and means angelic herb. American angelica grows wild in North America and is similar in appearance to European angelica, except that it has a purple root.

Special tips Angelica is a tall plant so place it at the back of an herbaceous border. In potpourris, the seeds act as a fixative.

Precautions Angelica is a suspected carcinogen. Can also cause skin allergies. Not given to pregnant women or people with diabetes.

Culinary uses Leaves eaten as a vegetable; leaf stems candied for cake decorations and desserts; also added to jam.

Medicinal uses For digestive problems, anorexia, pleurisy, rheumatism and migraines.

Other uses In potpourri; seeds used to flavor drinks, especially gin.

Other common names Wild celery, wild parsnip.

Other species American angelica *A. atropurpurea* has tiny white flowers in umbels 10 inches (25 cm) across; height to 6 feet (1.8 m). Chinese angelica *A. polymorpha* var. *sinensis* is a perennial with short rhizomes and pinnately divided leaves; greenish flowers are produced in umbels in late summer followed by notched seeds; height 2–5 feet (60–150 cm).

Gardener's trivia The name comes from the medieval belief that this plant would protect against evil and cure all ills.

Anthriscus cerefolium

CLIMATE AND SITE
Zones 6–10. Cool sun to partial shade.

IDEAL SOIL
Moist but well-drained garden soil rich with humus; pH 6.0–6.7.

GROWING HABIT
Annual with slender, hollow, slightly branching stems and lacy, fernlike leaves; height 1–2 feet (30–60 cm).

PARTS USED
Leaves.

CHERVIL

CHERVIL GROWS BEST AND RETAINS MORE FLAVOR WHEN TEMPERATURES ARE COOL IN SPRING AND AUTUMN. IT IS REPUTED TO IMPROVE MEMORY AND AID DEPRESSION.

Growing guidelines Sow fresh seed shallowly outdoors in early spring or autumn; thin to 9–12 inches (23–30 cm). Keep seedlings moist. Sow again at 2-week intervals until midsummer for continuous harvest. Chervil transplants poorly. Mulch to protect autumn-sown seed. Chervil can seed itself each year if flowers are left to mature in the garden.

Flowering time Summer; small, umbrella-like, white clusters.

Pest and disease prevention Usually free from pests and diseases.

Harvesting and storing Snip leaves continuously after 6–8 weeks; best used fresh.

Special tips Loses flavor quickly when heated, so add to recipes at the end.

Culinary uses Chervil has an aroma like anise and parsley combined. Use in soups and salads. Also added to potatoes, eggs and fish.

Medicinal uses For jaundice, eczema, conjunctivitis and rheumatism.

Other uses In floral arrangements.

Other common names Garden chervil.

Apium graveolens

CLIMATE AND SITE
Zones 5 and warmer. Full sun with protection from strong winds.

IDEAL SOIL
Rich, moist soil; pH 5.5–7.5.

GROWING HABIT
Aromatic perennial with bulbous, fleshy roots; ridged, branching stems and divided leaves; height 1–3 feet (30–90 cm).

PARTS USED
Whole plant, roots, seeds, oil.

WILD CELERY

WILD CELERY HAS BEEN USED AS A FOOD AND MEDICINAL PLANT SINCE EARLIEST TIMES AND WAS FOUND IN TUTANKHAMUN'S TOMB. CULTIVATED CELERY IS POPULAR TODAY.

Growing guidelines Sow seed in early spring. Wild celery germinates slowly and can be overtaken by weeds. In colder climates, start indoors 6–8 weeks before last spring frost. Set out 10–12 inches (25–30 cm) apart. Keep bed well weeded and watered. Apply fish emulsion or compost tea once a month.

Flowering time Tiny green-white clusters of flowers produced in late summer of second year followed by small, oval, aromatic, gray-brown ridged seeds.

Pest and disease prevention Rotate plantings of celery to avoid blights to which it is vulnerable. Also prone to slugs, celery-fly maggots and celery leafspot.

Harvesting and storing Harvest the roots in autumn and use fresh or dried in tinctures. Collect seeds as they ripen in autumn. Cut stems close to the roots and store like turnips in damp sawdust.

Culinary uses Wild celery is rarely used in cooking as it is bitter and toxic in large amounts.

Medicinal uses For rheumatoid arthritis, gout, indigestion and fungal infections.

Arctium lappa

CLIMATE AND SITE
Zones 3–10. Full sun but tolerates partial shade.

IDEAL SOIL
Deep, loose, moist, fertile soil; pH 5.0–8.5.

GROWING HABIT
A biennial grown as an annual; burdock is stocky and branched at the top; height 5 feet (1.5 m).

PARTS USED
Stems, roots, seeds.

BURDOCK

THIS BIENNIAL OR SHORT-LIVED PERENNIAL HAS LARGE, WOOLLY LEAVES, THISTLE-LIKE DAISY FLOWERS, AND A LONG, EDIBLE ROOT. SEEDS USED TO LOWER BLOOD SUGAR LEVELS.

Growing guidelines Sow seed shallowly in early spring or autumn outdoors or indoors. Burdock's deep taproot makes transplanting difficult. Thrives despite neglect. Burdock will self-seed.

Flowering time Summer, but only if plants are not harvested; individual purple to red thistle-like flowers mature to burrlike seed heads that cling to passersby.

Pest and disease prevention Usually free from pests and diseases.

Harvesting and storing At the end of the season, dig up roots, scrub them and slice to dry on paper in the sun. Store dried roots in airtight containers and use for tea. Harvest young leaf stalks in spring and summer and use as a vegetable.

Culinary uses Stalks cooked like celery; roots eaten raw in salads, added to stir-fries and cooked like carrots.

Medicinal uses For skin problems, eczema, psoriasis, rheumatism and colds. Seed extracts used to lower blood sugar levels.

Other common names Greater burdock, cuckold, beggar's buttons.

Arctostaphylos uva-ursi

CLIMATE AND SITE
Zones 4–9. Full sun but tolerates partial shade.

IDEAL SOIL
Acid, well-drained soil with plenty of organic matter; pH 4.5–5.5.

GROWING HABIT
Mat-forming perennial shrub with leathery, shiny leaves; height 3 inches (7.5 cm).

PARTS USED
Leaves.

BEARBERRY

BEARBERRY IS A PROSTRATE, CREEPING, EVERGREEN SHRUB WITH LONG SHINY LEAVES, PINK OR WHITE FLOWERS, AND RED BERRIES THAT ARE SAID TO APPEAL TO BEARS.

Growing guidelines Sow seed outdoors in spring or autumn into a mixture of peat and sand, or take cuttings from new growth in autumn. Stems may be layered in pots set close to the mother plant. Bearberry needs little care except for pinching away stem tips to encourage sideshoots.

Flowering time Spring to early summer; white or pink, waxy and drooping flowers followed by bright red berries in autumn.

Pest and disease prevention Usually free from pests and diseases.

Harvesting and storing Gather fresh green leaves in the morning during sunny autumn weather; dry thoroughly in the sun and store in airtight containers. Use the leaves to make a medicinal, diuretic tea to treat bladder infections.

Medicinal uses For urinary infections, such as cystitis, and kidney infections.

Other common names Bear's grape, hog cranberry, mountain box.

Other species Alpine bearberry *A. alpina* is a similar creeping shrub.

Armoracia rusticana

CLIMATE AND SITE
Zones 5–10.
Requires full sun.

IDEAL SOIL
Fertile, moist but
well-drained soil;
pH 6.0–7.0.

GROWING HABIT
Upright perennial
with a thick
taproot. Leaves are
stalked and oblong;
height 1–4 feet
(30–120 cm).

PARTS USED
Leaves, roots.

HORSERADISH

HORSERADISH IS A WEEDY HERB WITH A
WHITE PERENNIAL ROOT. ORIGINALLY IT WAS
CULTIVATED AS A MEDICINAL PLANT BUT
TODAY IS USED MAINLY AS A FLAVORING HERB.

Growing guidelines Plant straight,
young roots that are about 9 inches
(23 cm) long and ½ inch (1 cm)
wide so that the crown or growing
point is 3–5 inches (7.5–12.5 cm)
below the soil surface and plants
are 1–1½ feet (30–45 cm) apart.
Plant at a horizontal angle.

Flowering time Early summer;
small, white blossoms that do not
produce viable seed.

Pest and disease prevention Usually
free from pests and diseases.

Harvesting and storing Horseradish
is grown mainly for its large, white,
pungently spicy roots. Harvest roots
in autumn and winter, and scrub
them before storing in the refrigerator, or pack in dry sand in the
cellar for spring planting. Can also
leave roots in the soil and harvest
as required.

Special tips Harvest early for the
most tender roots.

Culinary uses Leaves can be added
to salads. Fresh roots are grated to
flavor meat or made into a sauce.

Medicinal uses For arthritis, gout,
urinary infections and as a poultice
for wounds.

Arnica montana

CLIMATE AND SITE
Zones 5–9. Full sun but tolerates partial shade.

IDEAL SOIL
Dry, sandy, acidic soil rich in humus; pH 4.0–6.5.

GROWING HABIT
Perennial with bright green leaves that form a flat rosette, from the center of which rises a flower stalk; height 2 feet (60 cm).

PARTS USED
Flowers.

ARNICA

ARNICA IS A HARDY PERENNIAL WITH SEVERAL FLOWER STALKS. THE FLOWERS ARE USED IN AN OINTMENT TO SOOTHE SPRAINS, BRUISES AND ACHING MUSCLES.

Growing guidelines Sow seed indoors in early spring; wait until after the danger of frost has passed before transplanting outdoors. Propagate by dividing the whole plant in spring.

Flowering time Midsummer; yellow-orange, daisy-like blossoms that are 2–3 inches (5–7.5 cm) across.

Pest and disease prevention Prone to aphids. To control, spray with water. Spray severe infestations with a botanical insecticide.

Harvesting and storing Cut flowers from the stalk after they have dried. In autumn, dig roots after the leaves have died.

Precautions In its natural state, arnica is poisonous. Only use internally under the supervision of a qualified practitioner. Can cause dermatitis in allergy-prone individuals. Its use is restricted in some countries.

Medicinal uses In creams and liniments for sprains, bruises, dislocations and aching muscles. Used in some countries to treat heart conditions.

Other common names Leopard's bane, mountain tobacco.

Artemisia abrotanum

CLIMATE AND SITE
Zones 5–9.
Requires full sun.

IDEAL SOIL
Well-drained
garden soil. Don't
fertilize; this plant
prefers a lean diet.

GROWING HABIT
Semi-evergreen
subshrub with
finely divided,
gray-green leaves;
height 3–6 feet
(90–180 cm).

PARTS USED
Leaves.

SOUTHERNWOOD

THIS ORNAMENTAL AND DROUGHT-TOLERANT
PERENNIAL WAS ONCE USED AS AN
APHRODISIAC AND TO STIMULATE THE
GROWTH OF MEN'S BEARDS.

Growing guidelines Propagate by
cuttings, or divide older plants in
spring or autumn. Space 2–4 feet
(60–120 cm) apart. Southernwood is
very difficult to grow from seed, but
cuttings root easily. In early spring,
prune to shape.

Flowering time Summer; small,
inconspicuous, button-like yellow-
white blossoms (rarely blooms in
cool summers).

Pest and disease prevention Usually
free from pests and diseases.

Harvesting and storing Collect
foliage anytime in summer and
hang in bunches to dry. Use dried
foliage to repel moths in stored
clothing, or as an aromatic backing
for herbal wreaths.

Special tips Plant as a living insect
repellent; its essential oils keep
moths and other pests away.

Precautions Not for pregnant or
breastfeeding women.

Medicinal uses For painful
menstruation, worms in children,
frostbite, extracting splinters and
hair loss.

Other common names The lover's
plant, old man, lad's love.

Artemisia absinthium
ASTERACEAE

CLIMATE AND SITE
Zones 4–9. Full sun to partial shade.

IDEAL SOIL
Ordinary, well-drained garden soil; pH 6.0–6.7.

GROWING HABIT
Hardy, woody-based perennial with gray-green, finely dissected foliage; height to 4 feet (1.2 m).

PARTS USED
Whole plant, leaves.

WORMWOOD

WORMWOOD IS A COMMON MEMBER OF SAND-DUNE COMMUNITIES. THE GRAY-GREEN FOLIAGE AND BUSHY GROWTH MAKE IT AN ATTRACTIVE PLANT FOR THE GARDEN.

Growing guidelines Sow seed shallowly outdoors in autumn; or sow seed indoors in late winter, planting outdoors in spring. Thin first-year plants to approximately 15 inches (38 cm), then to 3 feet (90 cm) the second year. Most plants last several years, with peak production during the third year.

Flowering time Summer; green-yellow flowers in panicles.

Pest and disease prevention This plant repels most pests.

Harvesting and storing Restrict harvests to the tops of plants when they flower in summer. Hang in bunches to dry, then store in airtight containers. Can withstand two harvests per season.

Precautions Take in small doses. Not given to children, pregnant or breastfeeding women.

Medicinal uses For worms, gall bladder problems, indigestion, bites and bruises.

Other uses Use in sachets to repel insects, or make a tea to repel aphids in the garden.

Other cultivars *A. absinthium* 'Lambrook Silver' has silvery foliage.

Artemisia dracunculus

CLIMATE AND SITE
Zones 4–9. Full
sun but tolerates
partial shade.

IDEAL SOIL
Well-drained
garden soil;
pH 6.0–7.3.

GROWING HABIT
Hardy perennial
with long, branched
green stems;
height 2–4 feet
(60–120 cm).

PARTS USED
Leaves, oil.

TARRAGON, FRENCH

TARRAGON'S HEAVY LICORICE FLAVOR HOLDS
WELL IN COOKING, MAKING IT AN EXTREMELY
USEFUL HERB IN THE KITCHEN. ORIGINALLY
USED FOR POISONOUS STINGS AND BITES.

Growing guidelines Seldom sets
seed. Take cuttings of new growth
in spring or autumn. Divide older
plants in late winter to spring every
3 years; space 1–2 feet (30–60 cm)
apart. Prune away flower stems
each year for most vigorous growth
and best flavor.

Flowering time Late summer; small
greenish yellow flowers. Will only
flower in warm summers.

Pest and disease prevention Usually
free from pests and diseases.

Harvesting and storing Clip foliage
as needed all summer. Foliage may
be harvested entirely twice each
summer. Fresh foliage lasts several
weeks in the refrigerator first
wrapped in paper towels, then
placed in a plastic bag. Or bunch
together and hang to dry away from
direct sunlight.

Culinary uses Leaves used to flavor
sauces, chicken and egg dishes.
Also used to flavor vinegar, oil
and mustard.

Medicinal uses For indigestion,
worms, toothache and rheumatism.

Other uses Oil is used in flavorings,
perfumes and detergents.

Artemisia vulgaris

CLIMATE AND SITE
Zones 5–9.
Requires full sun.

IDEAL SOIL
Light, well-drained,
organic soil;
pH 6.0–7.0.

GROWING HABIT
Perennial with
upright, purple
stems and deeply
cut, dark green
leaves that have
soft and downy
white undersides;
height 3–6 feet
(90–180 cm).

PARTS USED
Leaves.

MUGWORT

MUGWORT IS AN ATTRACTIVE ORNAMENTAL
FOR THE GARDEN AND FLORAL WREATHS.
THE LEAVES OF MUGWORT HAVE A SAGE-
LIKE SMELL AND ARE SAID TO REPEL INSECTS.

Growing guidelines Sow seed
outdoors after danger of frost. In
spring or autumn, divide older
plants. May be invasive.

Flowering time Late summer;
reddish brown or yellow ball-
shaped flower heads in panicles.

Pest and disease prevention Usually
free from pests and diseases.

Harvesting and storing Collect
leaves just before flowering in
summer. Dry in the shade and store
in airtight containers.

Precautions Unsafe when given
internally to pregnant or breastfeeding women. For use by
qualified practitioners only.

Culinary uses In English, German
and Spanish cooking and in stuffing
for meat and game dishes.

Medicinal uses For depression, loss
of appetite, worms and menstrual
problems. Used in traditional
Chinese medicine on the skin at
acupuncture points. Also used as
a wash for fungal infections.

Other uses In flower arrangements
and for making wreaths.

Other common names St John's
plant, felon herb.

Asparagus officinalis

CLIMATE AND SITE
Zones 3 and warmer. Full sun and cold winters.

IDEAL SOIL
Deep, fertile, well-drained, moist soil; pH 6.5–7.5.

GROWING HABIT
Perennial with creeping rhizomes and upright stems that appear in the spring as shoots; height 3–5 feet (90–150 cm).

PARTS USED
Young shoots, rhizomes.

ASPARAGUS

THIS CLASSIC SPRING VEGETABLE REQUIRES WELL-PREPARED, MOIST SOIL WITH HIGH FERTILITY. A WELL-MAINTAINED PATCH MAY YIELD FOR DECADES.

Growing guidelines Grow from seed or from 1-year-old crowns. Place the crowns in trenches that are 8 inches (20 cm) deep, fanning the roots in all directions. Cover with soil to half the depth of the trench. When foliage peeks above ground level, finish filling the trench with soil. Each autumn, cut back dead foliage and mulch heavily.

Flowering time Green-white, bell-shaped flowers in summer followed by red berries.

Pest and disease prevention Prone to asparagus rust in damp locations; use rust-resistant cultivars.

Harvesting and storing Young shoots are cut in late spring at ground level, leaving woody stems behind. Harvest while tips of spears are still tightly closed. Roots are lifted when plant is dormant and boiled before drying.

Culinary uses Young shoots are steamed and served as a vegetable. Also used in soups and salads. Popular canned vegetable.

Medicinal uses For kidney disease, cystitis, rheumatism, gout and as a diuretic.

Astragalus gummifer

CLIMATE AND SITE
Zones 9–10. Needs
hot, dry conditions.

IDEAL SOIL
Well-drained, sandy
and slightly alkaline
soil; pH 5.6–7.9.

GROWING HABIT
Perennial umbrella-
shaped shrub;
height 1 foot
(30 cm). Stems are
erect, branching
and cushion
forming, leaves
spiny and egg
shaped.

PARTS USED
Gum.

GUM TRAGACANTH

THIS EVERGREEN SHRUB IS ONE OF THE
SPECIES OF MILK VETCHES, WHICH HAVE
BEEN USED AS MEDICINES, FOOD AND
FODDER CROPS FOR COUNTLESS CENTURIES.

Growing guidelines Propagate by
scarified seed; rub seed with
sandpaper or place in a cup of
boiling water and wait for seed
to swell. Germinates slowly.

Flowering time Flowers are small,
white and pea-shaped and occur in
clusters in spring and summer.

Pest and disease prevention Usually
free from pests and diseases.

Harvesting and storing The gum is
collected from 2-year-old plants by
making an incision in the stem
base. Once collected, the gum is
dried for further use.

Special tips Some species of this
large group of herbs accumulate
minerals in their leaves from the soil
and have been used as indicators in
prospecting because of this.

Medicinal uses Stimulates the
immune system and suppresses
tumor growth.

Other uses As the thickening agent
in toothpastes, processed cheese
and confectionery; also to bind the
ingredients of pills.

Other species *A. membranaceus*
and *A. complanatus* are important
in Chinese medicine as tonics.

Avena sativa

CLIMATE AND SITE
Zones 3–9. Full sun with plenty of water and humidity.

IDEAL SOIL
Well-drained, fertile soil; pH 4.5–7.3.

GROWING HABIT
Erect, annual grass with flat leaves, smooth stems and spreading panicles of large, pendulous seed heads; height to 3 feet (90 cm).

PARTS USED
Seeds.

OATS

THIS POPULAR CEREAL IS CULTIVATED AROUND THE WORLD, WHERE ITS FOOD VALUE HAS BEEN KNOWN SINCE EARLIEST TIMES. OATS ARE RICH IN VITAMINS.

Growing guidelines Propagate by seed sown in spring.

Flowering time Nondescript flowers occur in summer followed by seed heads. Seeds are spindle shaped and pale gold.

Pest and disease prevention Can be prone to grasshoppers and other flying insects.

Harvesting and storing Plants are cut in summer and threshed to separate the grains, which are then dehusked and rolled.

Special tips Oats are a great source of vitamins as they contain protein, starch, minerals and oils. They are also rich in copper, cobalt, zinc and iron.

Culinary uses Important ingredient of breakfast cereals, breads, cakes and muesli snacks.

Medicinal uses For depression, herpes, shingles and for strengthening the body after a debilitating illness. Regular consumption of oat germ reduces blood cholesterol levels. Stimulates the central nervous system.

Other uses As a soothing skin wash for dry skin. Dried stalks are included in tonics.

Azadirachta indica

CLIMATE AND SITE
Zones 4–9. Full
sun; native to the
tropics of Eurasia
and Africa.

IDEAL SOIL
Tolerates poor
soil but must
be well drained;
pH 4.5–7.0.

GROWING HABIT
Fast-growing, ever-
green tree with
long, pinnate leaves;
height 40–50 feet
(12–15 m).

PARTS USED
Leaves, bark,
seeds, oil, resin.

NEEM

NEEM IS A FAST-GROWING, LONG-LIVING
TREE THAT IS POPULAR AS AN ORNAMENTAL
IN THE TROPICS. THE TIMBER IS HIGHLY
VALUED FOR ITS INSECTICIDAL PROPERTIES.

Growing guidelines Propagate from
fresh, ripe seed. Drought-tolerant.

Flowering time Small, yellow-white,
fragrant flowers appear from spring
to late autumn, followed by yellow
to red-brown berry-like fruit.

Pests and diseases Due to the
insecticidal and repellent properties
of this tree, it is rarely bothered by
pests and diseases.

Harvesting and storing Seeds
are harvested when ripe for oil
extraction. Leaves, bark and resin
are collected when required and
dried or used fresh.

Precautions Not given to the old or
very young.

Medicinal uses For malaria, intestinal
worms, arthritis, jaundice and skin
problems such as eczema, ringworm and fungal infections. Also
important as a detoxicant.

Other uses Resin is added to soap,
toothpaste and skin creams. Oil is
used in hairdressing products and
insecticides. Leaves used in libraries
to protect against insect damage.

Other common names Nimba,
margosa.

Berberis vulgaris

CLIMATE AND SITE
Zones 3–9. Full sun
to partial shade.

IDEAL SOIL
Moist, fertile,
well-drained soil;
pH 6.0–7.0.

GROWING HABIT
Deciduous,
ornamental shrub
with spiny stems;
height to 8 feet
(2.4 m). Provide
wind shelter in
winter.

PARTS USED
Leaves, bark, roots,
fruits.

BARBERRY

THIS WOODY ORNAMENTAL SHRUB MAKES
AN EXCELLENT HEDGE, AND IS EASILY
TRAINED TO TWIST AND TURN ATTRACTIVELY
IN KNOT GARDENS.

Growing guidelines Sow seed
indoors or outdoors in spring,
or plant fresh seed outdoors in
autumn. Take cuttings in late
summer and root suckers in autumn.
Prune and thin branches after
flowering. If plant becomes overgrown, cut growth to 1 foot (30 cm).

Flowering time Spring; hanging
yellow flowers are followed by
orange-red berries.

Pest and disease prevention Usually
free from pests and diseases.

Harvesting and storing Collect
berries in autumn and use fresh.
Dig roots in summer or autumn and
shave into slices. Strip bark from
stems anytime, then dry thoroughly.

Special tips Barberry quickly
becomes overgrown if neglected;
prune to control growth.

Precautions All parts except the
berries are harmful if eaten.

Culinary uses Fruits once used in
jelly for meat dishes.

Medicinal uses For gallstones,
dysentery, chemotherapy and as
a gargle for sore throats.

Other uses For a yellow dye.

Betula spp.

CLIMATE AND SITE
Zones 3–8. Full sun
to partial shade.

IDEAL SOIL
Fertile, ideally
neutral to acid
soil with good
drainage;
pH 5.0–6.0.

GROWING HABIT
Deciduous tree
that can live for
50–100 years or
more; height
40–90 feet
(12–27 m).

PARTS USED
Leaves, bark,
oil, sap.

BIRCH

BIRCHES ARE REGARDED AS EXCELLENT
MEDICINAL PLANTS. THE TWIGS, INNER BARK
AND FERMENTED SAP ARE USED AS THE MAIN
INGREDIENTS IN BIRCH BEER.

Growing guidelines Sow seed when
ripe in late summer or autumn.
Indoors, sow thickly in trays,
cover only lightly and keep moist.
Transplant seedlings when 1 year
old. Staking may be necessary to
maintain upright growth.

Flowering time Spring; catkins
of male and female flowers are
produced on the same tree before
the leaves.

Pest and disease prevention Watch
for borers on young, sappy limbs.

Harvesting and storing In spring,
collect the sap by boring holes in
the tree trunk, inserting a tube and
collecting the liquid. Collect leaves
in spring and use fresh, or dry and
store. Harvest bark as it peels off
the tree; dry the bark and twigs in
a cool, dry area. Keeps well.

Medicinal uses For arthritis, kidney
stones, rheumatism, psoriasis, gout
and eczema.

Other uses Sap is fermented to make
beer, wine, spirits and vinegar.
Birch twigs used to make strong
and effective brooms. The wood
is used for charcoal, paper, cotton
reels and to smoke fish. The bark
is used in the tanning industry.

Borago officinalis

CLIMATE AND SITE
Zones 6–10.
Full sun to
partial shade.

IDEAL SOIL
Fairly rich,
moist soil with
good drainage;
pH 6.0–7.0.

GROWING HABIT
Frost-hardy annual
with broad, hairy
leaves arising from
a central stalk;
height 2 feet
(60 cm).

PARTS USED
Leaves, flowers,
seeds, oil.

BORAGE

THIS GREEN, ROBUST AND BRISTLY PLANT,
WITH DROOPING CLUSTERS OF BLOSSOMS,
ATTRACTS HONEYBEES TO THE GARDEN.
THE LEAVES HAVE A CUCUMBER FLAVOR.

Growing guidelines Sow seed
½ inch (1 cm) deep outdoors after
danger of hard frost has passed.
Indoors, plant in peat pots to avoid
disturbing the sensitive taproot
when transplanting. Control weeds
to reduce competition for moisture.
To promote blooming, go easy on
the nitrogen. Self-sows well. Tall
plants may need support.

Flowering time Continuously from
midsummer until first frost; star-
shaped circles of pink, purple or
blue flowers with black centers.

Pest and disease prevention Mulch
with light materials, such as straw,
to keep foliage off the soil and
prevent rotting.

Harvesting and storing Harvest
foliage anytime for culinary use and
use raw, steamed or sautéed. Snip
blossoms just after they open and
candy, toss fresh in salads, or dry
with silica gel for floral arrangements.
The flowers and leaves deteriorate
rapidly after harvesting so should be
processed quickly.

Special tips Borage attracts bees to
the garden and is a favorite plant of
beekeepers. It is also an excellent
companion plant. Place near
strawberries as they stimulate each

Borage continued

Historically, borage had the reputation of making people happy and giving them courage. The bright blue, star-shaped flowers turn pink with age.

other's growth. Plant near tomatoes to control tomato hornworms and Japanese beetles.

Precautions Some sources suggest that borage is toxic when consumed in large quantities over long periods of time. Not given to pregnant women. This herb is subject to legal restrictions in some countries.

Culinary uses Leaves chopped in salads and used in cream cheese. Cooked as a vegetable in parts of Italy. Fresh flowers used as a garnish and candied for cake decorations. Leaves give a cucumber flavor to drinks such as Pimms and wine-based drinks.

Medicinal uses For bronchial infections, throat infections and as an alternative to evening primrose oil for skin problems. Also for mouthwashes, eyewashes and for poultices.

Other cultivars *B. officinalis* 'Alba' has the same bristly, cucumber-flavored leaves but has pure white flowers; height to 3 feet (90 cm). Similar culinary and medicinal uses.

Gardener's trivia Borage was used in the past to give people courage. It is high in calcium, potassium and mineral salts and recent research suggests that borage may stimulate the adrenal gland, which is where courage begins.

Boswellia sacra

CLIMATE AND SITE
Zones 8–10.
Full sun. Native
to the Middle East.

IDEAL SOIL
Well-drained to dry
soil; pH 5.0–7.9.

GROWING HABIT
Evergreen, resinous
tree with small,
divided leaves
and papery,
peeling bark;
height to 15 feet
(4.5 m).

PARTS USED
Gum resin.

FRANKINCENSE

IN CHRISTIANITY, FRANKINCENSE WAS GIVEN
TO BABY JESUS. THE GUM RESIN HAS BEEN
HIGHLY VALUED FOR ITS MEDICINAL AND
COSMETIC PROPERTIES SINCE ANCIENT TIMES.

Growing guidelines Propagate by
semihardwood cuttings in summer.

Flowering time Late spring and
summer. Dense heads of small,
white, occasionally blue flowers,
followed by red-brown seed capsules.

Pest and disease prevention Usually
free from pests and diseases.

Harvesting and storing Gum is
collected all year. Collection time
and season will determine quality
of harvest. The best-quality resin is
collected when the plant is growing
during the hottest months in the
driest season. Either used fresh or
dried for powders.

Medicinal uses For urinary and
bronchial infections, as an exhalant
for congested chests, and as a wash
for mouth and throat infections. Use
under medical supervision.

Other uses In cosmetics, incense
and perfumery.

Other common names Olibanum,
mastic tree.

Gardener's trivia Four thousand-
year-old stone carvings show
frankincense trees being grown in
pots and then being used to make
rejuvenating facemasks for royalty.

Brassica spp.

CLIMATE AND SITE
Zones 6–10.
Full sun. Winter
annuals can tolerate
cold conditions.

IDEAL SOIL
Rich, well-drained
soil; pH 4.2–6.0.

GROWING HABIT
Very hardy annual
or biennial with
leaves of various
shapes; height to
6 feet (1.8 m).

PARTS USED
Leaves, seeds,
flowers, oil.

MUSTARD

MOST MUSTARDS ARE ANNUALS OR BIENNIALS.
SOME ARE WINTER ANNUALS THAT REMAIN
GREEN WHEN BURIED IN SNOW. MUSTARD
CAN BENEFIT CROPS BY DETERRING PESTS.

Growing guidelines Easily grows
from seed sown outdoors from
early spring until autumn; thin to
9 inches (23 cm). Can self-sow.
Prepare beds with compost or well-
rotted manure, but avoid excessive
applications of manure, as this can
damage the roots.

Flowering time Summer; four-
petaled yellow flowers occur in
terminal racemes.

Pest and disease prevention Usually
free from pests and diseases.

Harvesting and storing Collect and
dry seeds when ripe.

Culinary uses Young leaves can be
cooked as a vegetable. Seedlings
can be added to salads. Seeds are
blended and ground for mustard;
also used in curries and pickles.

Medicinal uses In poultices, baths
for rheumatism, muscular pain and
respiratory tract infections.

Other species Black mustard
B. nigra is a branched annual
cultivated as the main source of
pungent table mustard.
White mustard *B. hirta* is an annual
cultivated for greens, and mustard-
and oil-producing seeds.

Calendula officinalis

CLIMATE AND SITE
Zones 6–10.
Full sun to
partial shade.

IDEAL SOIL
Average garden
soil with good
drainage;
pH 6.0–7.0.

GROWING HABIT
Annual; branched,
succulent stem
with fine hairs
and aromatic,
hairy leaves; height
1–2 feet (30–60 cm).

PARTS USED
Flowers, petals.

CALENDULA

CALENDULA IS A CHEERY, DEPENDABLE
BLOOMER IN THE GARDEN AND IS ONE OF
THE MOST VERSATILE HERBS. PLANT ENOUGH
TO MAKE LONG-LASTING BOUQUETS.

Growing guidelines Sow seed
outdoors in autumn or spring; thin
to 10–18 inches (25–45 cm). Work
in compost or aged manure before
planting. Deadhead old blooms for
continuous flowering.

Flowering time Spring or summer;
golden yellow to orange daisy-like
flowers, 3 inches (7.5 cm) across.

Pest and disease prevention Prone to
aphids, powdery mildew and rust.

Harvesting and storing Dry petals in
shade on paper to prevent sticking;
store in moisture-proof containers.
Preserve whole flowers in salad
vinegar. Dried, ground calendula
flowers can be used as a substitute
for saffron.

Culinary uses As a substitute for
saffron in rice and soups; infused to
color butter and cheese. Flowers
added to salads.

Medicinal uses For gastric problems,
hepatitis, eczema and athlete's foot.
Used also as a general antiseptic.

Other common names Pot marigold.

Other cultivars Hen-and-chickens
calendula *C. officinalis* 'Prolifera' is
grown for its curious flowers; small
flowers grow from the large.

Camellia sinensis

CLIMATE AND SITE
Zones 6–8. Prefers
sunny positions
with high humidity.

IDEAL SOIL
Light, humus-rich
soil; pH 4.5–6.2.

GROWING HABIT
Evergreen shrub;
height 3–20 feet
(90–600 cm).
Slender stems,
with yellowish
gray bark. Leaves
are leathery and
elliptical in shape.

PARTS USED
Leaves (shoot tips),
oil.

TEA

TEA HAS BEEN DRUNK FOR OVER 3,000
YEARS AND CONTAINS BENEFICIAL ANTI-
OXIDANTS, WHICH HELP PROTECT AGAINST
HEART DISEASE, STROKES AND CANCER.

Growing guidelines Propagate by
semiripe cuttings in summer or
by layering.

Flowering time White flowers with
yellow stamens in axils in autumn
or winter, followed by capsules of
large, oily seeds.

Pest and disease prevention Usually
free from pests and diseases.

Harvesting and storing Leaves are
picked during the year from bushes
over 3 years old and dried for use
in infusions; also dried for green

tea or dried and fermented for
black tea.

Special tips Tea contains high
concentrations of tannins, which
is a possible cause of esophageal
cancer. Drinking tea with milk
eliminates this risk because the milk
neutralizes the tannins.

Culinary uses Used worldwide as a
refreshing beverage. Also used in
cooking to flavor foods.

Medicinal uses For hepatitis,
diarrhea, insect bites, minor injuries
and tired eyes.

Other uses Oil used in perfumes,
hair oil and in food flavoring.

Cannabis sativa

CLIMATE AND SITE
Zones 9–10.
Full sun.

IDEAL SOIL
Average, moist soil;
pH 4.5–8.8.

GROWING HABIT
Strong-smelling
annual with a
long taproot; erect,
branched stem
and palmlike
leaves with downy
undersides; height
3–15 feet
(90–450 cm).

PARTS USED
Whole plant, seeds,
flowering tops.

HEMP

HEMP HAS BEEN GROWN IN ASIA FOR OVER
4,000 YEARS FOR ITS NARCOTIC AND FIBER
PROPERTIES. TODAY, ITS POSSESSION AND USE
IN MOST WESTERN COUNTRIES IS ILLEGAL.

Growing guidelines Grown from
seed and cuttings in summer.

Flowering time Small green flowers
appear in summer. Plants are either
male or female. Female plants have
green flowers in spikelike clusters
while males have small, rounded,
nondescript blooms. Fruit is small,
ash-colored and filled with seeds.

Pests and disease prevention Usually
free from pests and diseases.

Harvesting and storing Only female
flower heads are harvested in
summer and air-dried before
extraction of volatile oils. For hemp
fiber, stems are collected and
chemically treated.

Precautions This herb is subject to
legal restrictions in most countries.

Medicinal uses For nausea associated
with cancer chemotherapy, to reduce
eyeball pressure in glaucoma and
to help AIDS patients gain weight.
Also for skin disorders.

Other uses Source of fiber for rope
and clothes making.

Gardener's trivia Modern research
has proved the value of hemp for
a wide range of medical conditions
but its illegal status stops its use.

Capparis spinosa

CLIMATE AND SITE
Zones 8–10.
Full sun.

IDEAL SOIL
Well-drained
sandy soil;
pH 5.6–8.0.

GROWING HABIT
A prostrate shrub
with long, trailing
stems and ribbed,
oval leaves;
height 3–6 feet
(90–180 cm).

PARTS USED
Root bark, flower
buds.

CAPER

CAPERS ARE THE TINY, UNOPENED, GREEN
FLOWER BUDS OF A BRAMBLE-LIKE SPINY
SHRUB. THEY HAVE AN AROMATIC PUNGENCY
AND ARE USED IN REGIONAL COOKING.

Growing guidelines Propagate by
ripe wood cuttings in summer.

Flowering time Flowers occur in
summer to early autumn and are
white to pink with four petals and
long and numerous stamens.

Pest and disease prevention Usually
free from pests and diseases.

Harvesting and storing Pick flower
buds early in the morning and
pickle in salt or white vinegar.
Strip bark from roots harvested
in autumn and dry.

Culinary uses Pickled or dry-salted
capers feature in Mediterranean
cooking, especially in dishes from
Provence. They are often described
as having a "goaty" taste. The finest
capers are known as *non-pareilles*
and are round and hard. They are
of value in reducing oiliness in food
and have an affinity with garlic,
lemon, anchovies and olives.

Medicinal uses Root bark is used
internally for gastrointestinal
infections, diarrhea, gout and
rheumatism. The flower buds are
used to treat coughs and for eye
infections. Also used for skin
abrasions and as a renal disinfectant
and tonic.

Capsicum annuum

CLIMATE AND SITE
Perennial in Zone
10. Greenhouse or
very sheltered sites
in full sun in
cooler areas.

IDEAL SOIL
Light, well-drained
soil, not overly
rich; pH 6.0–7.0.

GROWING HABIT
Shrubby tropical
perennial, grown
as an annual in
cool areas; height
1–2 feet (30–60 cm).

PARTS USED
Fruits.

PEPPER

BELL PEPPERS (CAPSICUMS) ARE RICH IN
VITAMIN C. THEY ARE CRISP AND JUICY
WHEN GREEN, BUT SWEETER WHEN ALLOWED
TO RIPEN TO RED, YELLOW OR ORANGE.

Growing guidelines Sow seed in
warmth and light; set young plants
outdoors several weeks after last
frost. Plant 1–1½ feet (30–45 cm)
apart. Do not overwater seedlings
as they are vulnerable to root rot.
Young peppers will tolerate cool
spells but will not thrive until
warmer weather arrives. Do not
mulch until the soil is thoroughly
warm. Too much nitrogen will
produce lush foliage and few
peppers, but an application of fish
emulsion or compost tea when

plants are in flower can help
increase yield. Water in dry spells
as peppers are prone to blossom-
end rot if drought-stressed.

Flowering time Summer; flowers
followed by red, orange, brown or
yellow fruit.

Pest and disease prevention Pests
tend to avoid spicy pepper plants.
Check for powdery mildew or leafspot. Plants under cover may be
affected by spider mites, whiteflies
and aphids.

Harvesting and storing Pick
immature or green peppers when
they are large enough to use. Leave
some fruit on the plant to mature.

Pepper continued

The soul of many Asian and Mexican dishes, hot peppers come in many sizes, shapes and degrees of heat. The thinner-fleshed, elongated peppers hold their flavor better.

Fully ripe peppers will be yellow, orange, brown or red, depending on the cultivar. Pick mature peppers when 75-percent colored; they will finish ripening at room temperature. Fresh peppers will keep for 2 weeks or more, or freeze them for winter cooking. Freeze or pickle thick-fleshed hot peppers, such as jalapeño, and dry thin-fleshed ones, such as cayenne.

Special tips Hot peppers and bell peppers may cross-pollinate. Plant them well away from each other, especially if you intend to save the seed.

Precautions Accidental contact can cause eye irritation.

Culinary uses As a vegetable, in pickles and chutneys, and in salads. Ripe fruits dried to make cayenne pepper, chili powder and paprika.

Medicinal uses For fevers, asthma, sprains, chilblains, digestive problems, pleurisy and laryngitis.

Related varieties Hot peppers *C. annuum* Longum Group are also called chili peppers. Hot peppers come in a wide variety of shapes, sizes, and degrees of "heat." A medium cultivar, 'Poblano', is often served stuffed. Medium–hot peppers include jalapeño and Hungarian wax. Fiery peppers include cayenne and Thai types. Hot weather intensifies the flavor.

Pepper continued

Jalapeño peppers are a Mexican cultivar with very pungent, thick-fleshed, cylindrical fruits. One plant can yield more than 100 fruits per season. They are a medium–hot pepper.

Sweet bell peppers (capsicums) *C. annuum* Grossum Group are blocky in shape and thick fleshed, most often used fresh in salads, relish or for stuffing. Most cultivars turn red or yellow when fully ripe. Sweet peppers (other) *C. annuum* Grossum Group are frying peppers, also called sweet Italian. Banana peppers can be sweet or hot. They have elongated fruit up to 1 foot (30 cm) long. They are generally thinner fleshed and hold their flavor better in cooked dishes.

Other species Tabasco pepper *C. frutescens* is a perennial shrub grown in the tropics and sub-tropics; woody stem, elliptical leaves and starlike white flowers with yellow centers appearing in summer. Small, leathery, oblong fruits containing numerous pungent seeds develop in various shades of red and yellow.

Tree pepper *C. pubescens* is a sprawling, shrubby perennial with striped stems and wrinkled, hairy leaves; height 10 feet (3 m). Single violet flowers are followed by erect yellow, red or brown fruits. It is the most cold-tolerant species and can fruit for 15 years in cool climates.

Gardener's trivia The name capsicum comes from the Latin *capsa*, meaning "box," on account of the hollow fruits.

Carthamus tinctorius

CLIMATE AND SITE
Zones 6–10.
Full sun.

IDEAL SOIL
Well-drained soil
enriched with
organic matter;
pH 6.0–7.0.

GROWING HABIT
Tall annual with
upright, branching
stems and spiny,
oval leaves; height
2–3 feet (60–90 cm).

PARTS USED
Flowers, seeds, oil.

SAFFLOWER

THE ORANGE-YELLOW FLOWERS OF
SAFFLOWER ARE USED TO PRODUCE YELLOW
AND RED DYES, WHICH ARE USED IN ROUGE.
THE SEEDS ARE USED FOR A COOKING OIL.

Growing guidelines Sow seed
shallowly outdoors in spring; thin
to 6 inches (15 cm). Safflower
transplants poorly.

Flowering time Summer; orange to
yellow thistle-like flowers, followed
by small, shiny, white fruit.

Pest and disease prevention Handpick snails and slugs from seedlings.

Harvesting and storing Collect
flowers in the morning, before they
are fully open, and use fresh or
dried for infusions. To dry, hang

upside-down in a shaded, airy spot.
Flowers keep for 1 year only.

Special tip The seed of the
safflower plant is high in linoleic
acid, an essential fatty acid which
can help to lower cholesterol in the
blood and prevent heart disease.

Precautions Not given to pregnant
or breastfeeding women.

Culinary uses Oil is used in cooking
and in cholesterol-reducing diets.

Medicinal uses For coronary artery
disease, measles, jaundice and as a
laxative. Also for skin problems,
bruises and painful joints.
Other uses As a food coloring.
Flowers used in dyes.

CARAWAY

THE SEEDS OF THIS AROMATIC BIENNIAL HAVE BEEN USED FOR OVER 5,000 YEARS. IN THE PAST, CARAWAY WAS THOUGHT TO GIVE PROTECTION FROM WITCHES.

Growing guidelines Sow seed outdoors in spring or early autumn, or sow young plants in spring to late summer so that they can establish themselves over winter; thin to 6–12 inches (15–30 cm). Can also grow indoors in pots. Don't allow seedlings to dry out. A thick, long taproot makes transplanting difficult. Self-seeds in the right conditions.

Flowering time Spring or summer of the second year depending on when seed is sown. White to pink flowers in umbels on stalks followed by ribbed fruits containing the licorice-flavored seeds.

Pest and disease prevention Watch for pests in dried, stored seeds.

Harvesting and storing Snip tender leaves in spring and use fresh in salads, soups and stews. After blooming, cut plants when seeds are brown and almost loose, then hang seed heads upside down in paper bags to dry. Collect seeds and dry a few more days in the sun; store in a airtight container. Dig up roots in the second year.

Special tips Excessive pruning during the first year weakens the plant.

Caraway continued

CLIMATE AND SITE
Zones 6–10.
Full sun.

IDEAL SOIL
Fertile, light garden
soil; pH 6.0–7.0.

GROWING HABIT
Biennial with
glossy, finely
dissected foliage
resembling the
carrot plant and
slender, branching
stems; height to
2 feet (60 cm).

PARTS USED
Leaves, roots,
seeds, oil.

Caraway has been found in the remains of Stone Age meals, in Egyptian tombs and along ancient caravan routes on the Silk Road.

Culinary uses The most commonly used part of caraway in the kitchen is the dried seeds, which have a distinctive, pungent taste. Use these to flavor cakes and bread, especially rye bread. Also in meat dishes, such as Hungarian beef goulash, cheese, confectionery and liqueurs, such as schnapps. Seeds added to cabbage water to reduce cooking smells. Leaves are added to soups and salads; roots are cooked as a root vegetable.

Medicinal uses Caraway has been used in herbal medicine for centuries for colic in babies and small children, bronchitis, diarrhea, flatulence and indigestion.

Other uses Oil is used in food flavoring and perfumery. Also in mouthwashes and colognes.

Other species Ajowan *C. copticum* is an aromatic annual with a thyme-like aroma; branching stems, finely divided, pinnate leaves and small white flowers followed by tiny, aromatic fruits; height 1–3 feet (30–90 cm). The seeds are used to flavor curries and bread.

Gardener's trivia About 30 species make up this genus of biennials and perennials. Caraway was believed to prevent departures, so was used in love potions. It is mentioned in the Bible and Shakespeare refers to it in some of his plays.

Catharanthus roseus

APOCYNACEAE

CLIMATE AND SITE
Zones 9–10. Full
sun to partial
shade.

IDEAL SOIL
Moist, well-drained
soil; pH 6.0–7.0.

GROWING HABIT
Tender perennial
with glossy
evergreen leaves
on a compact
plant; height to
2 feet (60 cm).
Cut back in spring
to shape.

PARTS USED
Leaves.

MADAGASCAR PERIWINKLE

THIS TENDER PERENNIAL, WHICH CAN BE
GROWN AS AN ANNUAL, HAS PROPERTIES
THAT CAN REDUCE THE NUMBER OF WHITE
BLOOD CELLS. USED TO TREAT LEUKEMIA.

Growing guidelines Propagate by
seed sown shallowly indoors several
months before last frost date; plant
outdoors after danger of frost has
passed. Space at 10–12 inches
(25–30 cm). Can be propagated by
cuttings of non-flowering shoots in
spring. In cool climates, bring potted
plants indoors to overwinter. Pinch
tops for best growth and shape.
Can become weedy in warm areas.

Flowering time Late spring to
autumn; rosy pink to white
blossoms with darker centers.

Pest and disease prevention Prone to
fungal diseases in low temperatures.

Harvesting and storage Leaves are
picked before or during flowering
and dried for infusions, liquid
extracts and tinctures.

Precautions Toxic if eaten.

Medicinal uses Reduces blood
sugar levels, stimulates the uterus
and increases perspiration. Also
used for diabetes, constipation,
asthma and menstrual regulations.
Is used to treat cancer and leukemia
in children.

Other common names Rosy
periwinkle, cayenne jasmine.

Ceanothus americanus

CLIMATE AND SITE
Zones 4–9. Best in full sun; tolerates partial shade.

IDEAL SOIL
Light, well-drained soil; pH 6.0–7.0.

GROWING HABIT
Straggly, deciduous shrub with downy, dark green oval-shaped leaves; height 2–3 feet (60–90 cm).

PARTS USED
Leaves, roots.

NEW JERSEY TEA

THIS PLANT HAS SMALL, SPARSE LEAVES, SMALL WHITE FLOWERS, AND SEEDPODS RESEMBLING ACORNS WITH HORNS. AN ASTRINGENT TEA IS MADE FROM THE LEAVES.

Growing guidelines Take cuttings from new growth in spring or autumn. Roots are tough and difficult to divide. Plants tend to be short-lived and may need replacement every few years. Prune severely in winter to control growth.

Flowering time Late summer; panicles of small off-white flowers appear on long stalks followed by triangular seedpods.

Pest and disease prevention Usually trouble free. Check for scale.

Harvesting and storing Collect leaves anytime; use fresh or dried for tea. Roots are dug up and dried in late autumn or early spring when the red color is at its deepest.

Culinary uses As a substitute for tea.

Medicinal uses For colds, sore throats, bronchitis, tonsillitis, whooping cough and nosebleeds. Was used by Native Americans to treat skin cancer and venereal sores.

Other common names Redroot, mountain-sweet, wild snowball.

Gardener's trivia There are around 50–60 species of evergreen and deciduous shrubs or small trees in this North American genus.

Centaurea cyanus

CLIMATE AND SITE
Zones 3–8.
Full sun.

IDEAL SOIL
Well-drained soil;
pH 4.2–7.2.

GROWING HABIT
Dependable,
easy-care annual;
height 8–36 inches
(20–90 cm). These
bushy plants have
narrow, lance-
shaped, silvery
green leaves and
thin stems with
fluffy flower heads.

PARTS USED
Flowers.

CORNFLOWER

THIS PLANT WAS COMMON IN CORNFIELDS THROUGHOUT EUROPE. ITS BOTANICAL NAME COMES FROM THE CENTAUR CHIRON, WHO REVEALED THE FLOWER'S HEALING POWERS.

Growing guidelines Grows easily from seed sown directly into the garden in spring or autumn. To extend the flowering season from an early spring planting, sow again every 2–4 weeks until midsummer. Cornflowers will self-sow if you leave a few flowers to set seed.

Flowering time Thistle-like flowers in late spring and summer. Flower color can vary from occasionally white to shades of bright blue, purple, pink or red.

Pest and disease prevention Leaves can be affected by rust, and flowers can be attacked by petal blight.

Harvesting and storing Flowers are harvested as they open and used fresh or dried.

Culinary uses Flowers can be used fresh in salads and as garnishes.

Medicinal uses For minor wounds and ulcers of the mouth. Also used as an eyewash for eye inflammation.

Other uses In cosmetic and hair preparations. Also used in natural dyes. Flowers used in potpourri.

Other names Bluebottle, knapweed, bachelor's button.

Centella asiatica

CLIMATE AND SITE
Zones 9–10. Full
sun to partial shade.

IDEAL SOIL
Well-composted,
moist soil;
pH 5.5–7.8.

GROWING HABIT
Low-growing,
creeping perennial
with kidney-shaped
leaves; height to
8 inches (20 cm).
Thrives in humid,
wet places such as
adjacent to water-
ways and ponds.

PARTS USED
Whole plant, leaves.

GOTU KOLA

THIS HERB WAS TRADITIONALLY USED TO
TREAT LEPROSY IN INDIA AND AFRICA. IT
CLEARS TOXINS, REDUCES INFLAMMATION
AND IMPROVES HEALING AND IMMUNITY.

Growing guidelines Propagate from
cuttings or seed in spring.

Flowering time Tiny, pink flowers
occur in clusters in summer.

Pest and disease prevention Usually
free from pests and diseases.

Harvesting and storing Whole plant
or leaves are collected whenever
required and used fresh or dried in
infusions, powder or medicated oil.

Special tips Extracts are added to
cosmetics to firm the skin.

Precautions Can be a skin irritant
and cause headaches. Excess can
be dangerous. Subject to legal
restrictions in some countries.

Culinary uses Leaves are picked
fresh and added to curries.

Medicinal uses For varicose veins,
hemorrhoids, sore joints, ulcers and
to reduce scarring from wounds and
to quicken healing. Sap of leaves
has been used to treat prickly heat.
Important in Ayurvedic medicine to
aid meditation.

Other uses Added to face masks to
increase collagen and firm skin.

Other common names Indian
pennywort, tiger grass.

Chaenomeles speciosa

CLIMATE AND SITE
Zones 5–10. Full sun in an open position.

IDEAL SOIL
Well-drained, slightly acid to neutral soil; pH 6.0–7.0.

GROWING HABIT
Deciduous shrub or small tree with dense, spiny twigs and ovate leaves; height 6–20 feet (1.8–6 m).

PARTS USED
Fruits.

FLOWERING QUINCE

FLOWERING QUINCES ARE AMONG THE LOVELIEST OF EARLY SPRING-FLOWERING PLANTS WITH THE ADDED BONUS OF EDIBLE FRUITS. THEY ARE NATIVE TO CHINA.

Growing guidelines Propagate by seed sown in autumn or by layering shoots in early autumn. For plants grown in the open, thin out and prune after flowering or when cutting blossoms for vases. For wall-trained species, cut back after flowering to reduce the previous year's growth to three buds and cut back any outward-growing shoots.

Flowering time Scarlet, five-petaled flowers appear in late winter followed by aromatic, green-yellow, speckled fruits.

Pest and disease prevention Prone to fireblight. May suffer from chlorosis if grown in alkaline soil.

Harvesting and storing Fruits are collected when ripe in autumn and either eaten fresh or dried for use in decoctions.

Special tips Can be trained to grow along a wall or fence.

Culinary uses Fruits can be eaten fresh or are used as a substitute for quince *Cydonia oblonga* in jams.

Medicinal uses For arthritis, rheumatism, gout, swollen lower limbs, leg cramps and stomach cramps due to diarrhea, indigestion and vomiting.

Chamaemelum nobile

CLIMATE AND SITE
Zones 4–10. Full
sun to partial
shade.

IDEAL SOIL
Moist, well-drained
garden soil;
pH 6.7–7.3.

GROWING HABIT
Low-growing
perennial with
aromatic, lacy
foliage; height to
9 inches (22.5 cm).

PARTS USED
Flowers, oil.

CHAMOMILE, ROMAN

HERB GARDENS OF YESTERYEAR OFTEN
INCLUDED A LUSH LAWN OF CHAMOMILE
THAT RELEASED A SWEET, APPLE-LIKE SCENT
WHEN WALKED UPON. IT IS A POPULAR TEA.

Growing guidelines Sow seed in
spring and thin to 6 inches (15 cm).
Once established, it will self-sow.
Divide older plants in early spring.
In the first year, clip to prevent
flowering and encourage vegetative
growth while it becomes established.
Creeping runners spread the plant,
creating a carpet-like surface.
Chamomile is a poor competitor,
so weed often.

Flowering time Summer; small,
white, daisy-like flowers with
yellow centers.

Pest and disease prevention Usually
free from pests and diseases.

Harvesting and storing Collect
flowers at full bloom and dry on
screens or paper. Store in tightly
sealed containers.

Special tips Chamomile lawns can
be mowed like grass.

Culinary uses As an herbal tea.

Medicinal uses For digestive
problems, insomnia, hyperactivity
and stress-related illnesses. Also in
inhalations for bronchitis.

Other common names Garden
chamomile, ground apple and
Russian chamomile.

Chimaphila umbellata

CLIMATE AND SITE
Zones 5–8.
Partial shade.

IDEAL SOIL
Humus-rich, well-drained but moist soil; pH 4.8–6.7.

GROWING HABIT
Low-growing, evergreen, shrubby perennial that shoots from a creeping underground rootstock; glossy leaves and trailing stems; height 10 inches (25 cm).

PARTS USED
Whole plant, leaves.

PIPSISSEWA

PIPSISSEWA IS AN INGREDIENT IN ROOT BEER, AND HAS BEEN USED MEDICINALLY FOR HUNDREDS OF YEARS. IT MAINLY GROWS IN CONIFEROUS FORESTS.

Growing guidelines Propagate by division of older plants, or take root cuttings in spring or autumn. Mulch plants with pine needles to maintain acid pH and soil moisture. Not easy to grow.

Flowering time Early to late summer; long stalks topped by white or pink blossoms with five rounded petals in small terminal clusters. Followed by egg-shaped seed capsules.

Pest and disease prevention Usually free from pests and diseases.

Harvesting and storing Harvest leaves for medicinal and culinary uses in late summer or early autumn. Store in airtight containers.

Special tips Grow pipsissewa in rock gardens or woodland conditions with partial shade for its ground-covering foliage and waxy flowers.

Culinary uses A traditional ingredient in root beer.

Medicinal uses For arthritis and rheumatism. Tea made with pipsissewa leaves has a good reputation as a remedy for kidney problems and urinary infections.

Other common names Prince's pine, king's cure, ground holly.

Chrysanthemum (Tanacetum) parthenium   ASTERACEAE

CLIMATE AND SITE
Zones 6–10. Full
sun to partial
shade.

IDEAL SOIL
Well-drained
garden soil;
pH 6.0–6.7.

GROWING HABIT
Aromatic perennial
with erect stems
and foliage
that resembles
chamomile; height
to 3 feet (90 cm).

PARTS USED
Whole plant,
flowers, leaves.

FEVERFEW

DOUBLE-FLOWERED FEVERFEW MAKES AN
ATTRACTIVE BORDER PLANT. FOLKLORE STATES
THAT IT REPELS UNDESIRABLE INSECTS. IT IS
EFFECTIVE IN TREATING MIGRAINES.

Growing guidelines Sow seed
shallowly indoors in late winter,
then transplant outdoors 9–12 inches
(23–30 cm) apart 2 weeks after
danger of frost has passed. In mild
areas, sow directly outdoors when
danger of frost is past. Divide mature
plants or take cuttings in spring or
autumn, but best plants are grown
from seed. Avoid planting in wet
areas. For vigorous plants, pinch
blossoms before the seeds set; side-
dress with compost or well-rotted
manure in early spring.

Flowering time Summer to autumn;
loose clusters of daisy-like white
flowers with yellow centers.

Pest and disease prevention Usually
free from pests and diseases.

Harvesting and storing Pick leaves
and flowers anytime. Dry stems at
full bloom for floral arrangements.

Precautions Fresh leaves may cause
dermatitis and mouth ulcers if
eaten. Not for pregnant women.

Medicinal uses For migraines,
arthritis, muscle spasms, insect bites
and bruising.

Other uses Flowers are used for
crafts and floral arrangements.

Cichorium intybus   ASTERACEAE

CLIMATE AND SITE
Zones 3–9.
Full sun.

IDEAL SOIL
Neutral to alkaline,
deeply tilled, well-
drained garden
soil; pH 6.0–6.7.

GROWING HABIT
Deep-rooted
perennial with
bristly, branched
stem; height to
5 feet (1.5 m).

PARTS USED
Leaves, roots.

CHICORY

LOOK FOR CHICORY'S BRIGHT BLUE FLOWERS
ALONG ROADSIDES. THIS HARDY WILD PLANT
THRIVES UNDER HARSH CONDITIONS; IT
DOESN'T LIKE THE COZY WARMTH OF INDOORS.

Growing guidelines Sow seed outdoors in spring, thinning to 1 foot
(30 cm). Side-dress in midsummer
with compost or rotted manure, but
avoid heavy nitrogen applications.
Keep weeded and moist. In autumn,
witloof types can be "forced" indoors
away from light to produce chicons.
To do this, plant roots trimmed to
9 inches (23 cm) long in deep
containers and keep away from
light. Within about 3 weeks, cone-
shaped leaves, or chicons, are ready
to be sliced off and boiled.

Flowering time Early spring to
autumn; bright blue, dandelion-
shaped flowers open and close
each morning and evening.

Pest and disease prevention Few
pests bother this fast grower.

Harvesting and storing Collect the
roots in spring or autumn, and dry
them before grinding.

Culinary uses Fresh leaves used
in salads or cooked like spinach.
Radicchio kinds are cooked or
eaten raw. Sliced roots are roasted
and used as a coffee substitute.

Medicinal uses For liver complaints,
gout and hemorrhoids.

Citrus aurantiifolia

RUTACEAE

CLIMATE AND SITE
Zones 9 and
warmer. Prefers
tropical climates
with full sun and
wind protection.

IDEAL SOIL
Prefers light, well-
drained, fertile soil;
pH 4.6–7.0.

GROWING HABIT
Small, evergreen
tree with short,
spiny branches and
glossy leaves; height
15 feet (4.5 m).

PARTS USED
Leaves, fruits,
peel, oil.

LIME

LIMES ARE FAMOUS FOR THEIR AROMATIC,
TART FLAVOR AND ARE NATIVE TO THE WEST
INDIES. THEY HAVE VALUABLE CULINARY AND
MEDICINAL PROPERTIES.

Growing guidelines Propagate from
seed or by grafting. The Tahitian
lime will take cooler conditions
than the Mexican lime. Keep well
watered during spring and summer.

Flowering time Small, white flowers
appear in clusters of two to seven
during spring and summer, followed
by small, round, green fruit.

Pest and disease prevention Scale,
mealybugs and leafminers.

Harvesting and storing Harvest fruit
when ripe and use fresh. Peel can

be used fresh or dried and distilled
for oil. Harvest leaves as required
for infusions.

Culinary uses Fruits used in
marmalade, savory and sweet
dishes; also in drinks. Peel used to
flavor confectionery and cakes; used
in similar ways to lemon peel. Juice
used in South Pacific countries to
"cook" fish.

Medicinal uses For the treatment of
minor complaints such as diarrhea
and headaches. Juice used to soothe
coughs and sore throats.

Other uses Oil used in perfumes.
Also in potpourri and as a skin
tonic and astringent.

Citrus bergamia

CLIMATE AND SITE
Zones 9–10.
Full sun.

IDEAL SOIL
Prefers light, well-drained, fertile soil; pH 4.7–7.2.

GROWING HABIT
Rounded tree with slender, spined branches and glossy, oval, green leaves; height to 30 feet (9 m).

PARTS USED
Flowers, ripe fruits, peel.

BERGAMOT ORANGE

THE BERGAMOT ORANGE HAS A MORE AROMATIC RIND THAN OTHER ORANGES AND PROVIDES AN OIL THAT GIVES EARL GREY TEA ITS CHARACTERISTIC FLAVOR.

Growing guidelines Propagate from seed or by grafting.

Flowering time Fragrant, small, white flowers occur in spring and summer. Fruits are round to pear-shaped, pale to bright yellow, with an aromatic pulp. The thin peel yields oil.

Pest and disease prevention Scale, mealybugs, leafminers, caterpillars and possible root rot.

Harvesting and storing Pick fruit when ripe and use fresh. Peel can be used fresh, or dried and distilled for oil.

Culinary uses Eaten fresh and in fruit salads. Juice and rind used in sweet dishes and cakes. Orange-flower water is used in pastries and desserts, especially blancmange.

Medicinal uses Orange-flower water given to babies for colic; also for douches and skin conditions.

Other uses Bergamot oil is used to flavor Earl Grey tea.

Other species Seville orange *C. aurantium* is a rounded tree with slender, spined branches and round, orange-colored fruit with a sweet, aromatic rind.

Citrus limon

CLIMATE AND SITE
Zones 9–10. Prefers full sun with wind protection.

IDEAL SOIL
Prefers light, well-drained, fertile soil; pH 5.0–8.0.

GROWING HABIT
Evergreen, sub-tropical tree with gray bark and glossy, dark green, elliptical leaves; height 10–20 feet (3–6 m).

PARTS USED
Fruits, juice, rind, flowers, leaves, oil.

LEMON

CITRUS TREES HAVE BOTH CULINARY AND MEDICINAL USES AND ARE HIGH IN VITAMINS. THE LEMON IS A POPULAR ORNAMENTAL TREE FOR THE SUBURBAN BACKYARD.

Growing guidelines Choose container-grown grafted cultivars. Propagate by cuttings or grafting. Ample moisture must be available during spring and summer.

Flowering time Clusters of small, simple, white flowers occur at all times of the year but main flush is in spring and summer; followed by sour-tasting, bright yellow oval fruits.

Pest and disease prevention Scale insects, mealybugs, leafminers, caterpillars or fruit flies may attack.

Harvesting and storing Fruit harvested when ripe for juicing. Rind used either fresh or candied, or dried for potpourri.

Culinary uses Lemon juice is used extensively throughout the world as a souring agent in cooking. Its fresh, natural sharpness is used in savory and sweet dishes, and in drinks.

Medicinal uses Lemon fruit, juice and peel are rich in vitamins and minerals and are valued for their antioxidant properties. Used for colds, coughs, sore throats, fevers and headaches. Also as a diuretic.

Other uses Oil used in perfumes and soaps. Also as a skin tonic.

Coffea arabica

CLIMATE AND SITE
Zone 10. Full sun or greenhouse with a minimum winter temperature of 55–60°F (13–16°C).

IDEAL SOIL
Well-drained soil rich in humus; pH 6.0–7.0.

GROWING HABIT
Evergreen large shrub with glossy leaves; height 15–20 feet (4.5–6 m).

PARTS USED
Seeds.

COFFEE

COFFEE BEANS ARE ACTUALLY THE SEEDS INSIDE A PULPY FRUIT. TO PRODUCE THE SEEDS, THE PLANT REQUIRES A HOT, MOIST CLIMATE AND RICH SOIL.

Growing guidelines Sow seed shallowly in spring in a temperature of not less than 65°F (18°C). Coffee germinates quickly. Does well indoors in pots, but benefits from regular mistings with water to maintain humidity.

Flowering time Late spring; white, star-shaped blooms in clusters, followed by deep red berries which contain large seeds or beans.

Pest and disease prevention For healthy plants, keep coffee well watered during periods of hot and dry weather.

Harvesting and storing Collect the berries when they are deep red, and extract the seeds. Sun-dry for 7–10 days, then roast them.

Precautions Coffee contains caffeine, which is a stimulant that can cause irritability. It also contains a known allergen.

Culinary uses As a beverage and flavoring. Can be combined with chocolate to give a mocha flavor.

Medicinal uses For nausea, narcotic poisoning, vomiting and burns.

Other uses In commercial painkillers.

Convallaria majalis

CLIMATE AND SITE
Zones 3–9. Prefers partial shade.

IDEAL SOIL
Fertile, moist soil; pH 4.2–7.0.

GROWING HABIT
Hardy perennial that grows from creeping, horizontal rhizomes with deciduous leaves that turn brown in late summer; height 1 foot (30 cm).

PARTS USED
Whole plant, oil, leaves, flowers.

LILY-OF-THE-VALLEY

ESTABLISHED CLUMPS OF THIS PLANT COMPETE WELL WITH WEEDS AND CAN THRIVE IN THE SAME SPOT FOR DECADES WITH LITTLE OR NO CARE. THE FLOWERS ARE POISONOUS.

Growing guidelines Propagate by seed sown in spring, or by division in autumn. Plants need a winter with frost.

Flowering time Spikes of small, white, bell-shaped flowers appear in late spring. They are waxy in texture and are sweetly perfumed. Followed by poisonous, small, round, red berries.

Pest and disease prevention Botrytis (gray mold) affects the leaves in wet conditions; prone to caterpillars.

Harvesting and storing All parts are collected in spring and used fresh or dried.

Special tips Grows well in moist soil in the dappled shade of deciduous trees. The name comes from the plant's natural habitat.

Precautions All parts of the plant are poisonous if eaten. This plant is subject to legal restrictions in some countries.

Medicinal uses For use by qualified practitioners. Used for cardiac failure, hypertension and angina.

Other uses In perfumery and tobacco manufacture.

Coriandrum sativum

CLIMATE AND SITE
Zones 6–10. Full sun for seed but some shade for best leaves.

IDEAL SOIL
Fertile, well-drained soil; pH 6.0–7.0.

GROWING HABIT
Annual with graceful, glossy, finely dissected foliage; height to 3 feet (90 cm).

PARTS USED
Leaves, seeds, roots, oil.

CILANTRO (CORIANDER)

THIS HERB IS AN ANNUAL WITH STRONG-SMELLING AND TASTY LEAVES. THE SEEDS, WHICH ARE ALSO USED, BECOME MORE FRAGRANT WITH AGE.

Growing guidelines Sow seed ½ inch (12 mm) deep outdoors after danger of frost has passed; thin to 4 inches (10 cm). Can self-sow. Weed diligently to prevent delicate seedlings from being overcome by more vigorous weeds. Keep well watered; cilantro tends to bolt if too dry at the seedling stage, and during warm summers. To prevent sprawling, avoid heavy applications of nitrogen. Can be grown indoors on a sunny window sill, but it has a strong scent.

Flowering time Early to late summer, depending on when sown; tiny white to pale pink flowers in umbels followed by small, round, beige, highly aromatic seed cases.

Pest and disease prevention Usually free from pests and diseases.

Harvesting and storing Harvest foliage before seeds form and use fresh. Dried foliage is of lesser quality. Freezes poorly. Gather seeds as they ripen in midsummer. Dig up roots in autumn.

Special tips Sow every 2–3 weeks for a continuous supply of fresh leaves. Honeybees are attracted to the flowers. The seeds remain

Cilantro (coriander) continued

Cilantro was brought to Europe by the Romans, who combined it with cumin and vinegar and rubbed it into meat as a preservative. The Chinese believed it led to immortality.

viable for 5–7 years. Recommended as a companion plant to repel aphids and carrot fly. Choose from varieties that produce either a large quantity of leaves or flowers.

Culinary uses Leaves used to flavor Middle Eastern and southeast Asian food. Seeds and roots added to curries, stews, pastries and some wine. Seeds are one of the main ingredients of curry powder. Oil is used in liqueur.

Medicinal uses For sore joints, digestive problems and hemorrhoids. Seeds used in laxatives. Also used to flavor medicines.

Other uses Oil used in perfumery.

Seeds used in potpourri. Also used to flavor various medicines.

Other common names Chinese parsley.

Other cultivars *C. sativum* 'Cilantro' and *C. sativum* 'Santo'.

Gardener's trivia Cilantro is one of the oldest known herbs and has been cultivated for more than 3,000 years. It was used as an aphrodisiac in ancient Persia and was used in Roman times to preserve meat. The species name comes from the Greek, *koriannon*, a type of bedbug that is thought to have a similar smell to the cilantro leaves.

Crataegus laevigata   ROSACEAE

CLIMATE AND SITE
Zones 5–9. Frost
hardy and drought-
resistant; prefers a
sunny position.

IDEAL SOIL
Clay or loamy soils;
pH 4.5–8.2.

GROWING HABIT
Deciduous tree;
erect trunk, reddish
brown bark and
thorny branches;
height 15–20 feet
(4.5–6 m). Leaves
lobed and toothed.

PARTS USED
Fruits.

HAWTHORN

IN PAGAN TIMES, HAWTHORN WAS A SYMBOL OF HOPE AND AN OMEN OF DEATH. BECAUSE IT FLOWERS IN THE NORTHERN SPRING, IT IS ALSO KNOWN AS MAY OR MAYBLOSSOM.

Growing guidelines Grows easily from seed or by grafting. Sow ripe seed outdoors in early spring, or plant young trees from autumn to early spring.

Flowering time In spring; white scented flowers with pink or purple anthers appear, followed by dark red, egg-shaped fruit.

Pest and disease prevention Leaves attacked by caterpillars; also prone to leafspot, powdery mildew or rust. Honey fungus causes death of tree.

Harvesting and storing Fruits are collected when ripe and used raw, cooked or dried.

Special tips For a hedge, plant shrubs 1 foot (30 cm) apart and prune to shape.

Medicinal uses For circulatory disorders and heart disease. For use by qualified practitioners only.

Other common names May, quickset, midland hawthorn.

Other species Chinese haw *C. pinnatifida* is a hardy small tree; white flowers with pink anthers followed by red fruit. Used to treat irritable bowel syndrome. Fruits baked for digestive problems.

Crocus sativus

CLIMATE AND SITE
Zones 6–9. Best in full sun and sheltered from winds and frost.

IDEAL SOIL
Light, fertile, well-drained soil; pH 6.5–7.5.

GROWING HABIT
Perennial with grasslike leaves; height 4–6 inches (10–15 cm).

PARTS USED
Flower stigmas.

SAFFRON

THE FRAGRANT PINK, MAUVE AND PURPLE BLOOMS OF SAFFRON CROCUSES, WITH THEIR RED STIGMAS AND LONG, YELLOW ANTHERS, ARE A STRIKING ADDITION TO THE GARDEN.

Growing guidelines Plant saffron crocus corms 3–4 inches (7.5–10 cm) deep, with the rooting side down, in early autumn at 4-inch (10-cm) intervals. Lift and divide corms every 2–3 years, after the foliage has died down in spring or autumn. Saffron self-propagates. Mulch in severe winters.

Flowering time Autumn; flowers appear with or before the leaves.

Pest and disease prevention Usually free from pests and diseases.

Harvesting and storing Collect individual dark yellow stigmas and dry on paper away from breezes. Store in an airtight glass container in a cool, dry place away from light. The flowers can be dried whole.

Culinary uses As a flavoring and color agent for cakes, paella, risotto and bouillabaisse.

Medicinal uses In Chinese medicine for liver problems and depression.

Gardener's trivia Good-quality saffron is expensive because the crops yield very little in a short blooming period of 20 days. From 160,000 flowers only about 2 pounds (1 kg) of saffron is produced.

Cryptotaenia canadensis

CLIMATE AND SITE
Zones 3–7.
Temperate and
shady.

IDEAL SOIL
Rich, moist soil;
pH 4.3–6.7.

GROWING HABIT
Attractive, hardy
succulent perennial
with creeping
roots, hollow stalks
and leaves with
serrated edges;
height 3 feet
(90 cm).

PARTS USED
Leaves.

MITSUBA

MITSUBA IS ONE OF THE FEW CULINARY
HERBS TO FLOURISH IN SHADE AND AS SUCH
IS A WELCOME ADDITION TO THE HERB
GARDEN. COOK THE LEAVES AS A VEGETABLE.

Growing guidelines Grow from seed
in early spring through to midsummer or by division in spring.
Often grown as an annual.

Flowering time Small, white flowers
appear in clusters in the summer
and quickly turn to seed.

Pest and disease prevention Usually
free from pests and diseases.

Harvesting and storing Young
leaves picked as required and used
fresh. Plants are ready to harvest
about 7–8 weeks after germination.

Special tips Mitsuba is celery
flavored and found in woodland
ravines and riverbanks throughout
northern temperate and mountain-
ous regions of Japan and China. It
is widely cultivated as a pot herb
in Japan.

Culinary uses In Japan, mitsuba is
added fresh or cooked to soups,
salads, sukiyaki, sashimi, tempura
batter, custards and rice. Young
leaves are cooked as a green
vegetable. Leaf stalks are added to
stews and soups instead of celery.
Mitsuba turns bitter if overcooked.

Other common names Honewort,
Japanese wild chervil.

Cuminum cyminum

CLIMATE AND SITE
Zones 8–10. Full sun with wind protection.

IDEAL SOIL
Light, well-drained soil; pH 5.6–8.2.

GROWING HABIT
Small, tender annual with dark green leaves which are slightly fragrant and threadlike; height 10 inches (25 cm).

PARTS USED
Seeds.

CUMIN

CUMIN IS A SMALL AND DELICATE ANNUAL OF THE PARSLEY FAMILY. THE SEEDS HAVE BEEN USED FOR CENTURIES AS A PUNGENT ADDITION TO CURRIES AND SPICY DISHES.

Growing guidelines Propagate by seed sown in spring in a sheltered, sunny site. Seed may not ripen in cold climates.

Flowering time White or pinkish flowers appear in summer and are followed by aromatic seeds. These are similar in appearance to caraway seeds except they are bristly.

Pest and disease prevention Usually trouble-free. Watch out for pests in dried and stored seeds.

Harvesting and storing Seeds are collected when ripe and stored whole. They are used whole or ground for culinary use.

Culinary uses Powerfully flavored seeds are either roasted or crushed and added to lamb, curries and yogurt. Also used for pickling and flavoring liqueurs.

Medicinal uses For minor digestive problems, flatulence, colic and migraine. The oil is antibacterial.

Other uses Cumin oil is used in perfumery and veterinary medicine.

Gardener's trivia The Romans used ground cumin seeds in the same way we use pepper.

Curcuma longa

CLIMATE AND SITE
Zones 8–9. Prefers
full sun and high
humidity.

IDEAL SOIL
Rich, well-drained
soil; pH 4.0–7.5.

GROWING HABIT
Tall perennial
with large, lily-
like leaves;
height 3 feet
(90 cm). Rhizome
is large, aromatic
and tuberous;
inside is bright
orange-yellow.

PARTS USED
Rhizomes.

TURMERIC

A MEMBER OF THE GINGER FAMILY,
TURMERIC IS KNOWN FOR ITS PUNGENT,
MUSKY TASTE AND ITS AROMATIC AND
PEPPERY FRAGRANCE.

Growing guidelines Propagate by
root division when dormant or
by seed sown in autumn.

Flowering time Flowers appear late
spring to midsummer; pale yellow
and clustered in dense spikes with
pale green and pink bracts.

Pest and disease prevention Usually
free from pests and diseases.

Harvesting and storing The rhizomes
are lifted during the dormant
period. These are then boiled or
steamed, then dried and ground.

Culinary uses An essential ingredient
in curry powder and as a flavoring
ingredient in Asian dishes. Used
commercially in processed foods
and sauces as a natural coloring
agent. Often used as a substitute for
saffron; however, although its color
is similar, its taste is quite different.

Medicinal uses Used fresh or dried
as a tonic and remedy for liver
problems. Also used to improve
digestion and stimulate the
circulatory system.

Other uses As a source of yellow
and orange dye.

Gardener's trivia Used to dye the
robes of Buddhist monks.

Cymbopogon citratus

CLIMATE AND SITE
Zones 9–10. Full
sun to partial
shade.

IDEAL SOIL
Well-drained
garden soil
enriched with
organic matter;
pH 6.5–7.3.

GROWING HABIT
Tender perennial
that forms dense
clumps of typical
grass leaves; height
6 feet (1.8 m).

PARTS USED
Leaves, stems, oil.

LEMONGRASS

THIS CLUMP-FORMING PERENNIAL HAS SLIM,
GRASSY FOLIAGE AND PROVIDES A CONTRAST
TO BROAD-LEAVED GARDEN HERBS. USE IT IN
COOKING OR AS A SOOTHING TEA.

Growing guidelines Propagate
by division of older plants. Trim
leaves to 3–4 inches (7.5–10 cm)
before dividing.

Flowering time Seldom flowers.

Pest and disease prevention Usually
free from pests and diseases.

Harvesting and storing Snip fresh
foliage as needed. Harvest larger
amounts anytime in summer and
dry quickly for the best flavor. Use
the white base in cooking.

Special tips Lemongrass oil blends
well with the oils of geranium,
basil, jasmine and lavender; use in
oil burners and mixed into a base
oil for massage.

Culinary uses The bases of the
leaves are used in Southeast Asian
cooking, especially with meat and
fish. The leaves can be infused for
a tea. Also used as a food flavoring.

Medicinal uses For digestive
problems in children, athlete's foot,
scabies, ringworm and lice.

Other uses In soaps, hair oil, herbal
baths and cosmetics.

Other common names Oilgrass, West
Indian lemon.

Dendranthema × *grandiflorum*

CLIMATE AND SITE
Zones 4 and warmer; prefers a sunny, sheltered position.

IDEAL SOIL
Rich, well-drained soil; pH 6.0–6.7.

GROWING HABIT
Perennial with spreading stems and strongly scented leaves; height 1–7 feet (30–210 cm).

PARTS USED
Flowers.

CHRYSANTHEMUM

ALSO KNOWN AS FLORISTS' CHRYSANTHEMUMS, THESE ATTRACTIVE, EASILY GROWN PERENNIALS HAVE BEEN VALUED FOR THEIR MEDICINAL QUALITIES SINCE THE FIRST CENTURY.

Growing guidelines Grown from root divisions or cuttings in early spring; also by seed in late winter or early spring. Sow seed ½ inch (12 mm) deep and thin to 6 inches (15 cm). Pinching out plants encourages sideshoots.

Flowering time Clusters of single or double red, yellow, bronze, pink or white flowers appear in late summer.

Pest and disease prevention Prone to aphids, snails, mildew and viruses.

Harvesting and storing Flowers are harvested in late autumn and dried.

Special tips The edible leaves featured in Asian cooking come from *C. coronarium*, an annual with spicy foliage and yellow flowers.

Precautions Can cause skin allergies.

Culinary uses Flowers can be blanched and used in salads.

Medicinal uses For coronary artery disease, angina, colds and liver disorders. Increases blood flow.

Other common names Florists' chrysanthemum, mulberry-leaved chrysanthemum, garden mums.

Dianthus caryophyllus

CLIMATE AND SITE
Zone 8. Full sun to partial shade. Best where summers are cool and winters are not very cold.

IDEAL SOIL
Well-drained, slightly alkaline soil; pH 8.0–9.0.

GROWING HABIT
Small, upright, hardy perennial; height to 2 feet (60 cm). Slender, grayish green leaves.

PARTS USED
Flowers, oil.

CLOVE PINK

ALSO KNOWN AS THE WILD CARNATION, THIS COLORFUL AND FRAGRANT PLANT IS ONE OF THE FEW FLOWERS THAT TOLERATES DRY, ALKALINE CONDITIONS.

Growing guidelines Propagate by softwood cuttings in spring, by layering in summer or by seed sown in spring.

Flowering time Flowers appear in summer and have a clove-scented fragrance. Color usually pink but can vary from pearly white to purple. Snipping off the dead flowers can promote further flowering in the season.

Pest and disease prevention Affected by a number of diseases including botrytis (gray mold), powdery mildew, and leaf and stem rot.

Harvesting and storing Flowers are cut in the early morning after a few hours of sun. Use fresh or dried.

Culinary uses Flowers sometimes added to salads and as a garnish. Flowers used as flavoring for liqueurs, jams and vinegars.

Medicinal uses Has been used to reduce fevers; medicinal uses are now restricted to Chinese medicine.

Other uses Oil used in perfumery and flowers in potpourri.

Other common names Wild carnation, gillyflower.

Digitalis purpurea

FOXGLOVE

FOXGLOVE IS GROWN COMMERCIALLY BY THE PHARMACEUTICAL INDUSTRY AS IT IS A SOURCE OF DIGITALIS, AN IMPORTANT HEART STIMULANT.

Growing guidelines Sow seed in spring or autumn the year before the plant is to flower. Sow the seed on the soil surface, press in lightly, and keep moist until seedlings appear. Benefits from an application of compost or well-rotted manure.

Flowering time Tubular, bell-like flowers, often spotted internally, are produced on one side of a single spike in summer, followed by numerous seed capsules. Colors range from purple to rose, pink and white. To promote rebloom, remove spent flower stalks and water well in dry weather. Leave one stalk to self-sow.

Pest and disease prevention Is susceptible to crown and root rot in wet conditions.

Harvesting and storing Leaves are picked before flowering and dried for their active components.

Special tips Grow them in the back of borders or plant against a dark background. They look wonderful planted in masses.

Precautions All parts of this plant are poisonous and should not be eaten. Can cause nausea, vomiting and visual impairment. In some

Foxglove continued

CLIMATE AND SITE
Zones 5–9. Prefers
partial shade.

IDEAL SOIL
Well-drained, acid
soil; pH 4.5–7.0.

GROWING HABIT
Biennial or short-
lived perennial;
height to 5 feet
(1.5 m). One
stem with narrow,
lancelike leaves.
Leaves are downy
and can have a
reddish tint.

PARTS USED
Leaves.

Foxglove's genus name of *Digitalis* means "finger," referring to
the way the flower caps fit neatly over the finger.

countries, the growing of this plant
is restricted.

Medicinal uses The leaves contain
digitoxin and digitalin, which are
used to strengthen the contractions
of the heart and to treat heart
failure. For over 200 years,
D. purpurea was the main drug
source for treating heart problems.
Today a synthetic form of the drug
has been developed, but this plant
is still grown commercially for the
drug industry. Also used as a
diuretic and as a poultice to aid
healing of wounds.

Other names Dogs fingers, fairy
fingers, fingers, ladiesglove, dead
men's bells.

Other species Yellow foxglove
D. grandiflora is a hardy evergreen
perennial with creamy yellow,
tubular flowers all summer.
Woolly foxglove *D. lanata* is the
most commonly used foxglove in
medicine today. A spike of cream
to fawn flowers is produced in
summer, followed by seed capsules.
Also used for heart failure.
D. x *mertonensis* has lance-shaped
leaves and more luxuriant, showy
flowers than other species.

Gardener's trivia Foxgloves are
common wildflowers in Europe.
The medicinal properties of
foxgloves were discovered by an
English doctor in the 18th century.

Echinacea purpurea

CLIMATE AND SITE
Zones 3–8. Full sun. Drought-tolerant once established.

IDEAL SOIL
Average to humus-rich, moist but well-drained soil; pH 4.2–7.0.

GROWING HABIT
Tall, rhizomatous perennial; height 4 feet (1.2 m). Leaves are lance-shaped; stems are stout and hairy.

PARTS USED
Roots, rhizomes.

ECHINACEA

THE NAME ECHINACEA COMES FROM THE GREEK WORD *ECHINOS*, MEANING HEDGEHOG, AND REFERS TO THE PRICKLY SCALES ON THE FLOWER CONE.

Growing guidelines Propagate by division in autumn and winter, by seed sown in spring, or by root cuttings in winter. Plants grow from thick rootstocks with short rhizomes.

Flowering time Pinkish purple daisy-like flowers are produced in summer and early autumn. Flowers are honey scented and have a conical, orange-brown center. Echinacea gives a wonderful display of color in the garden during summer and autumn.

Pest and disease prevention Usually free from pests and diseases.

Harvesting and storing Plants are lifted in autumn and the roots and rhizomes are dried for use in powders, tablets and infusions.

Medicinal uses Research has recently shown that echinacea stimulates the immune system, promotes rapid healing of wounds, and has antiviral and antibacterial properties. Used for coughs, colds, venereal diseases, boils and other skin complaints.

Other names Purple coneflower, purple echinacea.

Elettaria cardamomum

CLIMATE AND SITE
Zone 10 or warmer. Does best in partial shade. Needs tropical conditions to fruit well.

IDEAL SOIL
Moist, humus-rich soil; pH 4.8–6.7.

GROWING HABIT
Tender perennial of the ginger family; height 6–10 feet (1.8–3 m).

PARTS USED
Seeds, oil.

CARDAMOM

CARDAMOM IS ONE OF THE MOST ANCIENT SPICES IN THE WORLD AND ALSO ONE OF THE MOST HIGHLY VALUED. IT IS A LARGE PERENNIAL AND IS RELATED TO GINGER.

Growing guidelines Propagate by division of rhizomes in spring or summer and by seed in autumn.

Flowering time In spring to early summer, spikes of white and pink flowers appear, followed by small oval fruits.

Pest and disease prevention Watch for thrip infestation.

Harvesting and storing The first harvest occurs 3 years after planting and from then on the plants bear for 10–15 years. The fruits are harvested every few weeks just before they ripen during the dry season. After picking, dry the capsules on open platforms in the sun. Store in airtight containers.

Culinary uses Cardamom is one of the main ingredients in curry powder. Also used in sweetmeats, pastries, bakery products, ice cream and mulled wine.

Medicinal uses For flatulence, indigestion and stomach disorders. Chewing the seeds cleanses the breath. Also used to detoxify caffeine and to counteract mucus-forming foods.

Other uses Oil used in perfumes.

Equisetum spp.

CLIMATE AND SITE
Zones 5–9. Full sun to partial shade.

IDEAL SOIL
Rich, moist soil with acid to neutral pH.

GROWING HABIT
Primitive spore-bearing perennial, with hollow stems impregnated with silica and a spore-producing cone; height 4–18 inches (10–45 cm).

PARTS USED
Stems.

HORSETAIL

A PRIMITIVE, SPORE-BEARING, GRASSLIKE PLANT CONTAINING SILICA, HORSETAIL HAS BEEN USED FOR CENTURIES TO ACCELERATE THE HEALING OF BROKEN BONES.

Growing guidelines Horsetail is rarely cultivated, since it is difficult to eradicate once established. Plant in buckets to prevent spreading. Propagate in the autumn by division of mature plants.

Flowering time Spring; spikes form at the top of the stalks, and terminal conelike structures release spores.

Pest and disease prevention Usually free from pests and diseases.

Harvesting and storing Cut stems just above the roots any time during the growing season, dry in the sun, and tie in bundles.

Special tips Dried stems are said to act as a garden fungicide. Steep the stems in boiling water, strain and spray on plants.

Medicinal uses The stems of horsetail contain large amounts of silica, which is used by the body in the production and repair of connective tissues and accelerates the healing of broken bones. Also used for incontinence, cystitis, conjunctivitis and hemorrhage.

Other common names Bottle brush, scouring rush, rough horsetail, shave grass.

Eucalyptus spp.

CLIMATE AND SITE
Zones 8–10. Full
sun to partial
shade. Tolerates
varying conditions.

IDEAL SOIL
Light, loamy soils;
tolerates wide
range of soil pH.

GROWING HABIT
Over 500 species
ranging from 5-foot
(1.5-m) shrubs to
300-foot (90-m)
trees. Hardiness
varies with species.

PARTS USED
Leaves, oil, resin,
bark, seedpods.

EUCALYPTUS

EUCALYPTUS ARE EVERGREEN TREES WELL
KNOWN FOR THEIR PUNGENT SCENT AND
SILVERY LEAVES. THEY ARE RICH IN VOLATILE
OILS AND ARE IMPORTANT MEDICINALLY.

Growing guidelines Best to
purchase container-grown trees,
but can easily be grown from seed
under cover in spring or autumn.
Cut back in spring only to restrict
size or to retain the juvenile foliage.

Flowering time Depends on species;
most with umbels of white, cream,
pink, yellow, orange or red flowers
in summer.

Pest and disease prevention Few
severe pest problems. Can be
injured by strong, cold winds.

Harvesting and storing Leaves are
cut as required and dried; oil is
distilled for medicinal and industrial
use. Branches and seedpods are
harvested throughout the year and
dried for use in crafts. All parts
retain their scent.

Special tips A spray made from
blended eucalyptus foliage may
deter garden pests.

Medicinal uses Most eucalyptus
have anti-inflammatory and
antiseptic properties. Use for diarrhea,
athlete's foot and arthritis. Also used
in inhalations for fevers, influenza
and bronchitis; in liniments for
bruises and sprains; in ointments for
cuts and wounds; and in vapor rubs.

Eucalyptus continued

The young leaves of the Tasmanian blue gum are oval and silvery blue; when mature they are long, glossy, green and narrow. The trunk is bluish white with bark that peels off in strips.

Other uses The lemon-scented gum is the richest known source of citronella, which is used in insect repellents, perfumes and detergents. Eucalyptus oil is used as a flavoring for pharmaceutical products, such as throat lozenges. Seedpods are used in herbal crafts.

Other species Tasmanian blue gum *E. globulus* is a large, spreading tree with smooth, creamy white to blue peeling bark and creamy flowers; height 100–160 feet (30–48 m). Used to treat bronchitis, muscular pains and abscesses.

Lemon-scented gum *E. citriodora* is a slender tree with white powdery bark and rough, pointy leaves. All parts are strongly lemon scented. Best known source of citronella.

Peppermint gum *E. dives* is a short-trunked tree with heart-shaped, blue-green leaves and small white flowers in summer. It is used mainly to manufacture menthol.

Red-flowering gum *E. ficifolia* syn. *Corymbia ficifolia* is a fast-growing tree with rough bark and lance-shaped leaves; pink or red flowers occur in spring to summer; height 40 feet (12 m).

White ironbark *E. leucoxylon* is a large gum with pendulous branches, grayish narrow leaves and flaking gray bark. It bears white, pink or red flowers from winter to spring; height 50–70 feet (15–21 m).

Eupatorium perfoliatum

CLIMATE AND SITE
Zones 3–9. Partial
shade or full sun.

IDEAL SOIL
Rich, marshy soil;
pH 4.5–7.0.

GROWING HABIT
Rhizomatous
perennial with
long, narrow leaves
that are dark green
and shiny above,
and white and
downy underneath;
height to 5 feet
(1.5 m).

PARTS USED
Whole plant,
roots, leaves.

BONESET

THIS PLANT'S GENUS NAME COMES FROM THE
ANCIENT KING OF PERSIA, EUPATOR, WHO
WAS FAMED FOR HIS HERBAL SKILLS. THIS
REFLECTS THE IMPORTANCE OF THIS HERB.

Growing guidelines Sow seed on
the surface of seed trays in autumn
or spring; divide mature plants in
spring and autumn, and grow in
damp or marshy soil. Cut stems
almost down to ground level in
autumn after flowering. Semihardwood cuttings can also be
taken in summer.

Flowering time Summer and
autumn; dense heads of small white
or occasionally purple flowers,
followed by feathery seed heads.

Pest and disease prevention Usually
free from pests and diseases.

Harvesting and storing Plants are
cut when in bud, and dried for use
in infusions, liquid extracts and
tinctures. Rhizomes and roots are
lifted in autumn and dried for use
in decoctions and tinctures. Leaves
used for an immune-boosting tea.

Medicinal uses For influenza, colds,
acute bronchitis and skin diseases.

Other common names Thorough-
wort, feverwort.

Other species Joe Pye weed
E. purpureum is a tall, frost-hardy
perennial with leaves that have a
vanilla scent when crushed.

Ferula assa–foetida

CLIMATE AND SITE
Zones 8–9. Full
sun. Frost hardy
but not fully hardy.

IDEAL SOIL
Rich, well-drained
soil; pH 4.3–7.3.

GROWING HABIT
Large, lacy
perennial; height
6 feet (1.8 m).
Finely divided
leaves, light green
in color, that emit
an unpleasant
smell when
crushed.

PARTS USED
Gum resin.

ASAFETIDA

THIS PLANT HAS THE DUBIOUS REPUTATION OF
BEING THE MOST FOUL-SMELLING OF ALL HERBS.
IT HAS A "ROTTEN-EGG" ODOR, AND IS USED
IN SMALL AMOUNTS TO FLAVOR FOOD.

Growing guidelines Propagate by
ripe seed sown in late summer.

Flowering time Tiny, yellow
flowers appear in summer after
5 years, followed by small seeds,
after which the plant dies.

Pest and disease prevention Usually
free from pests and diseases.

Harvesting and storing Stems and
roots are shallowly cut during the
growing season so that the resin
will exude and can be collected.
Whole plants are cut as soon as

flowering begins and gum resin is
scraped from the top of the root.
The resin is formed into lumps that
are then processed into pastes, pills
and powders.

Special tips Store asafetida in
an airtight container to avoid
contamination of other food.

Culinary uses Used in Indian
cuisine. Also to flavor vegetables,
sauces and pickles.

Medicinal uses For asthma, minor
digestive complaints and coughs.
Also for sore joints.

Other common names Giant fennel,
devil's dung.

Filipendula ulmaria

CLIMATE AND SITE
Zones 2–7. Full sun
to partial shade.

IDEAL SOIL
Rich, wet soil
with low acidity,
pH 6.3–8.1.

GROWING HABIT
Hardy, woody
perennial with
bright green oval
leaves. Rootstock
is aromatic when
cut; height 4 feet
(1.2 m).

PARTS USED
Whole plant,
flowers.

MEADOWSWEET

THIS PLANT HAS AN IMPRESSIVE PLACE IN
HISTORY. IT WAS FROM MEADOWSWEET THAT
THE COMPOUND OF SALICYLIC ACID, LATER
KNOWN AS ASPIRIN, WAS FIRST ISOLATED.

Growing guidelines Propagate by
division of rootstock in autumn or
spring, or by seed sown in early
spring. Needs wet soil to thrive.

Flowering time Big clusters of
creamy white, almond-scented
flowers occur from midsummer
through to autumn.

Pest and disease prevention Usually
free from pests and diseases.

Harvesting and storing Plant is
harvested as flowering begins and
is dried for use in tablets, liquid
extracts and other uses. Flowers
are picked when open and dried
for infusions.

Precautions Some people are
sensitive to salicylates.

Medicinal uses For peptic ulcers,
heartburn, digestive disorders,
rheumatic and joint pain, dysentery
and colds.

Other uses Used in potpourri. Also
as a natural dye; the plant produces
a greenish dye and the roots
produce a black dye. Meadowsweet
was an important strewing herb in
the Middle Ages due to its ability to
repel skin parasites, and was used
to fill mattresses and cover floors.

Foeniculum vulgare

FENNEL

GROW LICORICE-SCENTED FENNEL AS A TALL
ORNAMENTAL IN THE FLOWER GARDEN,
AND FOR ITS CULINARY PROPERTIES IN THE
KITCHEN. THE FLOWERS ATTRACT HOVER FLIES.

Growing guidelines Sow seed
shallowly outdoors in spring or
autumn and keep moist; thin to
6 inches (15 cm); transplants poorly.
Will self-seed once established. Do
not grow near dill as seeds will
cross-pollinate. Remove seed heads
if not required, to promote leaf
growth. Fennel is not suitable for
growing indoors.

Flowering time Summer to early
autumn; small, aromatic, flat, yellow
flowers in umbels.

Pest and disease prevention Usually
free from pests and diseases.

Harvesting and storing Snip leaves
before blooming for fresh use;
leaves can also be frozen. Collect
seeds when dry but before they
shatter by snipping the ripe seed
heads into a paper bag; dry them
on paper. Dig up roots in autumn.
Harvest swollen leaf bases of
Florence fennel before flowering.

Special tips Fennel's delicate flavor
is destroyed by heat, so add it at
the end of the cooking time. Try
the bronze-colored variety for
foliage contrast outdoors and on
the dinner plate as a garnish. The
flowers attract beneficial insects.

Fennel continued

Roman warriors ate fennel to keep in good health, while Roman women ate it to prevent obesity. Every part of the plant is edible.

Precautions Do not eat in excessive doses. Oil not given to pregnant or breastfeeding women.

Culinary uses Leaves and seeds used in fish dishes and soups; popular in the south of France. The anise-flavored leaf base, bulb and stem can be eaten raw in salads and cooked as a vegetable. Leaves and seeds can also by infused as a tea.

Medicinal uses For indigestion, colic, urinary problems and to aid lactation. Also as a mouthwash or gargle for sore throats and gum diseases. It was used in the past as an antidote for anyone who had eaten poisonous mushrooms.

Other uses Oil used in toothpaste, soap and air fresheners.

Other cultivars Florence fennel *F. vulgare* var. *azoricum* is smaller with a bulbous stalk base and is eaten as a vegetable; height to 2 feet (60 cm).
Bronze fennel *F. vulgare* 'Purpureum' has bronze-purple foliage and is hardier than the other cultivars; height 4–5 feet (1.2–1.5 m).

Gardener's trivia There is only one species in this genus. The name comes from the Latin *faenum*, meaning "hay," because of the scent of the leaves.

Fragaria vesca   ROSACEAE

WILD STRAWBERRY

THIS TASTY PERENNIAL IS FOUND NATURALLY IN NORTHERN TEMPERATE REGIONS. IT IS THE PARENT PLANT OF THE POPULAR CULTIVATED STRAWBERRY THAT IS LOVED FOR ITS FLAVOR.

Growing guidelines Sow seed in spring by scattering on the surface of potting soil in a container; transplant the seedlings when they are large enough to handle. To divide older plants, separate rooted runners from the outside of the clump; replant divisions immediately. Replace plants every few years.

Flowering time Five-petaled, white flowers with yellow centers occur throughout spring and summer; followed by bright red, conical fruits, with tiny seeds.

Pest and disease prevention Keep birds at bay with netting, or grow yellow-fruited cultivars, which birds tend to leave alone.

Harvesting and storing Harvest the fruits when they are soft and aromatic. They do not store well. Leaves are picked in summer and dried. Roots are lifted in autumn and dried.

Culinary uses Used in herbal teas. Fruit eaten fresh or cooked in jams and desserts. Also used to flavor wines, vinegars and confectionery.

Medicinal uses For digestive problems, skin inflammations, sunburn and diarrhea.

Galium odoratum

CLIMATE AND SITE
Zones 5–9. Prefers
shade; grows well
under trees. Leaf
color will fade in
full sun.

IDEAL SOIL
Moist, well-drained
soil rich in humus;
pH 5.0–8.0.

GROWING HABIT
Rhizomatous
perennial with
whorls of lance-
shaped leaves;
height 8–18 inches
(20–45 cm).

PARTS USED
Whole plant.

SWEET WOODRUFF

SWEET WOODRUFF IS A HARDY PERENNIAL
GROUNDCOVER THAT GROWS WELL IN FULL
SHADE AND SMELLS LIKE VANILLA WHEN
DRIED. HANG IT TO SCENT ROOMS.

Growing guidelines Sow ripe seed
shallowly outdoors in summer to
autumn; germination may take as
long as 200 days. Or purchase
plants from nurseries and plant
9 inches (23 cm) apart. Divide the
creeping rootstock of established
plants in spring or autumn.

Flowering time Late spring to early
summer; small, star-shaped, scented
white blossoms.

Pest and disease prevention Has
insect-repellent properties.

Harvesting and storing Gather
foliage and flowering stems anytime
in summer; hang in bunches to dry.

Precautions Can cause dizziness and
vomiting, and may be carcinogenic.

Culinary uses Used in wines and
other alcoholic beverages.

Medicinal uses For varicose veins,
hepatitis, jaundice and insomnia in
both adults and children.

Other uses In potpourris; also as a
tan-colored dye.

Gardener's trivia The leaves only
develop their sweet, distinctive
scent of vanilla or hay when dried.

Galium verum

CLIMATE AND SITE
Zones 3–9. Full sun to light shade.

IDEAL SOIL
Deep, light, fertile, well-drained soil; favors neutral to alkaline soil; pH 6.7–7.3.

GROWING HABIT
Hardy perennial with creeping rootstock; branched square stems with whorls of linear leaves; height to 3 feet (90 cm).

PARTS USED
Whole plant.

LADY'S BEDSTRAW

LADY'S BEDSTRAW NEEDS LITTLE ATTENTION AND SPREADS READILY BY SEED. HERBALISTS SEAL THE DRIED FOLIAGE IN PILLOWS THAT RELEASE A SLEEP-INDUCING SCENT.

Growing guidelines Sow seed shallowly in spring or divide roots of mature plants; space 2 feet (60 cm) apart. Self-sows; requires little attention.

Flowering time Throughout summer; sizeable clusters of small, bright yellow, honey-scented flowers are produced in panicles.

Pest and disease prevention Usually free from pests and diseases.

Harvesting and storing Harvest foliage anytime through the year and hang in small bunches in the sun to dry.

Culinary uses Used in cheese making. The yellow foliage is used as a food dye; used to color cheese and butter.

Medicinal uses For kidney and bladder complaints. Used as a diuretic and relaxes spasms.

Other uses Foliage once used to stuff mattresses. The roots provide a red dye. Leaves and flowers used in potpourri and herb pillows.

Other common names Our Lady's bedstraw, yellow bedstraw, maid's hair, cheese rennet.

Gardenia augusta

CLIMATE AND SITE
Zones 8–10. Full sun to partial shade but must be kept moist.

IDEAL SOIL
Well-drained, acid soil with high humus content; pH 4.2–5.6.

GROWING HABIT
Tender evergreen shrub with dark green, glossy leaves; height 5 feet (1.5 m).

PARTS USED
Fruits, flowers.

GARDENIA

A BEAUTIFUL AND HIGHLY FRAGRANT, ORNAMENTAL SHRUB, GARDENIA IS KNOWN AS THE "HAPPINESS HERB" AS IT IS SAID TO IMPROVE LIVER FUNCTION AND WELL-BEING.

Growing guidelines Plants like humid conditions. Propagate by semiripe cuttings in summer or greenwood cuttings in spring. Young plants will flower the best.

Flowering time Very fragrant single, semidouble or double white, waxy flowers occur in summer followed by oval fruit.

Pest and disease prevention Avoid damaging plants with gardening tools, as such wounds are a common entry point for pests and diseases. Check for mealybugs. If mealybugs, aphids or whiteflies attack, spray with insecticidal soap.

Harvesting and storing Fruits are picked when ripe and dried.

Culinary uses Fruits used in China to flavor tea.

Medicinal uses Fruits have been used for jaundice, hemorrhage, toothache, wounds, sprains and skin infections.

Other uses Volatile oil extracted from gardenia flowers is highly valued for its fragrance in the perfume industry.

Other common names Cape jasmine.

Gentiana lutea   GENTIANACEAE

CLIMATE AND SITE
Zones 5–7. Sun
to partial shade.

IDEAL SOIL
Moist, well-drained,
alkaline soil;
pH 5.5–8.9.

GROWING HABIT
Herbacious
perennial with
simple erect,
hollow stems, oval
veined leaves and
large fleshy roots;
height 3–6 feet
(90–180 cm).

PARTS USED
Roots, rhizomes.

GREAT YELLOW GENTIAN

GENTIAN CONTAINS ONE OF THE MOST
BITTER CHEMICALS KNOWN AND FORMS THE
BENCHMARK FOR GRADING OTHER BITTER
AGENTS. IT IS USED AS A STIMULATING TONIC.

Growing guidelines Propagate by
offshoots in spring, seed sown in
autumn, or by division in autumn.
This plant thrives with little care.
Needs afternoon shade to avoid
leaf browning.

Flowering time Small, tubelike
flowers with starry lobes occur in
clusters in summer. Color is usually
yellow. Flowers only appear on
mature (10 years and older) plants.

Pest and disease prevention Root rot
may be a problem in wet conditions.

Harvesting and storing Roots are
lifted in autumn and dried for use.
This is the main commercial source
of gentian root.

Precautions Not given to people
with stomach ulcers.

Medicinal uses For liver disorders,
gastric infections and for cleaning
wounds. Particularly useful in
anorexia associated with indigestion
as it stimulates the appetite.

Other uses Due to its bitter taste,
gentian is used in commercial
tonics, bitter aperitifs, vermouth
and schnapps.

Gardener's trivia Has been known
to survive for as long as 50 years.

Geranium robertianum

CLIMATE AND SITE
Zones 5–9. Full sun
to partial shade.
Thrives in rocky
soils and on walls.

IDEAL SOIL
Well-drained, sandy
soil; pH 4.3–7.0.

GROWING HABIT
Either annual or
biennial plant;
height 1⅔ feet
(50 cm). Stems are
hairy and can be
reddish in color.
Leaves are palm-
shaped and large.

PARTS USED
Whole plant.

HERB ROBERT

AN OLD MEDICINAL PLANT OF THE MIDDLE
AGES, ITS NAME COMES FROM ST ROBERT
OR POPE ROBERT AND REFLECTS THE
IMPORTANCE THIS PLANT HAS AS A CURE-ALL.

Growing guidelines Propagate with
seed sown in spring or summer.
Grows well. Benefits from an
application of nitrogenous fertilizer.
Plant has an unpleasant fragrance.

Flowering time Simple, pink flowers
are produced in summer through to
autumn. Petals have longitudinal,
white stripes.

Pest and disease prevention Prone to
slugs, snails and caterpillars.

Harvesting and storing Plants are
harvested as soon as flowering
begins and can be used fresh or
dried for decoctions.

Medicinal uses For diarrhea,
gastrointestinal infections, bleeding,
skin infections, ulcers, wounds
and inflamed gums. Leaves can
be chewed or used to treat
inflammation in the throat and
mouth. Also used as an eyewash.

Other common names Red Robin.

Other species American cranesbill
G. maculatum is a clump-forming
perennial with deeply divided,
palmate leaves and pink, round
flowers followed by beaked fruits.
Used for diarrhea and to control
bleeding and gum inflammations.

Ginkgo biloba

CLIMATE AND SITE
Zones 4–8.
Full sun.

IDEAL SOIL
Deep, moist,
humus-rich,
well-drained soil;
pH 5.3–6.9.

GROWING HABIT
Deciduous,
pyramidal-shaped
tree with fan-
shaped leaves
that turn yellow in
autumn; height to
120 feet (36 m).

PARTS USED
Leaves, seeds.

GINKGO

AN ANCIENT SPECIES OF PLANT THAT IS
OFTEN REFERRED TO AS A "LIVING FOSSIL,"
GINKGO CONTAINS A CHEMICAL THAT IS
IMPORTANT IN BLOCKING ALLERGIC RESPONSES.

Growing guidelines Plants are either
male or female; take cuttings of
male trees in summer. Female trees
bear evil-smelling fruit and are not
desirable as a garden tree. Seed can
be sown when ripe in autumn.

Flowering time Inconspicuous,
greenish flowers occur in early
spring on female plants, followed
by small, yellow, unpleasant-
smelling seeds. Fruiting only occurs
when male and female plants are
grown together and if conditions
are warm.

Pest and disease prevention Usually
free from pests and diseases.

Harvesting and storing Leaves are
picked in autumn as they change
color and are dried. Seed kernels
are cooked for use in medicinal
preparations.

Precautions Excess can cause
diarrhea and vomiting. The seed
pulp can cause dermatitis.

Culinary uses Nuts or inner kernels
are roasted and eaten.

Medicinal uses For allergic
inflammatory responses and asthma.
Helps to improve circulation by
dilating blood vessels.

Glycyrrhiza glabra

CLIMATE AND SITE
Zones 8–10.
Full sun.

IDEAL SOIL
Deep, rich, moist
soil; pH 6.5–7.8.

GROWING HABIT
Hardy stoloniferous
perennial with
long, narrow
leaflets; wrinkled
and brown
branching taproot
with yellow flesh;
height 2–5 feet
(60–150 cm).

PARTS USED
Roots, stolons.

LICORICE

THE BITTERSWEET LICORICE ROOT HAS BEEN ENJOYED AS A NATURAL CONFECTION FOR THOUSANDS OF YEARS. IT IS A PERENNIAL LEGUME AND NATIVE TO THE MEDITERRANEAN.

Growing guidelines Divide rootstocks or take stolon cuttings in autumn and spring, or propagate by seed in spring or autumn. Slow to grow from seed. Remove flower heads to encourage stronger roots and stolons.

Flowering time Pale blue or purplish flowers appear in summer followed by reddish brown pods.

Pest and disease prevention Usually free from pests and diseases.

Harvesting and storing Roots and stolons are lifted in early autumn 3–4 years after planting and dried for decoctions, liquid extracts, lozenges and powder.

Culinary uses Used as a flavoring in confectionery, ice cream and beverages. Roots are boiled to extract the familiar black substance used in licorice candy. It contains a substance many times sweeter than sugar and can be used by diabetics.

Medicinal uses For constipation, asthma, bronchitis, coughs, shingles and eczema.

Other uses Licorice is a basis for most commercial laxatives. Also used to flavor tobacco, beer, soft drinks and pharmaceutical products.

Hamamelis virginiana

CLIMATE AND SITE
Zones 5–9. Full sun to partial shade.

IDEAL SOIL
Moist, humus-rich garden soil; pH 6.0–7.0.

GROWING HABIT
Deciduous shrub or small tree with smooth, gray to brown bark; height 8–15 feet (2.4–4.5 m).

PARTS USED
Leaves, branches, twigs, bark.

WITCH HAZEL

THE FORKED BRANCHES OF WITCH HAZEL ARE USED AS WATER DIVINING RODS AND AN EXTRACT FROM ITS BARK HAS BEEN A POPULAR ASTRINGENT FOR CENTURIES.

Growing guidelines Propagate by seed planted outdoors in autumn. Germination is slow and erratic and can take 2 years. Or take cuttings or layerings from established plants.

Flowering time Autumn; yellow threadlike petals followed by black seed capsules.

Pest and disease prevention Usually free from pests and diseases.

Harvesting and storing Leaves are collected in summer; branches, twigs and bark in spring.

Precautions Can cause skin allergies.

Medicinal uses For dysentery, diarrhea, burns, sore throats and eye and skin inflammations. An infusion of the young, flower-bearing twigs can be used on a compress for bruises, sprains, muscle aches and insect bites.

Other uses In commercial eye drops, skin tonics and skin creams. Also used as an astringent.

Other common names American or Virginian witch hazel.

Gardener's trivia The twigs of witch hazel are often used for water divining.

Helianthus annuus

CLIMATE AND SITE
Zones 5 and
warmer. Full sun.

IDEAL SOIL
Rich, well-drained
soil; pH 6.0–7.5.

GROWING HABIT
Giant tender
annual with erect
stems and large,
drooping flower
heads; height
3–10 feet
(90–300 cm).

PARTS USED
Whole plant,
seeds, oil.

SUNFLOWER

ALL PARTS OF THE SUNFLOWER ARE USABLE.
EACH FLOWER CONTAINS MORE THAN
1,000 SEEDS WHICH HAVE BEEN USED
MEDICINALLY FOR MORE THAN 3,000 YEARS.

Growing guidelines Propagate by
seed sown in spring. Sow ½ inch
(12 mm) deep and 6 inches (15 cm)
apart. Thin to stand 1½–2 feet
(45–60 cm) apart. Cultivate or
mulch. Drought-tolerant, but regular
watering will produce larger seed
heads. Avoid planting near potatoes
as growth may become stunted.

Flowering time Yellow-petaled
flowers in summer with heads
up to 1 foot (30 cm) across; disc
flowers are red or purple, or
possibly brown, but cultivars vary.

Pest and disease prevention Provide
good air circulation to avoid
mildew. Stems may collapse
through *Sclerotinia* rot. Flowers
attract beneficial insects, such as
lacewings and parasitic wasps,
which eat such pests as aphids.

Harvesting and storing Whole plants
are cut as flowering begins. Seeds
are collected in autumn. Rub the
seed heads to dislodge the seeds
and store them in airtight containers
in a cool place. Keep well watered
and cut and dry the heads when
they start to droop.

Special tips Sunflowers bloom
relatively quickly but take a long
time to ripen their seeds. Very

Sunflower continued

The sunflower has always been revered as an emblem of the sun. The seeds are arranged in concentric spirals, forming stunning geometric patterns.

heavy heads may need support. Sunflowers tend to drop their leaves along the bottom half of their stem, so place them in the middle or back of borders where other plants will hide their bare bottom stems.

Precautions Contact with the leaves and stalks may cause skin allergies.

Culinary uses The oil is used for cooking and salads. Seeds are used in cereals and breads, either roasted or fresh.

Medicinal uses For tuberculosis, malaria, kidney inflammation, coughs and bronchial infections. Also as a massage oil. In China, flower parts used for arthritis.

Other uses The oil is used in the manufacture of margarine. Once the oil has been processed, the waste product is used for cattle feed. The flowers are used to make a yellow dye. The fibers of the stems are used to make paper.

Other cultivars *H. annuus* 'Italian White' has small, black-centered cream flowers; height 4 feet (1.2 m). *H. annuus* 'Teddy Bear' is a dwarf plant with yellow double blooms; height 2 feet (60 cm).

Gardener's trivia The flower head will rotate so that it always faces the sun. The botanical name comes from the Greek *helios*, meaning sun, and *anthos,* which means flower.

Humulus lupulus

CLIMATE AND SITE
Zones 5–9,
however may stand
temperatures that
are lower. Prefers
full sun.

IDEAL SOIL
Moist, rich soil;
pH 6.0–7.0.

GROWING HABIT
Prickly, herbaceous
climbing vine with
dark green, lobed,
grapelike leaves;
height 20–30 feet
(6–9 m).

PARTS USED
Leaves, shoots,
flowers, oil.

HOP

A PILLOW STUFFED WITH HOPS IS SOPORIFIC
AND RELAXING. HOP IS AN ATTRACTIVE
VINING PERENNIAL FOR ARBORS AND SCREENS,
AND AN ESSENTIAL INGREDIENT IN BEER.

Growing guidelines Take basal
cuttings in spring and grow singly
in pots for 1 year before planting
out, then plant in clumps, up to five
plants spaced 6 inches (15 cm)
apart. Place poles for the twining
stems at the base of plants. In
autumn, remove both poles and
old growth. Mulch with compost
or well-rotted manure each spring.
Seed is slow to germinate so is
not good for propagation.

Flowering time Late summer; bears
male and female flowers on separate
plants the third year; female flowers
resemble papery cones.

Pest and disease prevention Check
for aphids and mites.

Harvesting and storing Flowers are
picked in late summer when mature
and immediately dried. Young
shoots harvested in spring for
culinary use. Does not store well.

Culinary uses Hops are the main
flavoring in beer. Oil is used in soft
drinks and food flavoring. Young
shoots can be eaten.

Medicinal uses For insomnia,
irritable bowel syndrome, anxiety,
eczema, herpes and ulcers.

Hydrangea arborescens

CLIMATE AND SITE
Zones 5–9. Sun to
partial shade; frost-
resistant but
drought-tender.

IDEAL SOIL
Rich, moist soil;
pH 4.5–8.0. The
pH determines
color of flowers.

GROWING HABIT
Deciduous shrub;
height 3–10 feet
(90–300 cm). Stems
are numerous with
layered bark;
leaves toothed.

PARTS USED
Roots.

HYDRANGEA

HYDRANGEA'S CUP-SHAPED FRUITS ARE DESCRIBED IN ITS BOTANICAL NAME, WHICH IS ADAPTED FROM THE GREEK FOR "WATER VESSEL." THERE ARE 23 SPECIES.

Growing guidelines Propagate by softwood cuttings taken in summer and autumn. Prune back previous year's flowering shoots to pairs of plump buds in early spring. Remove dead flower heads.

Flowering time In summer, small white flowers sometimes tinged pink or purple occur in rounded or globular clusters.

Pest and disease prevention As long as hydrangeas receive regular watering, they are generally healthy.

Plants can be attacked by aphids, red spider mites and scales.

Harvesting and storing Roots are lifted in autumn and dried for use in extracts and tinctures.

Special tips Color of flowers in non-white common hydrangeas is determined by the pH of the soil. Flowers will be blue in acid soil; pink in alkaline soil.

Precautions Excess may cause dizziness and congestion.

Medicinal uses For kidney and bladder stones, arthritis and gout.

Other common names Sevenbark, hills of snow.

Hypericum perforatum

CLIMATE AND SITE
Zones 5–8. Full sun
to partial shade.

IDEAL SOIL
Well-drained to dry
soil; pH 4.5–8.0.

GROWING HABIT
Weedy perennial;
height 10–36 inches
(25–90 cm). Stem
branched; leaves
small and oval-
shaped with oil
glands on the
surface; small,
black dots on
the edges.

PARTS USED
Whole plant.

ST JOHN'S WORT

WHEN CRUSHED OR SOAKED IN OIL,
ST JOHN'S WORT FLOWERS EXUDE A BRIGHT
RED PIGMENT SIMILAR TO BLOOD, WHICH IS
A REASON FOR THIS PLANT'S SIGNIFICANCE.

Growing guidelines Set plants 2 feet
(60 cm) apart in spring or autumn.
Prune stems back in early spring.
Propagate by cuttings after flowering,
or by seed in spring and division
in autumn.

Flowering time Flowers occur in
summer and early autumn and are
five-petaled, golden-yellow with
glandular, black dots that exude
brown oil when pressed.

Pests and disease prevention Usually
trouble-free; watch for rust.

Harvesting and storing Plants are
harvested as flowering begins and
either used fresh or dried for use
in liquid extracts or medicated oils.

Precautions Use only under
professional supervision.

Medicinal uses For depression,
premenstrual tension, shingles and
sciatica; used recently in drug trials
for AIDS. Also for wounds, bruising
and burns.

Other uses As a red dye and in
cosmetics. Also used traditionally
in anointing oil.

Gardener's trivia This herb has been
valued for centuries for its reputed
ability to protect from evil.

Hyssopus officinalis   LAMIACEAE

CLIMATE AND SITE
Zones 3–9. Full sun
to partial shade.

IDEAL SOIL
Light, well-drained
soil; pH 7.0–8.5.

GROWING HABIT
Semi-evergreen
perennial with
woody base and
narrow, aromatic
leaves; height to
2 feet (60 cm).

PARTS USED
Whole plant,
leaves.

HYSSOP

THE BLOSSOMS OF THIS SHRUBBY PLANT
ATTRACT HONEYBEES AND OTHER BENEFICIAL
INSECTS. THE LEAVES HAVE A MINTY AROMA.
THE OIL IS USED IN LIQUEURS.

Growing guidelines Sow seed about
¼ inch (6 mm) deep in early
spring, thinning to 1 foot (30 cm).
Take cuttings or divide mature
plants in spring or autumn. Prune
to 6 inches (15 cm) in spring and
lightly mulch with compost. Trim
hedges and cut plants back hard in
spring. Replace every 4–5 years.
Hyssop can be grown indoors.

Flowering time Summer; dense
spikes of blue or violet flowers
in whorls along the stem tops.

Pest and disease prevention Usually
free from pests and diseases.

Harvesting and storing For
medicinal use, harvest only green
material. Cut stems just before
flowers open and hang in bunches
to dry; store in an airtight container.

Special tips Excellent border plant
in knot gardens. It is an excellent
plant for attracting beneficials to
the garden.

Precautions High doses of the
essential oil may cause convulsions.
This plant is subject to legal
restrictions in some countries.
Should not be taken by pregnant
or breastfeeding women.

Hyssop continued

Hyssop is an ancient herb that is mentioned several times in the Old Testament as being used for purification. It was once one of the best-known medicinal herbs.

Culinary uses The leaves are bitter and have a sage-mint flavor. Use sparingly in meat dishes and with legumes. Use also with game, fish, vegetables and kidneys. Serve with cranberries in fruit salads. Flowers can be added to salads.

Medicinal uses A hot tea of the leaves and flowers, or just the flowers, can be drunk at the early stages of colds and flu to promote sweating, or at any time there is chest congestion or coughing to promote expectoration. Also used for bronchitis, upper respiratory tract infections, flatulence, cuts, burns and bruises. Essential oil is used in aromatherapy for bruises.

Other uses To flavor liqueurs, such as Chartreuse.

Other cultivars White hyssop *H. officinalis* f. *albus* is an excellent plant for informal hedges, with flowers that are pure white; height 1½–2 feet (45–60 cm).
Rock hyssop *H. officinalis* subsp. *aristatus* is a low-growing, colorful, late-flowering shrub.

Gardener's trivia The mold that produces penicillin grows on the leaf of hyssop. Lepers were bathed in hyssop, which may have acted as an antibiotic. *Hyssopus* is the name that Hippocrates used for this herb and it is derived from the Hebrew *ezob*, which means holy herb.

Inula helenium

CLIMATE AND SITE
Zones 5–9. Full
sun to light shade.

IDEAL SOIL
Moderately fertile,
moist soil;
pH 6.5–7.0.

GROWING HABIT
Branched perennial
with large, elliptical
basal leaves and
smaller, oblong
top leaves; height
to 6 feet (1.8 m).

PARTS USED
Roots, flowers,
oil.

ELECAMPANE

OTHERWISE KNOWN AS WILD SUNFLOWER,
ELECAMPANE IS A TALL PERENNIAL WITH
HAIRY STEMS AND BRIGHT YELLOW DAISY
FLOWERS. IT IS USED IN WINES AND CORDIALS.

Growing guidelines Sow seed
outdoors in spring, or collect root
cuttings from mature plants in
autumn; winter them in frame pots,
setting plants out in the garden the
following spring.

Flowering time Summer months;
daisy-like yellow flowers 3–4 inches
(7.5–10 cm) across.

Pest and disease prevention Usually
trouble-free but can be vulnerable
to pests that suck juices from
leaves. Control with pyrethrin.

Harvesting and storing Collect roots
for medicinal and culinary use in
the autumn of the plant's second
season, after several hard frosts.
Dry them thoroughly before storing.

Special tips It is best propagated by
offsets taken in autumn from the
old root, with a bud or eye to each.

Culinary uses As a flavoring for
desserts and sweets. The roots can
also be candied. Also used in wine.

Medicinal uses As a remedy for
chest ailments, hay fever, asthma,
stomach aches and as a skin wash
for ulcers.

Other common names Wild
sunflower, scabwort, velvet dock.

Iris 'Florentina'

CLIMATE AND SITE
Zones 4–9.
Full sun.

IDEAL SOIL
Deep, rich,
well-drained soil;
pH 6.7–7.3.

GROWING HABIT
Perennial with
sword-shaped
leaves, overlapping
at the base; height
to 2½ feet (75 cm).

PARTS USED
Rhizomes.

ORRIS

THE DRIED ROOT OF ORRIS IS USED AS A
FIXATIVE IN PERFUMERY AND POTPOURRI AND
HAS A STRONG VIOLET FRAGRANCE. IT IS
ALSO USED IN DENTAL PRODUCTS.

Growing guidelines Plant after
flowering, leaving the top surface
of the rhizome above soil. Divide
the roots every 2–3 years in late
spring or early autumn, to promote
vigorous flowering. Half the divided
root should be left above the soil so
that it doesn't rot. The rhizomatous
roots smell of violets.

Flowering time Spring or early
summer; blossoms are large, white
and tinged with blue or purple,
with yellow beards.

Pest and disease prevention Usually
free from pests and diseases.

Harvesting and storing Harvest orris
at maturity. If using the roots for
their aroma, dig them up in
autumn. Wash and split them, then
cut them into small pieces before
drying. Grind them to a powder.
Store in a dark glass container for
at least 2 years; the violet fragrance
needs this time to mature.

Medicinal uses For coughs, excess
mucus, diarrhea and for deep cuts.
All iris species are harmful if eaten.

Other uses Added to breath
fresheners and dental products.
Used as a fixative in perfumery.

Jasminum officinale

CLIMATE AND SITE
Zones 7–10.
Full sun to
partial shade.

IDEAL SOIL
Moist, well-drained
soil; pH 4.2–6.5.

GROWING HABIT
Vigorous,
deciduous climber
with twining green
stems and soft,
pointed leaflets;
height 30 feet
(9 m).

PARTS USED
Flowers, oil.

COMMON JASMINE

THIS VIGOROUS, SEMI-EVERGREEN VINE OR
LOOSE SHRUB HAS DELIGHTFULLY FRAGRANT
WHITE FLOWERS AND IS AN EXCELLENT PLANT
FOR GROWING ON TRELLISES.

Growing guidelines Take cuttings
during active growth in spring
or autumn, or by layering in
autumn. Thin out shoots and
cut back after flowering. Keep
soil moist in summer.

Flowering time Very fragrant white
flowers occur in summer and early
autumn. Prune after flowering to
keep vigorous growth under control.

Pest and disease prevention Prone to
red spider mites (two-spotted mites),
aphids, whiteflies and mealybugs.

Harvesting and storing Flowers are
picked early in the morning and
used fresh for oil extraction or dried
for teas and powders.

Culinary uses Essential oil used to
flavor Maraschino cherries. Flowers
used to flavor tea.

Medicinal uses Mainly used in
aromatherapy for depression, weak
digestion and menstrual disorders.

Other uses Essential oil used in
perfume and soap.

Other species Arabian jasmine
J. sambac is an evergreen rambler
with white to purple-pink flowers.
Used mainly as a flavoring for
Chinese green tea.

Juglans regia

JUGLANDACEAE

CLIMATE AND SITE
Zones 4–8.
Full sun.

IDEAL SOIL
Deep, well-drained,
fertile soil;
pH 4.3–6.7.

GROWING HABIT
Hardy, deciduous
tree; height 100 feet
(30 m). Bark is a
silver-gray, and
leaves are dark
green, divided and
aromatic. Young
leaflets are bronze.

PARTS USED
Leaves, bark, fruits.

WALNUT

CULTIVATED SINCE ROMAN TIMES FOR THEIR
NUTS AND OIL, WALNUTS ARE THOUGHT TO
HAVE ANTICANCER PROPERTIES. THEY HAVE
BEEN WIDELY USED AS LAXATIVES.

Growing guidelines Propagate by
grafting or by seed sown in autumn.

Flowering time A tree has flowers
of both sexes; male flowers are
dark yellow catkins; female flowers
are upright spikes. Flowers appear
in late spring to summer and are
followed by dark green fruits,
which contain a woody nut.

Pest and disease prevention Prone
to bacterial walnut blight.

Harvesting and storing Fruits are
collected both ripe and unripe.

The kernels, or nuts, are pressed
for oil, and eaten fresh. Leaves are
picked through the growing season.
Bark is stripped anytime.

Culinary uses Nuts are popular as
a snack food; also used in cakes,
sweets, bread and regional dishes.
Oil is used in salad dressing and for
frying. Unripe fruits are pickled,
preserved and used in liqueur.

Medicinal uses For constipation,
asthma, eye problems and hair loss.

Other uses A highly valued wood
in furniture making. Oil is used in
paint manufacture and cosmetics.
Leaves and husks used to produce
a brown dye.

Juniperus communis

CUPRESSACEAE

CLIMATE AND SITE
Zones 3–9. Full sun
to light shade.

IDEAL SOIL
Tolerates different
soils, wet and dry,
acid and alkaline;
pH 4.2–8.2.

GROWING HABIT
Upright or prostrate
shrub with papery,
red-brown bark
and spiky, needle-
like foliage; height
to 20 feet (6 m).

PARTS USED
Berries, oil.

COMMON JUNIPER

JUNIPER IS AN EVERGREEN, CONIFEROUS
SHRUB THAT HAS BEEN USED FOR CENTURIES
FOR ITS MEDICINAL PROPERTIES. IT IS BITTER
WITH ANTISEPTIC AND DIURETIC PROPERTIES.

Growing guidelines Take heel
cuttings in late summer, autumn or
winter. Remove seed from its fleshy
covering and sow in autumn. Grow
seedlings in nursery rows outdoors
for 1 or 2 years before planting in
permanent positions. Both male and
female plants needed for berries.

Flowering time Inconspicuous
spring flowers, yellow on the male,
greenish on the female, followed by
small fruit on the female. Fruits are
green at first, turning dark blue
when ripe.

Pest and disease prevention Prone
to juniper scale, mites and blight.

Harvesting and storing Berries are
harvested by shaking the branches
and are used fresh for oil distillation
or dried for other uses.

Precautions May cause skin allergies.

Culinary uses Berries added to
game dishes, pickles, pork and ham.

Medicinal uses For poor digestion,
kidney inflammation, rheumatism
and rheumatic pain.

Other uses Oil distilled from the
berries and used to flavor the
alcoholic drink gin. Oil also used
in spicy fragrances.

Laurus nobilis

CLIMATE AND SITE
Zones 8–10, but needs a sheltered site in colder areas. Full sun to partial shade.

IDEAL SOIL
Rich, well-drained soil; pH 6.0–7.0.

GROWING HABIT
Evergreen tree; height up to 50 feet (15 m) but easily kept to any desired size with pruning. Slow growing.

PARTS USED
Leaves.

BAY, SWEET

BAY IS THE ONLY LAUREL THAT IS NOT POISONOUS. BAY LEAF GARLANDS REPRESENT VICTORY. USE LEAVES FOR FLAVOR IN SOUPS AND STEWS. ADD LEAVES TO POTPOURRI.

Growing guidelines Take cuttings from fresh green shoots in autumn and keep the soil in which you plant them moist, since rooting may take 3–9 months. In warm climates, sow seed outdoors; germination may require 6–12 months. Transplant to 4 feet (1.2 m) apart. Grows well in pots in cold areas if moved indoors during winter; survives moderate frost in the garden. Trim away roots from large, potbound plants and add fresh compost to stimulate new growth.

Flowering time Spring; inconspicuous, yellowish flowers; rarely flowers in pots.

Pest and disease prevention Usually trouble-free.

Harvesting and storing Best used fresh, but the leathery leaves can be dried and stored in airtight jars.

Culinary uses Add to sauces, soups, stews; in bouquet garni.

Medicinal uses For indigestion, colic, flatulence, sprains, rheumatism and scabies.

Other common names True laurel.

Gardener's trivia The family name means "crowned with laurels."

Lavandula angustifolia

LAVENDER, ENGLISH

MOST HERB GROWERS NEVER HAVE ENOUGH LAVENDER. THE SILVERY FOLIAGE AND PURPLE BLOSSOMS ARE STUNNING IN BORDERS, AND THE BLOSSOMS ATTRACT BEES.

Growing guidelines As seeds do not always produce plants identical to the original, the best way to propagate is by cuttings 2–3 inches (5–7.5 cm) long, taken from side-shoots in spring or autumn; space 1–2½ feet (30–75 cm) apart. Place cuttings in a well-drained medium; transplant them as soon as they root to avoid rot. Pinch away flowers on first-year plants to encourage vigorous growth. Provide shelter from winter winds; in areas with cold, wet winters, loose, well-drained soil is the secret to success. Some growers find that plants will weaken with age and may need replacing every 5 years. Remove old plants each spring, and lightly mulch before planting new, young plants. The hardiness of lavender varies with each species, but generally plants are extremely drought-tolerant. Prune immediately after flowering.

Flowering time Summer; lavender-blue blossoms on tall spikes.

Pest and disease prevention Usually free from pests and diseases.

Harvesting and storing For the most intense scent in fresh and dried

Lavender continued

CLIMATE AND SITE
Zones 5–9. Full sun
to light shade.

IDEAL SOIL
Light, well-drained,
ideally limey soil.
Neutral or slightly
alkaline is best;
pH 6.7–8.0.

GROWING HABIT
Small shrub with
downy, slender
leaves, white at
first turning gray-
green; height to
3 feet (90 cm).

PARTS USED
Flowers, oil.

Italian or spike lavender produces more oil than English lavender.
It is sometimes mixed with higher-quality lavender oil to add bulk.

arrangements, gather the flower stems just as the flowers are opening, preferably in dry weather. The leaves, which are bitter and sometimes used in European cooking, can be harvested after the first year of growth and then picked at any time. Hang bunches of lavender upside-down, away from sunlight, to dry.

Special tips Plant lavender as a hedge or border, or to configure knot gardens. In borders, combine lavender with other plants that need excellent drainage, such as yarrow and rosemary. Incorporate lavender into vegetable and ornamental gardens to increase populations of visiting beneficial insects. Excess soil fertility will make the silver-gray foliage fade to green.

Culinary uses Fresh flowers are crystallized; can be added to jams, ice creams and vinegar; as a garnish.

Medicinal uses For depression, anxiety, indigestion, migraines, bronchitis, sunburn, other minor burns, muscular pain, cold sores, halitosis and vaginal discharge.

Other uses Oil is used in perfumes, toiletries and cleaning products. Also added to baths for people suffering nervous tension and insomnia. Dried flowers are used in potpourris and herbal crafts.

Lavender continued

French lavender has attractive, fernlike leaves with a rosemary-like scent. It is less hardy than English lavender and makes an interesting and fragrant pot plant.

Other species French lavender *L. dentata* is less hardy than English lavender. It has a rosemary-like scent. Mainly grown as an ornamental, but the flowers can be dried for herbal crafts and potpourris.

Lavandin *L.* x *intermedia* is an aromatic herb with a camphoraceous lavender scent. Fresh flowers are crystallized; dried flowers are added to herb pillows. The oil is used in perfumes and cleaning products.

Italian lavender *L. latifolia* produces more oil of a lesser quality than English lavender. The oil is distilled from glands around tiny hairs on the flowers, leaves and stems.

Spanish lavender *L. stoechas* is an antiseptic herb with a balsam-like scent. It helps digestion, relaxes muscle spasms, repels insects and has a mild sedative property that can help the nervous system.

Giant lavender *L.* x *allardii* is a hybrid with broad, gray-green leaves and violet-purple flowers. It is used mainly in the perfume industry. Flowers used in potpourri.

Common lavender *L. angustifolia* 'Hidcote' is a compact plant with strongly scented, deep purple flowers. Popular cultivar for hedges.

Gardener's trivia The fresh, clean scent of lavender was the favorite additive to the bathwater of the Greeks and Romans and its name derives from the Latin "to wash."

Leptospermum scoparium

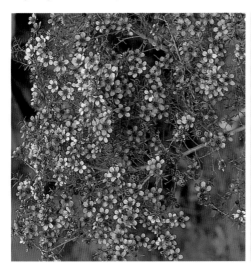

CLIMATE AND SITE
Zones 8–10. Prefers a warm temperate climate with full sun. Thrives in coastal gardens.

IDEAL SOIL
Tolerates most soils; pH 4.5–7.8.

GROWING HABIT
A compact evergreen shrub; height to 10 feet (3 m). Slow growing. Leaves needle-like and tapering; bark is brown-gray.

PARTS USED
Leaves.

NEW ZEALAND TEA TREE

THE TEA TREE GETS ITS NAME FROM EARLY NEW ZEALAND SETTLERS WHO USED THE LEAVES AS A SUBSTITUTE FOR TEA. IT IS NOW GROWN WORLDWIDE AS AN ORNAMENTAL.

Growing guidelines Propagate from seed or semihardwood cuttings struck in a sandy mix in summer.

Flowering time Profusion of small, scented, white to pale pink or purplish blooms from spring to summer.

Pest and disease prevention Prone to scales with associated black smut and webbing caterpillars.

Harvesting and storing Leaves are picked at any time of year; oil extracted by steam distillation.

Special tips Prone to transplant shock; do not allow to dry out when becoming established. This tree can resist drought as well as wind, including salt winds.

Medicinal uses Used by New Zealand and Australian settlers as an aromatic tea to combat scurvy. New Zealand Maoris used it for diarrhea, dysentery, coughs and fevers. Also used to relieve aches and pains and to relax tight muscles. The oil can be used neat on the skin for rashes and wounds. Also used for acne, athlete's foot, cold sores, warts, ringworm and insect bites.

Other common names Manuka.

Levisticum officinale

CLIMATE AND SITE
Zones 5–9. Prefers full sun to partial shade.

IDEAL SOIL
Fertile, moist, but well-drained soil; pH 6.0–7.0.

GROWING HABIT
Perennial with hollow, ribbed stems and toothed, divided green leaves; height 6 feet (1.8 m).

PARTS USED
Leaves, stems, roots, seeds, oil.

LOVAGE

IF YOU ARE UNSUCCESSFUL GROWING CELERY, TRY THIS EASY AND FLAVORFUL SUBSTITUTE. IT CAN ALSO IMPROVE THE GROWTH AND FLAVOR OF VEGETABLE CROPS.

Growing guidelines Sow ripe seed shallowly in late summer or early autumn; thin to 3 feet (90 cm) apart. Prune away flowers to encourage vegetative growth. Each spring, mulch with compost. Replace plants every 4–5 years.

Flowering time Summer; tiny green-yellow flowers in umbels.

Pest and disease prevention Usually free from pests and diseases.

Harvesting and storing Once established, harvest leaves as needed for fresh use. In autumn, bunch foliage and stems and hang to dry. Or blanch small bunches before freezing for winter use. Seeds are ripe and ready to harvest when the fruits begin to split open. Dig roots in late autumn, wash and slice before drying.

Culinary uses Blanch young shoots and eat as a vegetable. Stalks can be candied. Leaves added to soup, salads and savory dishes. They add a strong flavor so use cautiously at first. Oil is used in commercial food flavoring.

Medicinal uses For indigestion, flatulence, kidney stones, colic and sore throats.

Magnolia officinalis

CLIMATE AND SITE
Zones 8–10. Full
sun to partial shade
with shelter from
cold winds.

IDEAL SOIL
Moist, humus-rich,
well-drained soil;
pH 4.2–7.0.

GROWING HABIT
Deciduous tree
with gray, peeling
bark and tongue-
shaped leaves that
have a downy
underside; height
to 75 feet (22 m).

PARTS USED
Bark, flowers.

MAGNOLIA

THIS ORNAMENTAL TREE IS A FEATURE PLANT
WITH ITS BEAUTIFUL WATERLILY-LIKE FLOWERS
AND FRAGRANCE. IT IS AMONGST THE MOST
EXOTIC OF FLOWERING TREES.

Growing guidelines Remove seed
from its covering and sow in
autumn or take cuttings in summer.
Graft in winter.

Flowering time Strongly scented,
creamy white flowers appear in late
spring and early summer followed
by red-seeded, strawberry-like fruit.
Prune after flowering only if
necessary to shape the tree.

Pest and disease prevention Prone to
scales and root rot. If scales attack
causing yellow leaves, prune out
any badly affected growth and
spray the remaining stems with
horticultural oil.

Harvesting and storing Flower buds
are picked in spring while flowers
are collected in summer when
open. Bark is collected in autumn
and dried. Its aromatic properties
don't keep well, so the bark needs
to be collected on a regular basis.

Medicinal uses For asthma, coughs,
diarrhea and vomiting. Magnolia
contains a compound that has
important muscle-relaxant properties.

Other uses The Chinese used the
fibers from the wood of the
magnolia as a source of paper.

Marrubium vulgare

CLIMATE AND SITE
Zones 4–9. Full sun
to partial shade.

IDEAL SOIL
Average, well-
drained, fairly
neutral to alkaline
garden soil on
the dry side;
pH 6.7–7.5.

GROWING HABIT
Perennial with
branching, square
stems and round to
oval, woolly leaves;
height 2–3 feet
(60–90 cm).

PARTS USED
Whole plant.

HOREHOUND

PLANT THIS ORNAMENTAL, AROMATIC
PERENNIAL TO ATTRACT BEES. THE MENTHOL-
FLAVORED LEAVES ARE SAID TO SOOTHE
COUGHS WHEN TAKEN AS A SYRUP.

Growing guidelines Sow seed
⅛ inch (3 mm) deep in early
spring, and thin to 10–20 inches
(25–50 cm). Horehound germinates
slowly, then grows easily. Divide
mature plants in spring. Plant in
a well-drained location, because
horehound will die in winter in wet
soil. In good conditions it becomes
weedy. Thrives on roadsides.

Flowering time Summer; first
blooms are fairly insignificant white
flowers arranged in whorls around
the upper part of the stems, but
during the second year, small,
white, tubular blooms in dense
whorls are produced in the upper
leaf axils. The flowers die off,
leaving a spiny burr containing four
small brown or black seeds.

Pest and disease prevention Usually
free from pests and diseases.

Harvesting and storing Cut foliage
sparingly in the first year. In the
second year, harvest leaves when
flower buds appear.

Precautions Causes irregular
heartbeat if overused internally.

Medicinal uses For bronchitis,
asthma, coughs, skin problems and
minor cuts.

Melissa officinalis

CLIMATE AND SITE
Zones 4–9. Full sun to partial shade.

IDEAL SOIL
Any well-drained soil; pH 6.7–7.3.

GROWING HABIT
Perennial with branching square stems and oval, toothed, fragrant leaves; height 1–2 feet (30–60 cm).

PARTS USED
Whole plant, leaves, oil.

LEMON BALM

LEMON BALM HAS LEMON-SCENTED LEAVES AND IS A POPULAR TEA FOR ITS CALMING PROPERTIES. THE SMALL, WHITE FLOWERS ATTRACT MANY BENEFICIAL INSECTS.

Growing guidelines Sow shallowly in spring, thinning to 1½–2 feet (45–60 cm); slow to germinate; readily self-sows. Take cuttings or divide older plants in spring or autumn. Each autumn, cut away old stalks. Mulch each spring to keep the soil moist and weeds at bay. Small plants can be grown indoors.

Flowering time Summer to autumn; small, two-lipped, pale yellowish green maturing through to white tubular blossoms in bunches in the leaf axils.

Pest and disease prevention Thin dense plantings for best air circulation to prevent powdery mildew. Rarely bothered by insects.

Harvesting and storing Collect leaves in summer, use fresh, or dry quickly to prevent them from turning black. Their flavor is best when the flowers begin to open. Cut the entire plant, leaving about 2 inches (5 cm) of stem.

Special tips Lemon balm is said to repel insect pests.

Culinary uses Fresh leaves with a lemon flavor can be added to salads, soup, herb vinegar, game and fish. Add to fruit salads, jellies,

Lemon balm continued

Lemon balm's virtue of dispelling melancholy has been noted for centuries by herbal writers. It has been cultivated for more than 2,000 years and is still widely used today.

custards and fruit drinks. Infuse fresh leaves for tea. Also used in liqueurs, such as Benedictine and Chartreuse, and in wine.

Medicinal uses For indigestion, depression, headaches, insect bites, herpes, feverish colds and gout. Also as a sedative.

Other uses Dried leaves are added to potpourris and herb pillows. The oil is used in aromatherapy to relax and rejuvenate the body and to counter depression and nervous tension.

Other common names Sweet balm.

Other cultivars *M. officinalis* 'All Gold' has bright yellow foliage.

Plant it in damp, shady parts of the garden as it scorches in full sun; height 1–2 feet (30–60 cm). *M. officinalis* 'Aurea' is very similar to the species but it has yellow-variegated leaves. The color fades in summer, but to encourage a new crop of young foliage, cut back plants after flowering; height to 2 feet (60 cm).

Gardener's trivia The leaves lowest on the plant are said to be highest in essential oils. Lemon balm was originally grown as a bee plant, which is where its botanical name comes from—*Melissa* is the Greek word for "honeybee." It was once used as a strewing herb.

Mentha pulegium

CLIMATE AND SITE
Zones 7–9. Full sun
to partial shade.

IDEAL SOIL
Moist, loamy soil;
pH 6.0–7.0.

GROWING HABIT
Creeping perennial;
mat-forming with
flowering, square
stems; hairy,
grayish green
leaves that have a
strong peppermint
scent; height to
1 foot (30 cm).

PARTS USED
Whole plant,
leaves, oil.

PENNYROYAL

PENNYROYAL IS AN ATTRACTIVE AND LOW-MAINTENANCE GROUNDCOVER THAT HAS A PLEASANT, MINTLIKE FRAGRANCE AND REPELS INSECTS. GROW IT BETWEEN PAVING STONES.

Growing guidelines Sow seed shallowly and thickly outdoors in early spring; thin to 6 inches (15 cm). Or take cuttings from stems, which easily root at joints. Divide in spring or autumn. Spreads rapidly. Grows well in containers and can be grown in hanging baskets in shady spots.

Flowering time Summer and early autumn; reddish purple to lilac blossoms in whorls.

Pest and disease prevention Usually free from pests and diseases; pennyroyal growing in the garden will repel mosquitoes and ants.

Harvesting and storing Harvest foliage just before blooming, then hang in bunches to dry; store in an airtight container.

Special tips A powder made from the dried leaves keeps pets free from fleas. Place sprigs under a dog's mat or around the house during a flea plague. Crush the leaves and rub on your skin to repel insects while you work in the garden.

Precautions Should not be taken in excess. Not given to pregnant women or people with kidney problems. Can cause skin irritation.

Pennyroyal continued

Pennyroyal can be grown between paving stones in courtyards, in rockeries or as a lawn. When flowering has finished, the plants can be cut down with the lawnmower.

Culinary uses Pennyroyal is a spicy mint and the leaves can be used the same way as mint, but the taste is much stronger. The leaves can be added to blood sausage (black pudding) in England and sausages in Spain. Also used to flavor pâté. Small amounts can be chopped and added to hot potatoes.

Medicinal uses For indigestion, colic, colds, influenza, excessive menstrual bleeding, skin rashes and irritations. Also used to stimulate the uterus and increase perspiration. It is said to be a helpful herb to use to relieve menstrual cramping.

Other uses Traditionally used to repel mice and insects. Leaves added to potpourris. Oil used in soaps, bath salts and detergents.

Other common names Pudding grass, flea mint.

Other cultivars Creeping pennyroyal *M. pulegium* 'Cunningham Mint' is a low-growing cultivar with lighter, oval-shaped green leaves which are peppermint scented; 4–6 inches (10–15 cm). Can be used in a similar way to pennyroyal.

Gardener's trivia When growing wild in pastures, pennyroyal brings on abortions in cows. It was used in medieval times to mask the taste of rotten meat.

Mentha spp.

CLIMATE AND SITE
Zones 3–10; varies with species. Full sun to partial shade.

IDEAL SOIL
Rich, moist, well-drained garden soil; pH 6.0–7.0.

GROWING HABIT
Aromatic, mainly perennial, with square stems and smooth lancelike leaves; height to 2½ feet (75 cm).

PARTS USED
Whole plant, leaves, oil.

MINT

THE MINTS ARE HERBACEOUS PERENNIALS THAT THRIVE IN MOST LOCATIONS. THE FRESH AND DRIED FOLIAGE PROVIDE FLAVORING FOR BOTH SWEET AND SAVORY DISHES.

Growing guidelines Propagate from new plants that spring up along roots, or by cuttings in spring or autumn. Allow 1–1½ feet (30–45 cm) between plants. Mint is a rampant spreader. To control, plant in bottomless cans 10 inches (25 cm) deep, or in large pots. Cut frequently and severely, or the plant will become woody after several years. Large areas can be mowed frequently like a lawn. Top-dress with compost or well-rotted manure in autumn.

Flowering time Summer; tiny purple or pink blossoms in whorls on spikes along the stem.

Pest and disease prevention Thin crowded clumps for good air circulation to prevent root and foliage diseases. Watch for aphids, which stipple leaves; control them with a strong spray of water or with a botanical insecticide, such as pyrethrin or rotenone.

Harvesting and storing Harvest fresh leaves as needed. Just before blooming, cut the stalks and hang in bunches to dry; store in airtight containers. Leaves can also be frozen or infused in oil or vinegar.

Mint continued

Chocmint is a delightful addition to the garden. Its leaves, when crushed, emit a wonderful chocolate-mint odor very reminiscent of an after-dinner chocolate.

Special tips Mints are said to grow well when planted where water drips, such as near outdoor taps that are used often in summer. Mint oil has many medicinal uses and may have fungicidal or pest-repellent uses; try a homemade spray using the fresh leaves. Any of the mints makes a refreshing addition to ice-cold water in summer and chewing on the leaves will relieve bad breath or a foul taste in the mouth.

Precautions Mints have hairy leaves that can cause skin irritations and rashes. Handle them with care. Mint tea should not be drunk continuously over a long period.

Culinary uses Leaves used to accompany lamb, added to salads, used to flavor sausages, meat dishes, tomatoes and fruit salads. Mint is an important ingredient in Middle Eastern cooking. Also used in teas and ice drinks.

Medicinal uses Peppermint is used for indigestion, colic, colds, excess mucus and nausea. Mint is also used to treat skin irritations, upper respiratory tract infections, minor burns, ringworm and sinusitis.

Other uses Peppermint and eau-de-cologne mint oils are used in oral hygiene preparations, antacids, toiletries, candy, chewing gum, ice cream and liqueurs.

Mint continued

Peppermint is grown on a large scale in Europe, the US, the Middle East and Asia. Its leaves and extracted oil are used to flavor sweet foods as well as toothpastes and medicines.

Other species Apple mint *M. suaveolens* is apple-scented and has broader, hairy leaves. A variegated cultivar is sometimes called pineapple mint.

Corsican mint *M. requienii* has a creeping growth habit. It is good as a groundcover but is less hardy than most mints. It has tiny, bright green leaves with a strong peppermint flavor; also called crème-de-menthe plant.

Eau-de-cologne mint *M.* x *piperita* 'Citrata' has leaves which, when crushed, give off a lemony aroma; also called bergamot mint.

Peppermint *M.* x *piperita* has smooth, lancelike and purple stems; height 2–4 feet (60–120 cm).

Rampant grower with a strong peppermint flavor. Spreads quickly and likes lots of water but rarely bears fertile seeds. Must be started by cuttings or division.

Spearmint *M. spicata* is a creeping, aromatic perennial with bright green, lance-shaped, serrated leaves with a strong, sweet spearmint flavor; height to 3 feet (90 cm).

Water mint *M. aquatica* has lilac flowers and hairy leaves.

Gardener's trivia In Greek mythology, Minthe was a nymph who was a favorite of Pluto. He transformed her into this favorite herb when her husband became jealous of her friendship with Pluto.

Monarda didyma

CLIMATE AND SITE
Zones 4–9. Full sun to partial shade.

IDEAL SOIL
Rich, moist, light garden soil, pH 5.0–7.0.

GROWING HABIT
Aromatic perennial with erect stems and oval shaped, serrated leaves; height 3–4 feet (90–120 cm).

PARTS USED
Whole plant, leaves, flowers.

BEE BALM (BERGAMOT)

THIS NORTH AMERICAN NATIVE HAS A CITRUS FRAGRANCE AND BLOOMS IN A RANGE OF COLORS. A TEA MADE FROM ITS LEAVES WAS DRUNK DURING THE BOSTON TEA PARTY.

Growing guidelines Grow from seed, cuttings or division. Plants grown from seed flower in the second year. Divide established plants every 3 years and discard old growth. For autumn blooms, prune stems back after the first flowering. Grows in quickly spreading clumps.

Flowering time Summer for several weeks; tubular flowers clustered together with bracts that range in color from red and pink to lavender and white.

Pest and disease prevention Plant away from mint, since it attracts the same insect pests. Prune after flowering to discourage sites for foliage diseases.

Harvesting and storing Harvest leaves for tea just before blooming and dry them quickly for best flavor. Pull individual flowers for a fresh salad garnish.

Culinary uses Leaves infused as a tea; also added to fruit salads and stuffing. Flowers added to salads.

Medicinal uses For digestive problems, colds, headaches, sore throats and skin complaints.

Other common names Oswego tea.

Murraya koenigii

CLIMATE AND SITE
Zone 10. Full sun.
Deciduous in
cooler areas.

IDEAL SOIL
Well-drained,
rich, moist soil;
pH 5.2–7.8.

GROWING HABIT
Evergreen tropical
tree with large
pinnate leaves that
have a pungent,
spicy aroma when
fresh; height to
20 feet (6 m).

PARTS USED
Leaves, bark, roots,
seeds, oil.

CURRY LEAF

CURRY LEAVES COME FROM A SMALL,
ORNAMENTAL TREE THAT GROWS WILD IN
SOUTHERN INDIA AND SRI LANKA. THE
LEAVES GIVE OFF A DISTINCT CURRY-LIKE ODOR.

Growing guidelines Grows easily
from seed in tropical conditions,
or propagate by semiripe cuttings in
summer. Prune back excess growth
in late winter.

Flowering time Clusters of tiny
white flowers appear in summer
followed by small, blue-black,
peppery-tasting, edible berries.

Pest and disease prevention Usually
free from pests and diseases.

Harvesting and storing Leaves are
picked all year and used fresh.

Dried curry leaves lose flavor, and
are a poor substitute for the fresh
leaves. Bark and roots are collected
when required and used either fresh
or dried. Oil is extracted from seeds.

Culinary uses Leaves are used in
curries. Sprigs added to soups,
stews, vegetables, rice dishes and
pickles to give a mild curry flavor.

Medicinal uses For digestive
problems, constipation, flatulence,
colic and diarrhea.

Other species Orange jasmine
M. paniculata blooms on and off
all year round, producing white
flowers that smell strongly of
orange blossoms.

Myristica fragrans

CLIMATE AND SITE
Zone 10. Full sun
and high humidity.

IDEAL SOIL
Rich, well-drained,
sandy soil;
pH 4.6–7.0.

GROWING HABIT
Bushy, large,
evergreen tree with
long, shiny leaves
which can be
covered in silvery,
pungent scales
when young;
height 30–50 feet
(9–15 m).

PARTS USED
Seeds, oil.

NUTMEG

THIS UNASSUMING, AROMATIC SPICE WAS RESPONSIBLE FOR THE FIERCE COMPETITION IN THE 16TH CENTURY SURROUNDING THE OWNERSHIP OF THE MOLUCCAS ISLANDS.

Growing guidelines Propagate by hardwood cuttings in autumn, or by seed sown when ripe.

Flowering time Yellow flowers occur in spring, followed by yellow, round to pear-shaped fruits containing an aromatic, brown seed (nutmeg) surrounded by a red starchy material (mace).

Pest and disease prevention Dried seed prone to attack by insects.

Harvesting and storing Nutmeg fruit is picked and left to dry. When dry, the seed coat is removed and the whole nutmeg is then ground for use as a spice. It is best to grate nutmeg when needed, as the ground spice loses flavor with storage.

Culinary uses Widely used in both savory and sweet dishes, bakery products, puddings and drinks. Nutmeg is often used combined with other spices and blends well with a wide variety of flavors. Mace is also ground as a spice.

Medicinal uses For abdominal pains, labor pains, rheumatism, indigestion, vomiting and diarrhea.

Other uses Oil used in perfume, soap and candles.

Myrrhis odorata

CLIMATE AND SITE
Zones 5–9. Partial
shade.

IDEAL SOIL
Rich, moist, well-
drained soil with
humus; pH 6.0–6.7.

GROWING HABIT
Large perennial
with aromatic,
fernlike leaves that
are finely divided;
whitish and spotted
underneath; height
to 3 feet (90 cm).

PARTS USED
Leaves, roots,
seeds.

SWEET CICELY

SWEET CICELY HAS A SCENT LIKE LOVAGE
AND A SWEET LICORICE TASTE. THE LEAVES
CAN BE USED FRESH IN SALADS AND THE
ROOTS COOKED LIKE A VEGETABLE.

Growing guidelines Sow seed
shallowly outdoors in autumn or
spring, thinning to 2 feet (60 cm);
germination is slow; self-sows.
Divide older plants in spring or
autumn, leaving each new piece
with a bud. Mulch each spring with
compost or well-rotted manure.

Flowering time Spring to early
summer; numerous white blossoms
in umbels, followed by shiny,
chocolate-colored fruit 1 inch
(2.5 cm) long with ridged seeds
that have a licorice flavor.

Pest and disease prevention Usually
free from pests and diseases.

Harvesting and storing Collect fresh
leaves as needed all summer. Collect
seed heads and dry on paper in a
shady spot. Dig roots after the first
year, scrub them and dry.

Culinary uses Leaves added to
soups, salads and stews; used as a
low-calorie sweetener for desserts.
Roots are cooked as a vegetable
and added to salads. Seeds used
in salads and desserts.

Medicinal uses For minor digestive
problems and anemia.

Other common names Myrrh, anise,
sweet chervil.

Nasturtium officinale

CLIMATE AND SITE
Zones 6–10. Grow in shallow, flowing water in full sun. Water temperature should not go below 50°F (10°C).

IDEAL SOIL
Slightly alkaline water; pH 6.5–7.9.

GROWING HABIT
Aquatic perennial with rooting stems and glossy, green, pinnate leaves that grow from branch-like stems.

PARTS USED
Leaves.

WATERCRESS

A DARK GREEN HERB WHOSE IDEAL HABITAT IS SHALLOW, FREE-FLOWING WATER. WATERCRESS IS RICH IN VITAMINS AND MINERALS, AND IS A VALUABLE MEDICINAL PLANT.

Growing guidelines Propagate by root cuttings in water during the growing season. Can be grown in pots in a rich potting mix; pots must stand in water that is changed daily. Pinch out to encourage bushiness and delay flowering.

Flowering time Small white flowers occur in late summer.

Pest and disease prevention Prone to aphid attack.

Harvesting and storing Leaves cut as required. Eaten in salads or juiced.

Precautions Watercress should not be harvested from the wild due to the frequent occurrence of pollutants and bacteria in some watercourses.

Culinary uses Leaves add a sharp, peppery zest to salads and sandwiches. Also used in soups, juices and as a garnish.

Medicinal uses For catarrh, skin disorders, bronchitis, rheumatism and debility associated with chronic disease. Traditionally taken as a spring tonic.

Gardener's trivia Watercress leaves contain a volatile mustard oil, giving a characteristic burning tang.

Nepeta cataria   LAMIACEAE

CLIMATE AND SITE
Zones 3–10. Full
sun to partial
shade.

IDEAL SOIL
Dry, sandy garden
soil; pH 7.0–8.0.

GROWING HABIT
Height 1–3 feet
(30–90 cm); new
stems each season
from a perennial
root; heart-shaped,
toothed, grayish
green leaves.
Self-sows.

PARTS USED
Whole plant,
leaves.

CATMINT

CATMINT IS CLOSELY RELATED TO MINT. IT
GROWS WILD AMONG WEEDS NEAR HOMES,
IN GARDENS OR IN FIELDS. CATS FIND ITS
SCENT IRRESISTIBLE AND WILL RUB ITS LEAVES.

Growing guidelines Sow seed
outdoors when ripe or in early
spring; thin to 1½ feet (45 cm).
Take softwood cuttings in spring or
early summer. Transplants poorly.

Flowering time Summer to early
autumn bloomer; white-spotted,
blue-violet tubular flowers in
branching spikes.

Pest and disease prevention Planting
near vegetables, such as eggplants
and turnips, appears to reduce
infestations of flea beetles.

Harvesting and storing In late
summer, strip topmost leaves from
stems and spread them to dry on
a screen in the shade or hang
bunches upside down. Store in
tightly sealed containers.

Special tips Grow enough to share
with your cat, as the bruised foliage
releases a scent that turns cats into
playful kittens.

Culinary uses Leaves can be added
to salads, sauces, stews and fruit
dishes. Also used to infuse tea with
a mintlike flavor.

Medicinal uses For insomnia, colds,
influenza, palpitations and colic.

Other common names Catnip.

Ocimum basilicum

BASIL, SWEET

SWEET BASIL IS ONE OF THE MOST POPULAR HERBS IN HOME GARDENS, DUE TO ITS STRONG FLAVOR (WITH HINTS OF LICORICE AND PEPPER), WHICH IS SO USEFUL IN THE KITCHEN.

Growing guidelines Sow seed outdoors, after all danger of frost has passed, to a depth of ⅛ inch (3 mm), then thin to 6 inches (15 cm). Or sow indoors in seed trays in warmth, 6 weeks before last frost; transplant to small pots before setting outdoors. Mulch with compost to retain soil moisture, and prune away flowers to maintain best foliage flavor. Side-dress with compost in midseason to enhance production. Basil is easily damaged by low temperatures. In autumn, cover with plastic to prolong the season and protect from the earliest frosts.

Flowering time Continuous flowering beginning in midsummer; white blooms, carried on green spikes at terminal buds.

Pest and disease prevention Plant away from mint to prevent damage from common pests. Basil is a good companion plant because it repels aphids, mites and other pests.

Harvesting and storing Harvest leaves every week, pinching terminal buds first to encourage branching. Leaves can be used fresh or dried. Dried foliage loses color and flavor. Best preserved chopped

Basil continued

CLIMATE AND SITE
Zone 10. Needs a warm, sheltered site in colder areas. Thrives in hot, sunny conditions.

IDEAL SOIL
Rich, moist soil; pH 5.5–7.5.

GROWING HABIT
Aromatic annual or short-lived perennial with oval-shaped leaves; height to 2 feet (60 cm).

PARTS USED
Whole plant, stems, leaves, seeds, oil.

Thai basil is a variation on the popular sweet basil. It is a tropical plant with lancelike leaves and small mauve-pink flowers.

and frozen, or as pesto. If freezing pesto, leave out the garlic until you're ready to use it, as garlic has a tendency to become bitter after a few months. Basil keeps well in a glass jar covered with olive oil.

Special tips Plant near tomatoes and peppers to enhance their growth. Some gardeners plant a second crop to ensure a plentiful supply when older plants become woody.

Culinary uses Leaves are used in salads, with tomatoes, in pasta sauces, with vegetables, in soups and in meat and poultry stuffing.

Medicinal For colds, influenza, nausea, abdominal cramps, insomnia, migraine, acne, insect stings, skin infections, wounds and non-venomous snakebites.

Other uses Oil is used in perfumes and aromatherapy. Also used in dental preparations.

Other common names Basil, St Josephwort, common basil.

Other species There are many different species and cultivars of basil that range widely in foliage size, color, aroma and plant habit. Thai basil *O. basilicum* 'Horapha' grows to 1½ feet (45 cm); leaves have a sweet licorice scent; has purple-flushed foliage and pale mauve-pink flowers; easy to grow.

Basil continued

Dark purple basil has a gingery aroma and adds an exotic flavor and decorative air to any salad. Grow it near silver foliage in the flower garden as a contrast plant.

Dark purple basil *O. basilicum* var. *purpurascens* has lavender flowers with deep purple, shiny foliage. Germinates slowly.

Lemon basil *O. basilicum* x *citriodorum* has flowers and foliage with a strong lemony fragrance. Unlike sweet basil, it reseeds itself each season if left in the garden to flower and produce seed.

Purple ruffles basil *O. basilicum* 'Purple Ruffles' has slow-growing, delicate seedlings. Plant early indoors in peat pots to minimize disturbance. Several types offer a range of color and leaf texture.

Holy basil *O. tenuiflorum* syn. *O. sanctum* is a shrubby perennial with a spicy aroma. Violet to white flowers are produced in summer. The stems are used in rosaries, hence the name. The oil is used as an antibiotic and as an insect repellent. Also used to lower temperatures, mainly in children.

Tree basil *O. gratissimum* is a large, shrubby annual or perennial with a strong clove scent. Toothed leaves and pale green flowers appear in summer. The leaves are used as a tea and the oil in perfumery.

Gardener's trivia Basil was found growing around Christ's tomb after the resurrection. It is used today in some churches in holy water and pots of basil are sometimes found on church altars.

Oenothera biennis

CLIMATE AND SITE
Zones 4–10. Prefers full sun. Can tolerate coastal conditions.

IDEAL SOIL
Dry, sandy soil; pH 5.7–8.9.

GROWING HABIT
Tall biennial (sometimes annual) plant with erect stems and varying leaf shape and size; height 5 feet (1.5 m).

PARTS USED
Oil from seeds, roots.

EVENING PRIMROSE

OIL FROM THE EVENING PRIMROSE PLANT CONTAINS CHEMICALS THAT ASSIST THE BODY TO REGULATE HORMONAL SYSTEMS, ESPECIALLY IN WOMEN.

Growing guidelines Propagate by seed in spring and autumn. Self-seeds readily.

Flowering time Fragrant, bright yellow flowers occur in summer and scent the air heavily at night. Downy seed capsules contain many tiny seeds.

Pest and disease prevention Plants can be susceptible to root rot and powdery mildew.

Harvesting and storing Seeds are collected when ripe and processed for oil. Roots are dug up in the second year and used fresh.

Culinary uses Young roots can be boiled or pickled and eaten as a vegetable. Also used as an aperitif. All parts of the plant are edible.

Medicinal uses For premenstrual and menopausal disorders, acne, skin problems, coronary artery disease, asthma and dry skin.

Other uses Oil added to cosmetic preparations.

Gardener's trivia The evening primrose flower can emit a phosphorescent light at night, giving rise to the lesser-known common name of "evening star."

Origanum majorana

LAMIACEAE

CLIMATE AND SITE
Zones 7–10.
Full sun.

IDEAL SOIL
Light, well-drained
soil; pH 6.7–7.0.

GROWING HABIT
Bushy, tender
perennial with
square, hairy stems
and a dense,
shallow root
system; height to
2 feet (60 cm).

PARTS USED
Whole plant,
leaves, seeds, oil.

MARJORAM, SWEET

SWEET MARJORAM IS A BUSHY, AROMATIC
PERENNIAL WITH LUSH FOLIAGE AND A MILD
OREGANO TASTE. IT IS TRADITIONALLY USED
IN ITALIAN AND GREEK COOKING.

Growing guidelines The small seeds
are slow to germinate. Sow
shallowly indoors in spring. Set
plants out after danger of frost,
spacing 6–12 inches (15–30 cm)
apart. Cut back by half just before
blooming, to maintain vegetative
growth. In autumn, divide roots.

Flowering time Summer; white or
pink blossoms. The flowers have
knotlike shapes before blossoming.

Pest and disease prevention Usually
free from pests and diseases.

Harvesting and storing Cut fresh
leaves as needed for cooking and
hang in bunches to dry.

Precautions Not for pregnant women.

Culinary uses Leaves and flowers
are used in Italian and Greek
cooking in soups, tomato sauces,
and meat, cheese and bean dishes.
Used to flavor vinegar and oil.

Medicinal uses For insomnia,
headaches, bronchitis, arthritis,
sprains and stiff joints.

Other uses Oil is used in liqueurs,
perfumes, soap and hair products.

Other common names Knotted
marjoram.

Origanum vulgare

CLIMATE AND SITE
Zones 5–10. Full sun to light shade.

IDEAL SOIL
Well-drained, average garden soil; pH 6.0–7.0.

GROWING HABIT
Bush perennial with purple-brown stems and woody base; height 1–2½ feet (30–75 cm).

PARTS USED
Whole plant, leaves, oil.

OREGANO

THE SPRIGS OF OREGANO, WITH THEIR SMALL LEAVES AND MINIATURE BLOSSOMS, MAKE AN ATTRACTIVE GARNISH, ESPECIALLY THE GOLD-LEAVED VARIETY. USE IT AS A BORDER.

Growing guidelines Sow seed outdoors after danger of frost has passed and when soil temperature is above 45°F (7°C). Germination may be slow. Plant in clumps 1 foot (30 cm) apart. Prune regularly for best shape. Since seedlings will not always produce the same flavor as the original plants, take cuttings or divide roots in spring or early autumn for best results. Lightly mulch each spring with organic matter such as compost or well-rotted manure. May not overwinter outdoors in cold climates. Heat increases the oil content. Replace plants every few years.

Flowering time Summer; tubular, rose-purple, rarely white blossoms in broad terminal clusters.

Pest and disease prevention Usually free from pests and diseases.

Harvesting and storing Snip fresh sprigs as needed all summer; plants are cut when they begin flowering. Hang foliage in bunches to dry.

Special tips Like other strongly aromatic herbs, oregano has gained a reputation as a pest repellent in the garden. It is more often used dried than fresh.

Oregano continued

Oregano gets its name from the Greek *oros ganos,* meaning "joy of the mountain." It grows wild on the hillsides of Greece and fills the air with its scent.

Precautions Not given to pregnant or breastfeeding women. The oil may cause skin irritation.

Culinary uses Important in Mexican, Italian, Spanish and Greek cooking. Used in strongly flavored dishes.

Medicinal uses For colds, stomach upsets, bronchitis and asthma.

Other uses Oil used in food flavoring and toiletries. Leaves and flowers added to potpourris.

Other common names Wild marjoram.

Other species and cultivars Pot marjoram O. *onites,* syn. *Majorana onites* is a perennial with erect, hairy stems and downy leaves which have a thymelike aroma; height 2 feet (60 cm). Clusters of white, sometimes purple flowers occur in summer and early autumn. Can be used as a substitute for sweet marjoram or oregano but has less flavor.

O. *vulgare* 'Compactum' is a dwarf cultivar with small, rounded, green leaves and clusters of pink flowers; height 6 inches (15 cm). Ideal for rock gardens and containers.

Gardener's trivia Aristotle reported seeing a tortoise that had swallowed a snake eat oregano to prevent death, so the Greeks used oregano as an antidote to poisoning.

Paeonia lactiflora

CLIMATE AND SITE
Zones 6–8. Full sun to partial shade.

IDEAL SOIL
Rich, well-drained soil. Good drainage is important to avoid root rot; pH 4.3–7.8.

GROWING HABIT
Herbaceous perennial with erect, reddish stems, divided leaves and fleshy large roots; height 2 feet (60 cm).

PARTS USED
Roots.

PEONY

NAMED AFTER THE PHYSICIAN TO THE GREEK GODS, PEONY HAS BEEN CULTIVATED FOR CENTURIES FOR ITS MEDICINAL VALUE. IT IS A LOVELY GARDEN PLANT.

Growing guidelines Propagate by seed sown in autumn (can take up to 3 years to germinate); plant divisions in spring or autumn and root cuttings in winter. Plants have been known to live for more than 100 years.

Flowering time Large, fragrant flowers occur in spring and summer. Flowers range in color from white, cream and yellow, to pink, rose, burgundy and scarlet. Flowers may be single, semidouble or double.

Pest and disease prevention Prone to leafspot, nematodes, viruses and the gray mold called peony wilt.

Harvesting and storing Roots of mature plants over 4 years old are lifted in autumn and boiled and dried for use in powders and pills.

Precautions Should be used by qualified practitioners only. Not given to pregnant women.

Medicinal uses For disorders of the female reproductive system, skin conditions and liver disorders. It is important in Chinese medicine, where it is highly valued as a yin tonic for the liver and circulation.

Panax ginseng

CLIMATE AND SITE
Zones 6–10. Prefers a shady position with ample warmth and humidity.

IDEAL SOIL
Rich, moist, well-drained soil; pH 4.5–6.9.

GROWING HABIT
Perennial to height of 2⅓–3 feet (70–90 cm). Erect, upright stems bear whorls of divided leaves. Rootstock is carrot shaped.

PARTS USED
Roots, flowers.

GINSENG

GINSENG IS THE MOST FAMOUS OF ALL CHINESE MEDICINES AND IS CREDITED WITH PROPERTIES OF LONG LIFE, STRENGTH AND HAPPINESS. ALSO USED AS AN APHRODISIAC.

Growing guidelines Propagate by seed in spring. Germination is slow.

Flowering time Small, greenish white flowers occur in spring and summer followed by small, bright red berries.

Pest and disease prevention Usually free from pests and diseases.

Harvesting and storing Roots from plants over 5 years old are lifted and used fresh or dried for use in powders and pills. Flowers are picked fresh for use in tonics.

Precautions Can cause headaches and raised blood pressure.

Medicinal uses For regulation of blood pressure and debility associated with old age or illness. Ginseng relaxes and stimulates the nervous system, encourages secretion of hormones, improves stamina, lowers blood sugar and cholesterol levels, and increases resistance to diabetes. Taken as a tonic for nerves and reputedly as an aphrodisiac.

Gardener's trivia Ginseng is now rarely found in the wild. It was used extensively by the Vietcong during the Vietnam War to speed recovery from gunshot wounds.

Passiflora incarnata

CLIMATE AND SITE
Zones 6–10.
Full sun.

IDEAL SOIL
Fertile, well-drained soil;
pH 6.0–8.0.

GROWING HABIT
Height 25–30 feet
(7.5–9 m); hairy
vine grows from a
woody stem with
tendrils that wrap
around a support
to climb. Leaves are
deeply three-lobed.

PARTS USED
Whole plant, fruits.

PASSIONFLOWER

MISSIONARIES REGARDED THE FLOWERS
OF THIS PLANT AS SYMBOLS OF CHRIST'S
PASSION. IT IS A CLIMBING PERENNIAL WITH
EDIBLE FRUIT, WHICH IS USED MEDICINALLY.

Growing guidelines Propagate by
seed or summer cuttings. Mulch the
soil each spring with a thin layer of
compost. Prune away old growth in
winter or early spring.

Flowering time Early to late summer;
sweet-scented, white or lavender
petals and pink to purple banded
filaments. The flowers are followed
by an edible, oval fruit that ranges
in color from yellow to orange.

Pest and disease prevention Check
for thrips.

Harvesting and storing Collect the
fruit in summer when ripe. It is best
eaten fresh; the juice can be used
to flavor drinks. The leaves and
flowers are used medicinally but
should not be taken without
professional advice.

Precautions Not recommended
during pregnancy.

Culinary uses Fruits are eaten fresh
or pulped for jam; juice used to
flavor drinks.

Medicinal uses For insomnia, tension
headaches, asthma, hypertension,
premenstrual tension and shingles.

Other common names Maypops,
apricot vine.

Pelargonium spp.

GERANIUM, SCENTED

SCENTED GERANIUMS HAVE BEEN CULTIVATED IN EUROPE SINCE THE 17TH CENTURY. THEY ARE POPULAR FOR THEIR AROMATIC LEAVES AND SOFT COLORING.

Growing guidelines Softwood cuttings root quickly and easily from spring to autumn. Scented geraniums grow well in pots near a sunny window. Apply a liquid plant food, such as fish emulsion or compost tea, but hold back on the nitrogen for the best fragrance. Plants more than a year old tend to get straggly; take new cuttings and discard the old plants. Remove dead foliage regularly.

Flowering time Three or more months from rooting; flowers are sometimes inconspicuous. Fragrant pink, red or white blooms depending on the species or cultivar.

Pest and disease prevention Prone to aphids and whiteflies. Vacuum whiteflies from foliage or control with weekly sprays of insecticidal soap or a botanical insecticide. Garlic sprays may help to repel pests. Avoid overwatering so you don't cause root rot and use fast-draining potting mixes. The showy flowering types of geranium are reputed to repel some caterpillars, corn earworms and Japanese beetles. The scented ones are thought to deter red spider mites and cotton aphids. Some gardeners believe that

Geranium, scented continued

CLIMATE AND SITE
Zones 9–10.
Full sun.

IDEAL SOIL
Rich, well-drained,
loamy soil;
pH 6.0–7.0.

GROWING HABIT
Foliage and growth
habit vary with
species or cultivar;
leaves are frilly,
variegated, ruffled,
velvety or smooth.
Height up to 3 feet
(90 cm).

PARTS USED
Whole plant,
leaves, oil.

Apple-scented geranium is a low-growing perennial with trailing stems and small, white, red-veined flowers. The name comes from the pronounced apple aroma of its leaves.

the white-flowered geraniums are effective as a trap crop for Japanese beetles; handpick the beetles from the leaves or destroy the plants.

Harvesting and storing Pick leaves throughout the summer and dry them, storing in an airtight container, to use in winter potpourris.

Special tips Keep a pot of scented geraniums near walkways; passers-by will brush against the foliage and release the fragrance.

Culinary uses Use fresh leaves in jellies, fruit dishes and tea, or as an aromatic garnish. Some species are used to flavor sauces, ice cream, cakes and vinegar.

Medicinal uses For gastroenteritis, nausea, tonsillitis, skin complaints, acne, lice and ringworm.

Other uses Dried leaves used in potpourris and herb pillows.

Other species Lemon-scented geranium *P. crispum* is a lemon-scented subshrub; height to 3 feet (90 cm). Leaves are small and three-lobed, with crinkled margins. Petals are rose or rosy white.
Rose geranium *P. graveolens* is a rose-scented subshrub; height to 3 feet (90 cm). Leaves are softly hairy, five- to seven-lobed and toothed. Flowers are white to pale pink, marked purple. Also called sweet-scented geranium.

Persicaria bistorta

CLIMATE AND SITE
Zones 3–8. Full sun to partial shade.

IDEAL SOIL
Rich, moist soil; pH 4.5–7.5.

GROWING HABIT
Hardy perennial; height 2 feet (60 cm). Broad, oval leaves with prominent central veins; knobbly, twisted black-brown rhizomes.

PARTS USED
Rhizomes, leaves.

KNOTWEED

REGARDED AS A WEED, THIS UNUSUAL SMALL PLANT GETS ITS NAME FROM THE SHAPE OF ITS CONTORTED, "KNOTTED" RHIZOMES. IT IS AN IMPORTANT TONIC HERB.

Growing guidelines Propagate by seed or by division in spring or autumn. Semiripe cuttings can also be taken in summer. The plant grows from creeping stems and rapidly forms wide clumps. Frequent removal of some parts is necessary to keep this plant under control.

Flowering time Small, pink flowers tightly packed into dense, erect spikes appear late spring to early summer, followed by numerous hard, nutlike seed capsules.

Pest and disease prevention Aphids are prone to attack young growth.

Harvesting and storing Plants are lifted in autumn and the rhizomes collected and dried.

Culinary uses Young raw leaves can be added to salads. Used in a traditional Easter herb pudding.

Medicinal uses For digestive disorders, catarrh, diarrhea and kidney infections. Also used for sore throats and inflammations of the gums and mouth.

Other species Flowery knotweed *P. multiflorum* is a deciduous climber with small, white or pink-tinted flowers. Used to lower cholesterol.

Petroselinum crispum

CLIMATE AND SITE
Zones 5–10.
Full sun but
tolerates partial
shade.

IDEAL SOIL
Moderately rich,
well-drained soil;
pH 6.0–8.0.

GROWING HABIT
Aromatic biennial
grown as an annual
with a taproot and
finely divided
leaves; height to
1 foot (30 cm).

PARTS USED
Leaves, roots,
seeds, oil.

PARSLEY

PARSLEY IS REQUIRED IN SO MANY RECIPES
THAT IT IS A FEATURE OF MOST HERB
GARDENS. GROW IN THE GARDEN OR
ON A SUNNY PATIO OR WINDOW SILL.

Growing guidelines Sow parsley
seed shallowly outdoors in early
spring when soil temperature
reaches 50°F (10°C), thinning to
8 inches (20 cm) apart; germinates
slowly. Alternatively, soak seeds
overnight in warm water before
sowing in peat pots indoors in
early spring; transplants poorly.
Remove all flower stalks that form
and prune away dead leaves. For
productive plants, side-dress with
compost in midseason. Usually
survives the winter, but quickly

goes to seed in spring. In order
to attract beneficial insects to the
garden, let a few plants flower and
go to seed. Plants may be grown
in pots to bring indoors for winter
cooking and harvests.

Flowering time Early spring of
second year; tiny, greenish yellow
umbels followed by tiny, ribbed
oval fruits.

Pest and disease prevention Follow
proper spacing guidelines for best
air circulation to prevent diseases.
Carrot pests can attack parsley.

Harvesting and storing Cut leaf
stalks at the base for fresh foliage
all summer. Hang in bunches to dry

Parsley continued

The flat, dark green foliage of Italian or flatleaf parsley (pictured on page 249) has a stronger flavor than the curly variety (pictured above) and is also hardier.

in the shade, or freeze whole or chopped. Roots are lifted in late autumn and dried. Seeds are collected when ripe.

Special tips May go to seed prematurely if the taproot is damaged during transplanting. Dried parsley quickly loses flavor.

Precautions Excess can cause abortion, liver and kidney damage and gastrointestinal hemorrhage. Not given to pregnant women or people with kidney problems.

Culinary uses Parsley is one of the most widely cultivated herbs around the world. The leaves are used to garnish and flavor savory dishes,

soups, sauces, stuffing and meat dishes. It is eaten as a vegetable in some countries.

Medicinal uses For menstrual problems, cystitis, anemia, anorexia, indigestion and arthritis. Used after delivery to help contract the uterus and promote lactation.

Other uses Oil is used in food flavoring; leaves and seeds used in perfumery.

Other cultivars Italian parsley *P. crispum* 'Italian' has flat, dark green foliage, not curly, with a strong flavor. Plants are hardier, more resistant and larger than the curly varieties.

Pimpinella anisum

CLIMATE AND SITE
Zones 6–10.
Prefers full sun.

IDEAL SOIL
Thrives in poor,
light, well-drained
soil; pH 6.0–6.7.

GROWING HABIT
Annual with lacy
foliage that
resembles Queen
Anne's lace; height
to 2 feet (60 cm).

PARTS USED
Leaves, seeds, oil.

ANISE

USE THESE LICORICE-SCENTED LEAVES AND
SWEET, SPICY SEEDS IN SALADS, ESPECIALLY
WHEN COMBINED WITH APPLES, OR USE THE
SEEDS IN POTPOURRIS OR TO FLAVOR CAKES.

Growing guidelines Sow seed
outdoors in spring where plants will
stand, then thin to 1 foot (30 cm)
apart. Or sow several seeds in peat
pots several months before the last
frost. Transplants poorly. Stake to
prevent sprawling.

Flowering time Summer; dainty
white blossoms in umbels.

Pest and disease prevention Anise
oil is said to have insect-repellent
properties; the strong smell of the
plant may repel aphids and fleas.

Harvesting and storing Seeds are
ready to harvest when they fall
easily from the head. Clip off the
seed heads into a bag before the
seedpods shatter, but leave a few
on the plant so it will self-sow for
next year. Dry seeds then store in
airtight containers.

Special tips Enhances the growth
of cilantro (coriander).

Culinary uses Leaves added to
salads; seeds used to flavor candy;
oil used to flavor drinks, such as
Pernod and ouzo.

Medical uses For indigestion and
flatulence. Also used for lice and
as a chest rub for bronchitis.

Piper nigrum

CLIMATE AND SITE
Zone 10. Prefers a protected, warm position with high humidity.

IDEAL SOIL
Rich, moist soil; pH 4.7–7.9.

GROWING HABIT
Tropical woody-stemmed climber; height to 12 feet (4 m).

PARTS USED
Fruits.

BLACK PEPPER

UNDOUBTEDLY ONE OF THE MOST FAMILIAR AND INDISPENSABLE OF COOKING HERBS, BLACK PEPPER COMES FROM A VINE NATIVE TO THE TROPICS.

Growing guidelines Propagate by semiripe cuttings in summer or by seed when available. Remove weak stems in early spring before new growth appears. Cut back young plants several times a year to stimulate shoot growth.

Flowering time Small, white flowers occur in spring followed by long strings of berries, which ripen from green to dark red. The vine takes 7–8 years to reach maturity and then bears fruit for 15–20 years.

Pest and disease prevention Usually free from pests and diseases.

Harvesting and storing The berries are harvested in spring and summer. Different varieties vary in flavor and pungency. Black peppercorns are the dried, unripe berries; white peppercorns are the ripe red berries, which have been fermented, the skin and flesh removed and the corns dried; green peppercorns are fresh, unripe berries, pickled or freeze-dried. Tree-ripened red peppercorns are rarely found outside their country of origin. White and black peppercorns should be kept in an airtight container in a cool, dark place.

The term pepper originally meant vine pepper from various plants of the genus *Piper*. The name was borrowed for hot and sweet peppers because of their similar pungency.

Whole peppercorns will retain their pungency for much longer than ground pepper, which should also be stored in an airtight container away from light. Green peppercorns should be stored in an airtight container in the refrigerator. Various other seasonings commonly called pepper are unrelated to *Piper nigrum*. The berries known as pink peppercorns are the almost-ripe berries of a South American tree, *Schinus terebinthifolius*; Sichuan pepper is the dried berry of a Chinese variety of a small ash tree.

Culinary uses Pepper is used universally, both ground and whole, as a seasoning and condiment.

Medicinal uses As an aid to digestion and for nasal congestion.

Gardener's trivia Pepper production accounts for one-fourth of the world spice trade. India is the main producer; pepper is also cultivated in Indonesia, Malaysia and Brazil. Once literally worth its weight in gold, pepper probably changed the course of history. It was the single most important reason for the European search for sea routes in the East; much of the exploration and colonization of new lands might not have occurred but for the European craving for pepper.

Plantago major   PLANTAGINACEAE

CLIMATE AND SITE
Zones 5–10. Full
sun to partial
shade. Plantain is a
cool-climate herb.

IDEAL SOIL
Well-drained, moist
soil; pH 5.0–8.0.

GROWING HABIT
Weedy perennial
with broad, oval,
ribbed leaves;
height 6–18 inches
(15–45 cm). It forms
basal rosettes and
spreads quickly.

PARTS USED
Leaves, roots.

PLANTAIN

PLANTAIN IS A COMMON ROADSIDE WEED.
TRY ITS TENDER, YOUNG LEAVES IN SALADS,
OR EAT THEM LIKE SPINACH. IT WAS ONCE
CONSIDERED AN INDISPENSABLE CURE-ALL.

Growing guidelines Sow seed
shallowly outdoors in early spring
or autumn. It is short lived and
grows quickly from seed so can
be treated as an annual.

Flowering time Summer; tall
cylindrical spikes of many small,
purplish green to yellowish flowers.
Bloom is followed by the appearance
of small capsules, which may
contain as many as 25 seeds.

Pest and disease prevention Usually
free from pests and diseases.

Harvesting and storing Dig roots in
autumn, scrub them well and allow
to dry until brittle.

Culinary uses Use fresh leaves in
salads; steam and eat leaves like
spinach. Was eaten as a pot herb.

Medicinal uses For diarrhea, cystitis,
bronchitis, asthma, hay fever, catarrh,
hemorrhage and sinusitis. Root was
chewed to relieve toothache. Also
for bee stings, eye inflammations,
insect bites, shingles and ulcers.

Other uses Root and plant used for
a gold or camel-colored dye.

Other common names Rat-tail
plantain, white man's foot.

Portulaca oleracea   PORTULACACEAE

CLIMATE AND SITE
Zones 4 and
warmer. Full sun.

IDEAL SOIL
Not fussy; will even
grow in sand and
is drought-resistant;
pH 6.0–7.0.

GROWING HABIT
Annual, with
trailing stems and
fleshy leaves;
height 8–18 inches
(20–45 cm).

PARTS USED
Whole plant,
leaves.

PURSLANE

POPULAR IN EUROPE AS A SALAD GREEN, CULTIVATED PURSLANE IS TALLER AND MORE SUCCULENT THAN ITS COUSIN THE WEED. IT IS A RICH SOURCE OF OMEGA-3 FATTY ACIDS.

Growing guidelines Grown from seed sown in spring. Keep moist until seeds germinate. Thin to 4–6 inches (10–15 cm) apart; use thinnings in salads. Water frequently.

Flowering time Small, yellow flowers occur in summer.

Pest and disease prevention Prone to aphids and slugs.

Harvesting and storing Harvest fresh leaves and stems with scissors as needed, leaving 1 inch (2.5 cm) above ground to sprout new leaves. May be harvested four or five times. Best used fresh; does not store well.

Special tips Cultivated purslane has a superior flavor to the common, weedy variety. Common purslane is also edible. Collect seeds from the best wild plants to grow in the garden, saving seeds each year from plants with the best flavor.

Culinary uses Leaves cooked as a vegetable and added to sauces, soups and salads. Can also be pickled in vinegar.

Medicinal uses For mastitis, bee stings, dysentery, hemorrhoids, appendicitis and boils. Also used to prevent heart disease.

Primula vulgaris

CLIMATE AND SITE
Zones 6–9. Sun to partial shade.

IDEAL SOIL
Moist, humus-rich soil; pH 5.7–7.8.

GROWING HABIT
Small, clump-forming perennial with broad, crinkled leaves rising directly from stout crowns; height 6 inches (15 cm). Thick, short rhizome.

PARTS USED
Whole plant, roots, flowers, leaves.

PRIMROSE

PRIMROSE IS A PRETTY GARDEN PLANT. IT WAS USED BY THE ANCIENT ROMANS FOR PARALYSIS, GOUT AND RHEUMATISM, AND ALSO BY CULPEPER AS A WOUND HEALER.

Growing guidelines Easy to grow from fresh seed sown in autumn. Also by division in late spring or early autumn. Mulch plants in summer and winter. Divide clumps after flowering.

Flowering time Flat, five-petaled, fragrant, yellow flowers occur in late winter to spring.

Pest and disease prevention Affected by rust, botrytis, leafspot and other fungal diseases. Aphids, caterpillars and weevils can attack the leaves.

Harvesting and storing Flowers are picked in spring and used fresh or dried. Whole plant cut when in flower and dried for use in infusions. Roots are lifted in autumn of second year and dried for use in decoctions.

Precautions Can cause allergies and skin irritations. Not given to pregnant women.

Culinary uses Young leaves and flowers are used in salads and as a garnish. Flowers are used to flavor desserts.

Medicinal uses For respiratory disorders, coughs, colds, insomnia, joint pain, minor wounds and tension headaches.

Pulsatilla vulgaris

CLIMATE AND SITE
Zones 3–8. Full sun to partial shade.

IDEAL SOIL
Average to humus-rich, well-drained soil; pH 6.7–8.3.

GROWING HABIT
Deciduous perennial with bell-shaped flowers and rosettes of divided, pinnate leaves clothed in soft hairs; height to 1 foot (30 cm).

PARTS USED
Flowering plants.

PASQUE FLOWER

THE NAME OF THIS HERB COMES FROM ITS PROPENSITY TO FLOWER AROUND EASTER TIME—*PASQUE* MEANING EASTER. THE FLOWERS WERE USED TO COLOR EASTER EGGS.

Growing guidelines Sow seed in autumn or spring. Self-sown seedlings are plentiful. Plants grow from deep, fibrous roots.

Flowering time Flowers appear in spring and are pale or dark purple with five starry petals surrounding a central ring of fuzzy, orange-yellow stamens. The flowers are followed by feathery seed heads. After seed is set, plants go dormant unless conditions are cool. Seldom needs division.

Pest and disease prevention Usually free from pests and diseases.

Harvesting and storing Harvest plants when flowering.

Precautions Harmful if eaten. For use by qualified practitioners only. Can cause vomiting, convulsions and skin irritations.

Medicinal uses For insomnia, skin infections, coughs, menstrual problems, asthma and bronchitis.

Other uses Flowers used to produce a green dye.

Other species Prairie pasque flower *P. pratensis* has pale to dark violet flowers. Used in homeopathy.

Rhamnus purshiana

CLIMATE AND SITE
Zones 7–9. Full sun
to partial shade.

IDEAL SOIL
Fertile, moist
garden soil;
pH 6.0–6.7.

GROWING HABIT
Deciduous shrub
with reddish gray
bark and thin,
elliptical leaves;
height 10–20 feet
(3–6 m).

PARTS USED
Bark.

CASCARA SAGRADA

IN SPANISH, *CASCARA SAGRADA* MEANS
"SACRED BARK." THIS PLANT YIELDS AN
EXTRACT THAT IS USED IN LAXATIVES FOR
BOTH PEOPLE AND THEIR PETS.

Growing guidelines Propagate by
seed sown in autumn, by layering
in late winter or early spring, or
by semiripe cuttings from the plant
in summer. Thin out branches and
remove dead wood in late winter
or early spring.

Flowering time Spring; tiny greenish
yellow flowers in clusters, followed
by small, poisonous red berries that
blacken when ripe.

Pest and disease prevention Usually
free from pests and diseases.

Harvesting and storing In spring
and autumn, strip bark from wood.
Dry well before storing.

Special tips The bark must be aged
for at least 1 year before use.

Precautions All parts are harmful if
eaten. Infusions made from fresh
bark tend to cause vomiting and
intestinal cramping. Not given to
pregnant or breastfeeding women.

Medicinal uses For constipation,
digestive problems, jaundice and
hemorrhoids. Used to stop nail
biting due to its bitter taste.

Other uses Contains an active
ingredient that is used in several
commercial laxatives.

Rheum palmatum

CLIMATE AND SITE
Zones 6–9. Full
sun. Native of Asia.

IDEAL SOIL
Moist, deep,
humus-rich soil;
pH 5.0–7.0.

GROWING HABIT
Large, robust
perennial with
thick rhizome and
round stalks with
palmlike leaves;
height 6 feet
(1.8 m).

PARTS USED
Rhizomes.

CHINESE RHUBARB

THERE ARE TWO MAIN MEDICINAL SPECIES OF
RHUBARB. THEY BOTH CONTAIN LAXATIVE
PROPERTIES AND ARE WIDELY USED IN
CHINESE MEDICINE.

Growing guidelines Propagate by
root division and root cuttings in
colder months or (less effectively)
by seed sown in spring. Need to
water frequently. Rhubarb is a
heavy feeder and needs regular
fertilizing during the growing
season. Compost and mulch often.

Flowering time Deep red flowers
occur in summer followed by three-
winged fruits.

Pest and disease prevention Usually
free from pests and diseases.

Harvesting and storing Rhizomes are
harvested in autumn from plants
that are at least 3 years old.

Precautions Leaves are poisonous
if eaten as they contain high levels
of oxalic acid and tannins. Roots
not given to pregnant or breastfeeding women.

Medicinal uses For constipation,
diarrhea, hemorrhoids, burns and
skin problems.

Other uses Used in commercial
food flavoring.

Other species Edible rhubarb
R. x *hybridum* has edible stems
only; the rhizomes are not used for
medicinal purposes.

Ribes nigrum

CLIMATE AND SITE
Zones 5–8. Full sun to partial shade. Protect from cold or hot winds and late frost.

IDEAL SOIL
Moist, well-drained, average soil; pH 4.3–7.2.

GROWING HABIT
Aromatic shrub; height 6 feet (1.8 m). Leaves are lobed and a deep green in color.

PARTS USED
Leaves, fruits.

BLACKCURRANT

BLACKCURRANTS ARE AN IMPORTANT SOURCE OF VITAMIN C AND HAVE BEEN USED AS A TREATMENT FOR SORE THROATS AND COLDS FOR CENTURIES.

Growing guidelines Propagate by hardwood cuttings in winter. Add compost and a potassium-rich fertilizer in early spring. Water regularly in dry weather. In the first season, cut the weakest stems to the ground in autumn. Remove one-quarter of the older growth each year to maintain vigor in plant.

Flowering time In spring, non-descript greenish white flowers occur in hanging clusters, followed by edible black berries.

Pest and disease prevention Prone to damage by aphids, birds and mites. Check for leafspots and mildews.

Harvesting and storing Fruits are picked in the summer when ripe. Leaves are picked during spring and summer.

Culinary uses Fruits eaten fresh or frozen; made into jams, cordials and desserts. Leaves can be used as a substitute for tea.

Medicinal uses For colds, and mouth and throat infections. Also in gargles for sore throats.

Gardener's trivia The berries of this plant were once thought to breed worms in the stomach.

Rosa spp.

CLIMATE AND SITE
Zones 3–10 and warmer. Full sun. Avoid windy sites.

IDEAL SOIL
Well-drained but moist, organic-rich soil; pH 6.0–7.5.

GROWING HABIT
Deciduous shrubs; height varies with species and cultivars; stems thorned and upright to spreading.

PARTS USED
Petals, fruits (hips).

ROSE

THE AROMATIC FRUITS OF THESE SHRUBS HAVE MEDICINAL PROPERTIES. THE FRAGRANT FLOWERS ARE USED FOR MAKING PERFUME. THEY BLOOM IN VARYING COLORS.

Growing guidelines Propagate from seed in autumn, by hardwood cuttings in autumn or by budding in summer. Purchase nursery stock for best results. Work in plenty of compost or well-rotted manure when planting, and mulch each spring. Plant 2½ feet (75 cm) apart in beds. Roses will be damaged if left standing in water, so they need good drainage. They need at least half a day of sun along with regular watering and feeding. Prune in winter to maintain shape.

Flowering time Spring to winter depending on type; single or double flowers, often clustered, with colorful hips ripening in autumn. Most species and old roses generally flower on older wood and should not be pruned back hard. Colors vary with species.

Pest and disease prevention Prone to blackspot, rust, mildew and aphids. Deadhead regularly to remove possible disease sites.

Harvesting and storing Pick the buds when formed. Gather the petals when flowers are opening; distill for oil and rosewater, or dry them quickly. Collect rosehips in autumn when ripe.

Rose continued

Roses were once called "gift of the angels." Roses, such as the apothecary's rose, were used medicinally by the ancient Greeks, Romans and Persians.

Culinary uses As a tea made from the fruit of roses (rosehip tea). Petals can be added to salads. Rosewater used to flavor candy, especially Turkish delight and jellies. Petals crystallized and made into preserves.

Precautions Seeds contain irritant hairs that can cause allergies. Most roses have sharp thorns.

Medicinal uses For colds, influenza, scurvy, diarrhea, sore throats, eye irritations and minor infectious diseases. Also used to treat burns.

Other uses Used to flavor medicine, cough medicine and nutritional supplements. Fruit extracts added to vitamin C tablets.

Other species Apothecary's rose *R. gallica* var. *officinalis* is a bushy deciduous shrub with prickly stems and leathery divided leaves. Flowers in summer with pink-red fragrant semidouble blooms, followed by dark red hips; height 3 feet (90 cm). Cherokee rose *R. laevigata* is a vigorous climbing rose with large, white, single flowers in spring or early summer, followed by orange-red hips; height 30 feet (9 m).

Gardener's trivia Never plant a new rose in an old rose's "grave." Disease pathogens or allelopathic substances that hinder the growth of a new plant of the same genus may still be in the soil.

Rosmarinus officinalis

CLIMATE AND SITE
Zones 7–10. Full sun to partial shade.

IDEAL SOIL
Light, well-drained soil; pH 6.0–6.7.

GROWING HABIT
Evergreen shrub with scaly bark and aromatic, needle-like leaves; height 2–6 feet (60–180 cm).

PARTS USED
Leaves, flowering tops, oil.

ROSEMARY

THE FLOWERS AND LEAVES OF THIS HIGHLY SCENTED HERB ARE USED TO SEASON AND GARNISH MEAT, FISH AND POULTRY. ALSO USED AS AN INSECT REPELLENT.

Growing guidelines Sow seed shallowly indoors in early spring, then transplant to pots outdoors; plant out in the garden for second season, spacing 3 feet (90 cm) apart. Or take cuttings from new growth in autumn, or layer young shoots in summer. Overwintering success varies with local conditions and cultivar; larger plants may overwinter better outdoors than small ones. Potted plants may be brought into a sunny greenhouse for the winter; or keep them at 45°F (7°C) in a sunny garage or enclosed porch, watering only occasionally. Prune after flowering to encourage bushy growth.

Flowering time Spring and summer, according to climate and cultivar. Whorls of small pale blue to lilac or pink tubular flowers in clusters.

Pest and disease prevention With indoor plants, watch for scale pests and wipe them from foliage with a cloth soaked with rubbing alcohol. Can also be susceptible to mildew, so provide good air circulation, especially in winter.

Harvesting and storing Leaves and flowering tops are collected in

White-flowered rosemary is an aromatic and ornamental herb with glossy green, needle-like leaves. Use it in cooking as you would other types of rosemary.

spring and early summer and distilled for oil or dried for extracts, spirits and infusions. Snip fresh foliage for culinary use as needed throughout the year.

Special tips Rosemary is a popular, attractive shrub for the garden. It is a good companion for cabbage, broccoli and related crops, as well as carrots and onions. The fragrance is said to repel insects; companion gardeners use it to discourage cabbage flies, root maggot flies and other flying pests. The small flowers will attract bees.

Culinary uses Fresh or dried leaves are used to flavor meat, especially lamb; used in soups and stews and with vegetables; small amounts added to biscuits, bread and jam. Fresh sprigs used to flavor oil, vinegar and wine. Leaves can be used for a tea.

Medicinal uses For headaches, poor circulation, nervous tension, dandruff, depression, arthritis, neuralgia, muscular injuries and digestive problems. Use as an antiseptic gargle and mouthwash.

Other uses In cosmetics, and hair, skin and bath preparations. Also used in potpourri. Scatter on a barbecue to discourage insects.

Other cultivars Prostrate rosemary *R. officinalis* Prostratus Group has

Rosemary continued

As well as being a popular culinary herb, rosemary can be used as an insect repellent, a hair and scalp tonic, and a breath freshener. It also makes an excellent garden hedge.

deep blue flowers almost all year; good for rock gardens and hanging baskets; not very winter-hardy. Gilded rosemary *R. officinalis* 'Aureus' is an unusual cultivar with variegated yellow foliage that adds interest to both the garden and container herbs; height 6 feet (1.8 m). Use flowers in potpourris. White-flowered rosemary *R. officinalis* var. *albiflorus* is a white-flowered rosemary and an excellent plant for white gardens, containers and floral tributes. Said to be the hardiest variety to frost. *R. officinalis* 'Pinkie' is an American cultivar with pinkish flowers and short gray-green leaves; height to 4 feet (1.2 m).

R. officinalis 'Severn Sea' is a semi-prostrate cultivar with violet blue flowers and fine leaves on arching branches. It is an excellent cultivar for containers, walls or rock gardens.

Gardener's trivia Rosemary is the herb of friendship and remembrance, and is supposed to stimulate the mind. Greek scholars wore garlands of rosemary to aid memory and concentration. It is traditionally carried at remembrance services and funerals. The genus name *Rosmarinus* is Latin and means "dew of the sea," referring to the dewlike appearance of its pale blue flowers, especially when viewed from a distance.

Rubia tinctorum

CLIMATE AND SITE
Thrives in full sun.

IDEAL SOIL
Fertile, deep, well-drained soil with a neutral pH; pH 6.7–7.0.

GROWING HABIT
Perennial with reddish brown rhizomes and weak stems that lie along the ground without support; prickles help the plant to climb; height to 4 feet (1.2 m).

PARTS USED
Roots, leaves.

MADDER

THE FOLIAGE AND ROOTS OF MADDER ARE USED TO PRODUCE BROWN, ORANGE, PINK AND RED NATURAL DYES. IT NEEDS SPACE TO SPRAWL BUT IS ALSO A PLANT THAT CLIMBS.

Growing guidelines If planting from seed, sow shallowly indoors in spring and set out in the garden in late spring or early autumn 1 foot (30 cm) apart. Once established, new plants will spring up from roots. Plant near a fence as the prickles on the stems and leaves will help the plant climb.

Flowering time Summer; loose spikes of small, yellow-green or honey-colored, starry flowers in second or third year, followed by small, round, red to black berries.

Pest and disease prevention Usually free from pests and diseases.

Harvesting and storing Dig the roots of the plant after about 3 years and after flowering; use the roots fresh or dry to make red to orange and pink dyes.

Medicinal uses As a diuretic and laxative for kidney problems and bladder stones; also for minor cuts and wounds.

Other uses The roots are used as a source of natural dyes. The prickly leaves can be used in facial scrubs.

Other species Indian madder *R. cordifolia* is a perennial climber with tiny flowers and black fruits.

Rubus fruticosus

CLIMATE AND SITE
Zones 6–10. Full sun and good air circulation.

IDEAL SOIL
Fertile, well-drained soil that hasn't been used to grow related plants, such as roses or quinces.

GROWING HABIT
Semi-evergreen shrub. Biennial canes grow the first season and flower the next.

PARTS USED
Leaves, roots, fruits.

BLACKBERRY

RICH IN VITAMIN C, SUGARS AND PECTINS, BLACKBERRIES HAVE BEEN AN IMPORTANT PART OF THE HUMAN DIET SINCE PREHISTORIC TIMES. USE THEM TO TREAT STOMACH ACHES.

Growing guidelines Can be grown from seed sown in spring, cuttings in summer or by tip layering in summer. However, due to the prevalence of viruses, it is best that only certified disease-free or quality nursery plants be used. Each year, cut out the fruited canes and tie in the new ones. Pruning will prevent an inhospitable bramble.

Flowering time Small, white to pink flowers occur in spring followed by red to black fruits in late summer.

Pest and disease prevention Prone to aphids, botrytis and viral diseases. Birds eat the fruits.

Harvesting and storing Leaves are picked just before flowering. Roots are harvested in summer and the fruits harvested when they turn black at the end of summer.

Culinary uses Fruits eaten fresh or cooked, or made into syrups, cordials and wine. Leaves are used for herbal teas.

Medicinal uses For stomach aches, dysentery, hemorrhoids, cystitis, gum and mouth inflammations and as a tonic. Tea made from the leaves used for premenstrual disorders.

Rubus idaeus

CLIMATE AND SITE
Zones 3–9. Full sun
with good air
circulation in a
sheltered position.

IDEAL SOIL
Fertile, well-
drained soil;
pH 4.5–7.0.

GROWING HABIT
Deciduous shrub;
has suckering
canes, prickly
stems and dark
green leaves.
Remove old stems
after fruiting.

PARTS USED
Leaves, fruits.

RASPBERRY

THIS DECIDUOUS, WOODY-STEMMED
SCRAMBLER IS NATIVE TO THE NORTHERN
HEMISPHERE. RASPBERRIES HAVE HERALDED
THE ONSET OF SUMMER FOR CENTURIES.

Growing guidelines Propagate by
division or layering of healthy stock.
Due to the prevalence of diseases,
it is advisable to only buy new,
certified disease-free plants.

Flowering time Small, white flowers
occur in drooping clusters in spring
and summer followed by copious
amounts of delicious, conical, red
or orange-red berries.

Pest and disease prevention Botrytis
(gray mold) can cause a gray
coating on fruit. Cane blight can
cause wilted shoot tips and dark
spots on the canes. Anthracnose can
cause red-bordered spots on canes
and leaves. Viruses can cause
stunted growth; curled, yellow
leaves; and malformed berries.

Harvesting and storing Pick leaves
just before flowering. Harvest
berries when they are ripe.

Culinary uses Fruits are eaten fresh
or made into cordials, syrups, wines
and vinegars. Fruit syrup can be
used as a flavoring agent.

Medicinal uses For digestion
disorders, childbirth preparations,
mouth and gum infections, minor
wounds and eye infections.

Rumex acetosa

CLIMATE AND SITE
Zones 5–9. Full sun
to light shade.

IDEAL SOIL
Fertile, moist
garden soil.

GROWING HABIT
Hardy perennial
with wavy, green
leaves; height
2 feet (60 cm).
Replace every
3 or 4 years by
letting a good
plant run to seed.

PARTS USED
Leaves.

SORREL

WHEN GROWN IN MEADOWS, THE SUMMER
STALKS OF SORREL'S REDDISH GREEN
FLOWERS WILL MAKE THE WHOLE AREA
APPEAR TO BE TINTED RED.

Growing guidelines Sow seed
shallowly outdoors in late spring,
thinning to 1½ feet (45 cm). Or
divide older plants in early spring
or autumn. If planting late, try to
plant about 2 months before the
first frost, to give the roots enough
time to establish before the soil
freezes. Water regularly.

Flowering time Midsummer;
greenish to red flowers.

Pest and disease prevention Prone
to snails and slugs.

Harvesting and storing Harvest the
outside leaves regularly to promote
new growth. Sorrel leaves are best
eaten fresh, but may also be
blanched and frozen.

Precautions Sorrel is acidic and
should not be eaten by people with
rheumatism, arthritis or gout.

Culinary uses Fresh leaves added to
salads, soups, cream cheese and
egg dishes. Sorrel leaves can be
cooked like spinach.

Medicinal uses Seldom used
medicinally.

Other uses Juice from the leaves
used to remove rust, mold, grass
and ink stains from linen and wood.

Rumex crispus

CLIMATE AND SITE
Zones 5–9.
Full sun.

IDEAL SOIL
Any soil which
is slightly acidic;
pH 6.0–6.7.

GROWING HABIT
Perennial with
long, lance-shaped,
wavy leaves; forms
a rosette the first
year, then develops
a large taproot;
height 1–4 feet
(30–120 cm).

PARTS USED
Roots.

DOCK, CURLED

CURLED DOCK IS A PERENNIAL WEED WITH
A LARGE TAPROOT, FOUND IN PASTURES AND
HAYFIELDS. THE SEED STALKS MATURE TO A
RUSTY COLOR IN LATE SUMMER.

Growing guidelines Sow seed
shallowly in spring, then thin to
6 inches (15 cm). Weedy and hard
to control, dock thrives despite
neglect. Control its growth to
prevent a future weed problem.

Flowering time Inconspicuous,
greenish yellow flowers in spreading
panicles are produced in summer
followed by rusty brown seed
capsules in autumn.

Pest and disease prevention Usually
free from pests and diseases.

Harvesting and storing Dig roots in
spring or autumn; clean and slice
them before drying in the sun.

Special tips Each plant produces
over 3,000 seeds. Most dock seeds
fall close to the parent and soil
movement may distribute the seeds.
Cultivation of the soil may create
root fragments, allowing new plants
to form from each fragment.

Precautions Excess use may cause
nausea and dermatitis.

Medicinal uses As an infusion,
laxative, astringent tonic and to
treat skin problems. Also used for
jaundice, liver disorders and to
treat anemia.

Ruta graveolens

CLIMATE AND SITE
Zones 5–9.
Full sun.

IDEAL SOIL
Poor, well-drained
soil; pH 6.0–7.0.

GROWING HABIT
Perennial with
woody stems and
greenish blue
foliage; height
to 3 feet (90 cm).
Grows well in a
pot, and continues
growing when
wintered indoors.

PARTS USED
Leaves.

RUE

RUE HAS A PUNGENT, SKUNKLIKE ODOR. IN THE GARDEN, ITS BLUISH, DELICATE FOLIAGE CONTRASTS WELL WITH THE GREENS OF OTHER PLANTS. GROW IT TO REPEL PESTS.

Growing guidelines Sow seed shallowly indoors in late winter, transplanting outdoors in late spring 1½–2 feet (45–60 cm) apart. Take cuttings from new growth or divide older plants. Mulch with compost or well-rotted manure each spring and prune away dead stems.

Flowering time Summer to early autumn; yellow-green blossoms in terminal clusters.

Pest and disease prevention Usually free from pests and diseases.

Harvesting and storing Can be harvested several times each season, bunching foliage to dry.

Precautions Rue can be toxic when taken internally and excess can affect the central nervous system. Can cause skin irritation.

Medicinal uses Externally for earache, sore eyes and rheumatism.

Other uses Leaves used to flavor the Italian liqueur grappa. Dried seedpods and leaves are sometimes used in flower arrangements.

Gardener's trivia According to folklore, rue slows the growth of basil, sage and members of the cabbage family.

Salvia officinalis

CLIMATE AND SITE
Zones 5–10.
Full sun to
partial shade.

IDEAL SOIL
Well-drained
garden soil;
pH 6.0–7.0.

GROWING HABIT
Perennial shrub
with woody stems
that have wrinkled
gray-green foliage;
height 1–2 feet
(30–60 cm).

PARTS USED
Leaves, oil, flowers.

SAGE

SAGE IS AN EASY-TO-GROW, SHRUBBY
PERENNIAL WITH AROMATIC FOLIAGE THAT IS
USED BOTH FRESH AND DRIED IN COOKING
AND IN HERBAL MEDICINES.

Growing guidelines Sow seed
shallowly outdoors in spring or
indoors in late winter; plant at
1⅔–2-foot (50–60-cm) intervals.
Trim back existing plants in spring
to encourage vigorous, bushy new
growth. Plants may decline after
several years; take cuttings or divide
in spring or autumn to have a
steady supply. Yellowing leaves
can mean roots need more space.
Remove flowering spikes when
young. Sage may improve the
growth and flavor of cabbages,

carrots, strawberries and tomatoes;
it is also thought to grow well with
marjoram. It may, however, stunt
the growth of some plants, such as
cucumbers, rue and onions.

Flowering time Spring; tubular pink
to purple flowers in whorled spikes.

Pest and disease prevention Small
green caterpillars can eat the leaves;
remove by hand or prune off.
Rarely bothered by other pests and
diseases except snails and slugs.

Harvesting and storing Snip fresh
leaves as needed, or bunch them
and hang to dry for use during
winter months. A branch of strongly
aromatic sage is a fragrant addition

Sage continued

Purple sage is grown and used like common sage. Sage was so valued by the Chinese in the 17th century that they would trade three chests of tea for one chest of sage.

to a clothes drawer or blanket box, as it helps keep moths away. Refrain from harvesting the first year.

Special tip Use sage as a border plant, or dot amongst other plants as it is fast growing and reaches an appreciable size in just one season. The flowers attract bees and other beneficial insects.

Culinary uses Leaves used in stuffing for poultry and meat; made into tea and used in Italian cooking. Also used to flavor vinegar, cheese and butter. Sage is an antioxidant.

Medicinal uses For indigestion, flatulence, depression, menopausal problems, insect bites and skin

infections. Sage tea and sage wine are nerve and blood tonics; also used to reduce sweating.

Other uses In cosmetics as an astringent cleanser and facial wash. Oil used as a fixative for perfumes and added to toothpaste. Used as a rinse to darken gray hair.

Other cultivars Golden sage *S. officinalis* 'Icterina' has variegated gold and green leaves; makes an excellent bushy border plant.
S. officinalis 'Tricolor' produces gray-green to cream foliage with tints of pink and purple; not quite so frost hardy as other cultivars.
S. officinalis 'Purpurascens' has leaves flushed red purple.

Salvia sclarea

CLIMATE AND SITE
Zones 5–10.
Full sun.

IDEAL SOIL
Average, well-drained soil;
pH 4.8–7.5.

GROWING HABIT
Biennial or short-lived perennial with upright, branched, square stems and broad, oblong, aromatic leaves; height to 5 feet (1.5 m).

PARTS USED
Leaves, flowers, seeds, oil.

CLARY

FRESH CLARY HAS A BITTER, WARM AROMA AND FLAVOR AND MAKES AN ATTRACTIVE FLOWERING GARDEN PLANT. IT HAS THE SAME CULINARY USES AS SAGE.

Growing guidelines Sow seed outdoors in spring; thin to 9 inches (23 cm). Can be propagated by division of 2-year-old plants in early spring, but best raised from seed annually.

Flowering time Spring and summer after first year; small cream and lilac to blue flowers that resemble sage.

Pest and disease prevention Usually free from pests and diseases.

Harvesting and storing Snip leaves for fresh use. Strip leaves and dry on screens for potpourri. Oil can be distilled from the flowering tops.

Special tips Clary can be used as a substitute for garden sage.

Precautions Clary may cause drowsiness and headaches. Not given to pregnant women.

Culinary uses Leaves cooked into fritters; also in seasoning. Flowers added to salads and used as a tea.

Medicinal uses For vomiting, nausea, menstrual complaints, ulcers, cuts and as an eyewash to remove foreign bodies.

Other uses As a massage oil and a fixative in perfumes; in potpourris.

Sambucus nigra

CLIMATE AND SITE
Zones 5–9. Full sun
to partial shade.

IDEAL SOIL
Moist, rich soil;
pH 6.5–8.1.

GROWING HABIT
Large, deciduous
shrub or tree; leaves
are dull green,
pinnate and emit
an unpleasant
odor when crushed.
Bark is corklike
in texture; height
30 feet (9 m).

PARTS USED
Leaves, bark,
flowers, fruits.

ELDER

THE ELDER HAS BEEN HIGHLY VALUED FOR
CENTURIES AND HAS BEEN TERMED "THE
MEDICINE CHEST OF THE PEOPLE" DUE TO
ITS MEDICINAL PROPERTIES.

Growing guidelines Propagate by
softwood cuttings in summer or by
seed sown in autumn. Prune back
hard in winter to ensure good
foliage for next season.

Flowering time Very small, highly
scented white flowers occur in early
summer, followed by black berries.

Pest and disease prevention Prone
to attack by aphids.

Harvesting and storing Leaves are
picked in spring and summer and
used fresh. Bark is stripped off the
trunk in winter and dried for further
use. Flowers are picked when fully
open and dried. Fruits are picked
when ripe and used fresh or dried.

Precautions Leaves, bark and raw
berries are harmful if eaten.

Culinary uses Flowers are used to
add flavor to stewed fruits, jellies
and jams; also used to make wine.
Fruits are made into sauces and
wine. Juice is used to make liqueurs.

Medicinal uses For fevers, colds,
arthritis, sore eyes, chilblains, minor
burns and mouth infections. Also
used to reduce inflammation.

Other uses In cosmetics, skin
lotions, oils and ointments.

Sanguinaria canadensis

CLIMATE AND SITE
Zones 3–9.
Dappled to
partial shade.

IDEAL SOIL
Well-drained,
humus-rich soil;
pH 4.5–6.9.

GROWING HABIT
Perennial spring
wildflower with a
single, deeply cut,
palmately lobed
leaf that emerges
around a single
flower bud; height
6 inches (15 cm).

PARTS USED
Rhizomes.

BLOODROOT

NAMED FOR THE BLOOD RED LIQUID
EXTRACTED FROM THE ROOT, BLOODROOT
IS A SOURCE OF SANGUINARINE, A DENTAL
PLAQUE INHIBITOR.

Growing guidelines Propagate by
seed sown in autumn or by plant
division after flowering. Self-sows
easily. Plants grow from a thick,
creeping rhizome with red sap.

Flowering time Solitary, snow white
to pink flowers appear in spring,
with a striking cluster of yellow-
orange stamens. Flowers last only a
few days and are followed by an
oblong seed capsule.

Pest and disease prevention Usually
free from pests and diseases.

Harvesting and storing Rhizomes
are dug up in autumn and dried.

Precautions Excess can cause
nausea and vomiting. For use by
qualified practitioners only.

Medicinal uses For respiratory tract
and throat infections, skin lesions
and chilblains. Bloodroot acts as a
local anesthetic and is effective
against pathogenic organisms.

Other uses Added to toothpaste and
mouthwash as an antiplaque agent.

Other common names Red puccoon,
red Indian paint.

Gardener's trivia Was used by Native
Americans as a dye for coloring skin.

Santolina chamaecyparissus

CLIMATE AND SITE
Zones 7–10.
Full sun.

IDEAL SOIL
Poor, well-drained soil. If soil is rich, growth will be slow; pH 7.0–8.0.

GROWING HABIT
Evergreen shrub with pinnately divided, narrow, highly aromatic, silver-green leaves; height to 2 feet (60 cm).

PARTS USED
Leaves, flowering stems.

SANTOLINA

SANTOLINA IS AN EVERGREEN SHRUB WITH YELLOW FLOWERS. THOUGH IT IS ALSO CALLED LAVENDER COTTON, IT IS A MEMBER OF THE DAISY FAMILY. USE IT AS AN INSECT REPELLENT.

Growing guidelines Sow seed in late spring; germinates slowly. Take cuttings in late summer to early autumn; layer or divide older plants in spring. Set 2 feet (60 cm) apart; less for hedging. Shear or clip the plant in spring or summer, never in the colder months. Pinch off fading blooms; don't overwater.

Flowering time Summer; clusters of yellow button-like blooms rise above the foliage on 6-inch (15-cm) stalks, followed by brownish fruit. May not flower the first year.

Pest and disease prevention Usually free from pests and diseases.

Harvesting and storing Harvest and bunch together the top 8–10 inches (20–25 cm) of foliage in summer and hang to dry. Collect flowers with the stems when they are at full bloom; hang to dry.

Precautions Do not take internally.

Medicinal uses For poor digestion, worms, stings and skin inflammations.

Other uses As a backing for making aromatic wreaths and for potpourris.

Other common names Lavender cotton.

Gardener's trivia Use in knot gardens.

Saponaria officinalis

CLIMATE AND SITE
Zones 5–9. Full sun to light shade.

IDEAL SOIL
Average to poor, well-drained soil; pH 6.0–7.0.

GROWING HABIT
Rhizomatous perennial with branching stems; leaves contain a sap that creates a lather when boiled; height to 3 feet (90 cm).

PARTS USED
Leaves, leafy stems, flowers, rhizomes.

SOAPWORT

THIS PERENNIAL, ALSO CALLED BOUNCING BET, IS A ROADSIDE AND GARDEN WEED. IT HAS WHITE OR PINK BLOSSOMS IN SPRING AND THE SAP LATHERS AND CLEANS LIKE SOAP.

Growing guidelines Divide plants in autumn or spring. Or sow soapwort indoors, about 6 weeks before last frost. Water regularly until the plants are established. Once established, soapwort self-sows and spreads rapidly; it is very drought-tolerant once matured. Clip back after flowering to encourage a second bloom. Don't plant next to fishponds as its lathering properties may seep into the water and poison the fish.

Flowering time Summer to autumn; single pink to white, five-petaled flowers in terminal clusters. The flowers have a sweet fruit scent.

Pest and disease prevention Usually free from pests and diseases.

Harvesting and storing Pick flowers, leaves, stems and roots in autumn or as required. Clean, chop and boil the roots to make a sudsy solution.

Precautions Soapwort is poisonous and should not be taken internally. Excess can destroy red blood cells. Can cause eye irritation.

Medicinal uses For eczema, acne, psoriasis and other skin problems.

Other uses As a soap substitute; used in museums to clean precious fabrics.

Sassafras albidum

CLIMATE AND SITE
Zones 5–9. Full sun
to partial shade.

IDEAL SOIL
Well-drained acid
to neutral soil;
pH 6.7–7.3.

GROWING HABIT
Aromatic deciduous
tree with deeply
fissured bark and
downy, mostly
three-lobed leaves;
height 20–60 feet
(6–18 m).

PARTS USED
Leaves, roots, oil.

SASSAFRAS

SASSAFRAS IS A TALL, DECIDUOUS TREE
THAT PRODUCES AN OIL ONCE USED AS A
FLAVORING FOR COLD AND HOT BEVERAGES.
IT HAS STRIKING FOLIAGE IN AUTUMN.

Growing guidelines Propagate by
seed, suckers or root cuttings. Only
very small, young trees transplant
successfully because the mature
trees develop long taproots. The
young foliage smells of citrus; the
roots and bark have a spicy scent
like that of root beer.

Flowering time Spring; clusters
of small, inconspicuous greenish
yellow blossoms appear with the
leaves. Male and female flowers are
unisexual. The fruit that follows is a
pea-sized, dark blue-black berry.

Pest and disease prevention Can be
affected by Japanese beetles and
gypsy moths.

Harvesting and storing Leaves are
picked in spring; roots are lifted in
autumn. Root bark and bark are
used to produce oil.

Precautions Excess can cause
vomiting. May be carcinogenic.

Culinary uses Leaves are dried and
powdered to thicken soup.

Medicinal uses For fevers, colic,
arthritis, rashes and insect bites.

Other uses An extract is used as a
flavoring for root beer; also used as
a perfumery ingredient.

Satureja montana

CLIMATE AND SITE
Zones 6–9.
Full sun.

IDEAL SOIL
Poor, well-drained
soil, pH 6.7–7.3.

GROWING HABIT
Evergreen
perennial with
woody stems and
oblong, needle-like
leaves; height
6–12 inches
(15–30 cm).

PARTS USED
Leaves, shoots.

SAVORY, WINTER

THIS AROMATIC, BUSHY PERENNIAL HAS A
PEPPERY FLAVOR AND HAS BEEN USED IN
COOKING FOR MORE THAN 2,000 YEARS. IT
IS SOMETIMES USED AS A SALT SUBSTITUTE.

Growing guidelines Sow seed
shallowly outdoors in late spring,
thinning to 1 foot (30 cm); winter
savory germinates slowly. Take
cuttings, or divide older plants in
spring or autumn. Tip-prune to
encourage bushiness.

Flowering time White to pale
purple flowers in summer.

Pest and disease prevention Usually
free from pests and diseases.

Harvesting and storing Harvest fresh
as needed, or cut the foliage just

before flowering and dry. Use as a
flavoring in a variety of dishes, teas,
herb butters and vinegars.

Culinary uses Leaves used to flavor
processed meats, sausages, salami
and Provençal dishes.

Medicinal uses For indigestion,
colic, nausea, diarrhea, sore throats
and insect bites.

Other uses Extracts used in liqueurs
and as a salt substitute.

Other species Summer savory
S. hortensis is an aromatic annual
with linear, downy leaves and pale
lavender or white blossoms; height
1–1½ feet (30–45 cm). Used as an
antiflatulent.

Simaba cedron

CLIMATE AND SITE
Zone 10 or more.
Full sun.

IDEAL SOIL
Well-drained soil;
pH 4.5–7.8.

GROWING HABIT
Deciduous tree;
height 15–50 feet
(4.5–15 m). Slender
and erect with
spreading branches;
leaves up to 3 feet
(90 cm) in length,
divided into
narrow leaflets.

PARTS USED
Seeds.

CEDRON QUASSIA

CEDRON QUASSIA AND THE RELATED
QUASSIA AMARA (ABOVE) ARE VALUED FOR
ANTIMALARIAL AND OTHER MEDICINAL
COMPOUNDS EXTRACTED FROM THEM.

Growing guidelines Propagate by
division of suckers or hardwood
cuttings at the end of summer; also
by seed when ripe.

Flowering time Dark yellow, fragrant,
simple, five-petaled flowers appear
in summer, followed by oval fruits
each bearing one seed.

Pests and disease prevention Usually
free from pests and diseases.

Harvesting and storing Collect seeds
when ripe and use fresh or dried,
or powder for use in infusions.

Special tips Once used to treat
roundworm and lice, it is used
today as a bitter or to denature
alcohol. Generally, quassia refers to
a bitter compound extracted from
the wood of a related tree species,
Quassia amara, not from *Simaba
cedron*. Quassia chips, used to repel
animals, are also from a related tree.

Precautions Sale and use of cedron
extracts are subject to legal
restrictions in certain countries.

Medicinal uses To lower fevers,
reduce inflammation and to relax
muscle spasms.

Gardener's trivia Native to Central
America and north Brazil.

Solidago spp.

CLIMATE AND SITE
Zones 5–9. Thrives in full sun but tolerates partial shade.

IDEAL SOIL
Average to poor, well-drained garden soil; pH 6.5–7.5.

GROWING HABIT
Unbranched perennial with simple leaves; height 3–7 feet (90–210 cm).

PARTS USED
Leaves, flowering tops.

GOLDENROD

USE THE DRIED FLOWERS OF GOLDENROD FOR FLORAL ARRANGEMENTS OR TO MAKE A YELLOW DYE. IT OFFERS ATTRACTIVE SHELTER TO PRAYING MANTIDS AND BENEFICIAL INSECTS.

Growing guidelines Easily grown from seed sown in early spring. Divide mature plants in spring or autumn. Can become weedy if the soil is too rich, so hold off on the nitrogen.

Flowering time Late summer and autumn; yellow blossoms occur in the second year.

Pest and disease prevention Usually free from pests and diseases.

Harvesting and storing Collect the leaves and tops during the flowering period and dry in bunches or on screens; quickly turns black without adequate air circulation. Store in airtight containers.

Special tips Plant in masses or weave clumps into ornamental plantings near the vegetable garden to attract beneficial insects. Its blooming plumes are tightly clustered with small flowers rich in pollen and nectar. Many species self-sow freely or spread quickly by creeping roots, so thin regularly.

Medicinal uses For urinary tract infections, catarrh, wounds, insect bites, skin problems, ulcers and sore throats. The leaves are used in a tea to treat flatulence.

Stachys officinalis   LAMIACEAE

CLIMATE AND SITE
Zones 5–9. Full
sun but tolerates
partial shade.

IDEAL SOIL
Average soil with
good drainage;
pH 5.5–7.0.

GROWING HABIT
Rosette-forming
perennial with
deeply veined
and toothed leaves;
height up to
3 feet (90 cm).

PARTS USED
Whole plant.

BETONY

PLACE BETONY, AN ATTRACTIVE PERENNIAL,
BETWEEN THE TALLER HERBS AND BORDER
PLANTS THAT FLOWER IN MIDSUMMER,
FOR A PRETTY GARDEN ARRANGEMENT.

Growing guidelines Easily started
from seed sown outdoors in early
spring. Spring cuttings will quickly
root. Or divide established root
systems for new plants. Control
summer weeds. Every 3 or 4 years,
dig up the plant and divide into
several new clumps, adding
compost to the soil.

Flowering time Summer; tubular
red-purple flowers in dense spikes.

Pest and disease prevention Usually
free from pests and diseases.

Harvesting and storing Collect
leaves in summer or just before
blooming; dry them quickly and
store in an airtight container. Use
the leaves to make a chartreuse dye.

Precautions Excessive internal use
causes diarrhea and vomiting. Not
given to pregnant women.

Medicinal uses For headaches,
anxiety, hypertension, bruises and
menopausal problems. Used on
wounds to stop bleeding. Gargle
tea made from the astringent leaves
to treat throat irritations.

Gardener's trivia People in the
Middle Ages believed betony kept
evil spirits away.

Stellaria media

CLIMATE AND SITE
Zones 5–10. Full
sun but tolerates
partial shade.

IDEAL SOIL
Easy to grow but
prefers moist soil;
pH 5.8–7.9.

GROWING HABIT
Vigorous, creeping
annual, 4–16 inches
(10–40 cm) long
with a slender
taproot. Succulent,
oval leaves grow
on brittle, hairy,
branched stems.

PARTS USED
Whole plant.

CHICKWEED

CHICKWEED HAS BEEN USED AS A HEALING
HERB FOR CENTURIES. THE LEAVES ARE A
RICH SOURCE OF VITAMIN C, AND DOMESTIC
BIRDS AND FOWLS FIND IT IRRESISTIBLE.

Growing guidelines Propagate by
seed sown at any time; self-seeds
readily and is a serious weed
problem in some areas.

Flowering time Small, starlike white
flowers with deeply notched petals
appear throughout the year.

Pest and disease prevention Usually
free from pests and diseases.

Harvesting and storing Plants are
cut and used fresh or dried for
infusions. Also used in liquid
extracts, medicated oils, ointments
and tinctures. It is an easy herb to
use as it is available throughout the
year and is readily infused in oil to
use as a lotion.

Culinary uses Leaves contain
vitamin C and phosphorus. Sprigs
can be added to salads and used
as a vegetable.

Medicinal uses For rheumatism and
constipation. Fresh leaves can be
used as a poultice to relieve ulcers
and inflammation. Use whole plant
to treat piles and sores. Use leaves
in an ointment to relieve eczema,
psoriasis and other skin diseases.

Other uses Sprigs used as food for
domestic fowls and pet birds.

Symphytum officinale

CLIMATE AND SITE
Zones 5–10.
Full sun to
partial shade.

IDEAL SOIL
Rich, moist garden
soil; pH 6.7–7.3.

GROWING HABIT
Perennial with
broad leaves;
height 2–4 feet
(60–120 cm).
New leaves sprout
each spring from
the roots.

PARTS USED
Leaves, roots.

COMFREY

COMFREY HAS A COLORFUL MEDICINAL
HISTORY, AND WAS ONCE THOUGHT TO HELP
REPAIR BROKEN BONES. IT HAS LARGE,
BROAD LEAVES AND TUBULAR FLOWERS.

Growing guidelines Propagate by
seed, division or cuttings; space
new plants 3 feet (90 cm) apart.
Establishes easily and requires little
care. Remove dead leaves during
the autumn cleanup. Divide every
few years to prevent crowding.

Flowering time Spring to late
summer; terminal clusters of
drooping, bell-shaped purple,
pink, white or cream flowers.

Pest and disease prevention Usually
free from pests and diseases.

Harvesting and storing Use the
leaves fresh or dried. Leaves for
drying are best picked in spring.
Dig up the roots when the plant has
died down in autumn and dry.

Special tips Shaded plants will be
smaller, with few blossoms.

Precautions Comfrey is a suspected
carcinogen and should not be taken
internally. If used excessively, it
may cause liver damage. Can also
cause skin irritation.

Medicinal uses For bronchitis,
arthritis, fractures, sprains and sore
breasts during breastfeeding.

Other common names Knitbone,
slippery root.

Tagetes patula

CLIMATE AND SITE
Zones 9–10. Full sun. Afternoon shade can help prolong blooms.

IDEAL SOIL
Average, well-drained soil; pH 4.2–7.2.

GROWING HABIT
Bushy annual; height to 1 foot (30 cm). Leaves are divided, toothed, and aromatic when crushed.

PARTS USED
Whole plant, leaves, flowers, oil.

FRENCH MARIGOLD

THE GENUS IS NAMED AFTER AN ETRUSCAN GOD, TAGES, WHO PRACTICED THE ART OF WATER DIVINATION. MARIGOLDS ADD COLOR TO ANY SUNNY GARDEN.

Growing guidelines Propagate by seed sown in spring; readily self-sows. Deadhead regularly.

Flowering time Yellow to orange or red-brown flowers appear from spring to autumn.

Pest and disease prevention Usually free from pests and diseases.

Harvesting and storing Whole plants are harvested when flowering and dried for further use. Leaves and flowers are picked in summer and used fresh or dried. Oil is extracted from leaves picked during the growing season.

Special tips This plant is an excellent companion plant for vegetables as it is effective in repelling pests, such as soil nematodes, slugs and whiteflies, which target tomatoes and other vegetables. Effectiveness varies with different cultivars.

Culinary uses Leaves used in salads and to flavor food. Oil is used as a food flavoring.

Medicinal uses For stomach upsets, eye inflammations, indigestion and rheumatic pain.

Other uses Flowers are used to give color to dairy products.

Tamarindus indica

TAMARIND

THE NAME TAMARIND COMES FROM THE
ARABIC WORD FOR "DATE OF INDIA" AND
REFERS TO THE DATELIKE PULP INSIDE THE
PODS. TAMARIND IS A GRACEFUL TREE.

Growing guidelines Propagate by
seed sown when the temperature
reaches 70°F (21°C) or by air
layering or grafting.

Flowering time Pale yellow, red-
veined, fragrant flowers occur in
summer, followed by brown fruit
containing kidney-shaped seeds in
an acid, sticky, brown pulp.

Pest and disease prevention Usually
free from pests and diseases.

Harvesting and storing Fruits are
picked when ripe and used fresh
or dried. Young, tender pods are
used as seasoning.

Special tips Tamarind fruits are
available compressed into a block.
To use, place in boiling water to
soften. Strain and use the liquid;
discard the debris.

Culinary uses Fruits are used freshly
picked and made into drinks. Pulp
is used fresh or dried in curries,
chutneys and sweets; also as a
souring agent similar to lemon juice.
Used in Worcestershire sauce.

Medicinal uses For fevers, asthma,
dysentery, ulcers and to improve
digestion. Has antiseptic effects.

Other uses In laxatives.

Tanacetum balsamita

ASTERACEAE

CLIMATE AND SITE
Zones 6–9. Full sun
though some shade
is tolerated.

IDEAL SOIL
Well-drained,
fertile, loamy soil;
pH 6.0–6.7.

GROWING HABIT
Perennial with
large, gray-green,
silvery, hairy
foliage; dies back
in cold climates
during winter;
height to 3 feet
(90 cm).

PARTS USED
Leaves.

COSTMARY

IN THE SUMMER, ENJOY COSTMARY'S MINT-
SCENTED LEAVES IN YOUR GARDEN AND ADD
THEM TO SALADS AND VEGETABLE DISHES.
HARVEST IN AUTUMN FOR HERB BASKETS.

Growing guidelines Plants produce
little or no seed, so propagate by
dividing older plants in spring.
Space at 2-foot (60-cm) intervals.
Divide plants every 2–3 years,
since they spread quickly. Avoid
shade, since costmary will not
flower without sun. For more
foliage production, discourage
flowering by pruning away buds.

Flowering time Late summer; very
small, white daisy flowers in loose
clusters with yellow button centers.

Pest and disease prevention Usually
free from pests and diseases.

Harvesting and storing Collect the
leaves and dry as needed. To
harvest foliage for baskets, cut
whole stems in late summer or
autumn and hang to dry.

Culinary uses Fresh leaves added
to salads, meat and vegetable
dishes. Dried leaves infused as tea.

Medicinal uses No longer used
medicinally but once popular as
a liver tonic and for insect stings.

Other uses Mainly for weaving into
fragrant herb baskets and for
potpourri. Also used for scenting
drawers and cupboards.

ASTERACEAE

CLIMATE AND SITE
Zones 6–10.
Full sun.

IDEAL SOIL
Average, well-
drained soil;
pH 6.0–6.7.

GROWING HABIT
Perennial with
slender, hairy stems
and leaves that
are fine and
heavily divided;
height 1–2½ feet
(30–75 cm). Plant
can become woody
and shrublike.

PARTS USED
Flowers.

PYRETHRUM

THIS HERB CONTAINS VOLATILE OILS THAT ARE
EXTREMELY EFFECTIVE IN REPELLING AND
KILLING INSECTS. DRIED FLOWERS RETAIN
THEIR INSECTICIDAL PROPERTIES INDEFINITELY.

Growing guidelines Propagate by
seed in spring to summer. Divide
plants in spring. Spreads quickly,
so prune back to control growth.

Flowering time Simple, small, daisy-
like white flowers with bright yellow
centers appear from early summer
to autumn.

Pest and disease prevention Due
to its insecticidal properties, rarely
bothered by pests and diseases.

Harvesting and storing Flowers are
picked as they open, dried and
powdered. They contain volatile oils
and other compounds.

Special tips Pyrethrum, which
contains pyrethrin, deters all
common insect pests, such as
bedbugs, aphids, mosquitoes and
ants. Also kills beneficial insects, so
spray at dusk when beneficials are
not active. Also toxic to fish.

Precautions Wear protective clothing
when using. Can cause dermatitis.

Other uses Extracts from dried
flowers are used in fumigants and
insecticides. The active constituent,
pyrethrin, is less toxic as it degrades
quickly and is valued as a natural
alternative to chemical pesticides.

Tanacetum vulgare

CLIMATE AND SITE
Zones 4–10.
Full sun to
partial shade.

IDEAL SOIL
Well-drained
garden soil;
pH 6.0–7.5.

GROWING HABIT
Erect perennial
with branched
stems and fernlike,
aromatic leaves;
height 3–4 feet
(90–120 cm). Tansy
grows very fast,
even in poor soil.

PARTS USED
Leaves, flowers.

TANSY

THIS EASY-TO-GROW, AROMATIC PERENNIAL
HAS BRILLIANT GREEN FOLIAGE AND YELLOW
BUTTON-LIKE FLOWERS. IT IS AN EXCELLENT
COMPANION PLANT FOR ROSES.

Growing guidelines Sow seed
indoors in late winter; transplant
outdoors after danger of frost, 4 feet
(1.2 m) apart. Divide established
plants in spring or autumn. Spreads
easily. Prune vigorously in midsummer for lush growth in late
autumn. Plants may need support.

Flowering time Summer to autumn;
button-like, yellow blossoms in
terminal clusters.

Pest and disease prevention Prone to
aphids; control with a spray of water.

Harvesting and storing Collect
foliage anytime during summer and
dry. Flowers dry well but lose their
bright yellow color.

Special tips Tansy repels certain
pests and was used in the past as
a flea and moth repellent.

Precautions The oil is highly toxic
for both internal and external use
and may prove fatal. It is subject to
legal restrictions in some countries.

Culinary uses Leaves were once
added to custard and tansy cakes.

Other uses Flowers used in dried
arrangements. Leaves and flowers
used to make a green-gold dye.

Taraxacum officinale

CLIMATE AND SITE
Zones 3–10.
Full sun to
partial shade.

IDEAL SOIL
Any moderately
fertile, moist soil;
pH 6.0–7.5.

GROWING HABIT
Perennial with
jagged leaves
arising from a basal
rosette; height
6–12 inches
(15–30 cm).

PARTS USED
Whole plant,
leaves, roots,
flowers.

DANDELION

SOME GARDENERS HAVE LEARNED TO ENJOY
THIS LAWN WEED. IF YOUR THUMB IS OTHER
THAN GREEN, TRY PLANTING DANDELIONS TO
BOOST YOUR SELF-CONFIDENCE!

Growing guidelines It is best to
obtain seed from a large-leafed
variety from a specialist seed
catalog and sow shallowly in early
spring. For large roots that are easy
to dig, work in plenty of compost
or rotted manure each spring to
help loosen the soil.

Flowering time Late spring; the
familiar golden yellow flowers
mature to puffballs of seed.

Pest and disease prevention Usually
free from pests and diseases.

Harvesting and storing Leaves can
be picked throughout the year. Dig
roots in autumn, and cut or slice
them into small pieces, then air dry
or roast in a slow oven.

Special tips Dandelion can become
a problem in gardens if allowed to
grow unchecked. Thin plantings
regularly to control.

Culinary uses Use dried, roasted
and ground roots for a caffeine-free
coffee substitute. Harvest young,
fresh leaves for salads and soup.
The flowers are used for wine.

Medicinal uses For jaundice, urinary
tract infections, cirrhosis, gallstones
and constipation.

Teucrium chamaedrys

Climate and site
Zones 6–9. Full sun to partial shade.

Ideal soil
Well-drained garden soil; pH 6.0–8.0.

Growing habit
Perennial with short, dark green, oval, hairy leaves; square, hairy stalks which are very weak; height to 2 feet (60 cm).

Parts used
Whole plant, leaves.

Germander

Germander is grown for its boxy, ornamental shape, and is well suited to the formal herb garden. The foliage is aromatic and is used to treat gout.

Growing guidelines Best propagated by cuttings, layering or division, since seed-raised plants are slow to germinate. Plant 1 foot (30 cm) apart; does well in pots. Can be pruned and trained like a dwarf hedge in knot gardens. Not fully frost-hardy in severe winters. Variegated germander is great for edging a perennial border.

Flowering time Early to late summer; small purple to purple-red flowers on leafy spikes, followed by egg-shaped nutlet fruits.

Pest and disease prevention Usually free from pests and diseases.

Harvesting and storing Harvest the leaves during spring and early summer. Dry and store them in an airtight container.

Precautions May cause liver damage.

Culinary uses Leaves used to flavor alcoholic drinks, such as liqueurs, wine and vermouth.

Medicinal uses For loss of appetite, rheumatoid arthritis, jaundice, bronchitis, snakebite, skin problems and gum disease.

Other common names Poor man's box, wall germander.

Thymus vulgaris

CLIMATE AND SITE
Zones 6–9. Full sun
to partial shade.

IDEAL SOIL
Ordinary, well-
drained, neutral
to alkaline soil;
pH 6.0–8.0.

GROWING HABIT
Variable shrub with
gray-green leaves;
height to 1½ feet
(45 cm). Most
species are ever-
green, aromatic,
woody perennials.

PARTS USED
Whole plant, leaves,
flowering tops, oil.

THYME, COMMON OR GARDEN

EASY-TO-GROW THYME IS A FAVORITE OF
COOKS AND GARDENERS. PRETTY IN LEAF
AND FLOWER, A CARPET OF THYME MAKES
A BEAUTIFUL UNDERPLANTING FOR ROSES.

Growing guidelines Sow seed
shallowly in late winter indoors,
keeping the soil at 70°F (21°C) for
best germination. Plant outdoors
in late spring in clumps, 1 foot
(30 cm) apart. Divide older plants
in spring or take cuttings in late
summer or autumn. In winter,
mulch with a light material such
as straw. Replace plants every
3–4 years to control woody growth.
There are more than 350 species of
thyme. Grow shrubs for low hedging
and creepers for aromatic carpets.

Flowering time Midsummer; flowers
vary in color (lilac, rose-purple,
mauve, white, pink, purple)
depending on the species and
cultivar; blossoms in clusters.

Pest and disease prevention Usually
free from pests and diseases if soil
is well-drained.

Harvesting and storing Snip foliage
as needed during the summer, or
harvest entirely twice per season,
leaving at least 3 inches (7.5 cm) of
growth. Best harvested while in
bloom. Bunch sprigs together and
hang to dry. Thyme foliage freezes
well. Place in airtight containers for
use during winter months.

Thyme, common or garden continued

The name comes from the Greek work *thymon,* meaning "courage." Lemon thyme is one of the most common species and has pale lilac flowers.

Special tips Thyme is said to benefit the growth of vegetables such as potatoes, eggplants (aubergines) and tomatoes; it repels caterpillars and whiteflies. Thyme is ideal for rock gardens and containers. The tiny, numerous flowers produce copious nectar that attracts beneficial insects. Thyme is rich in volatile oil, which has powerful antiseptic properties. Can be used as a household disinfectant.

Precautions Not recommended for pregnant or breastfeeding women. The oil may cause skin irritations and allergic reactions.

Culinary uses Thyme, when mixed with parsley and bay, is an essential ingredient of bouquet garni. It is important in French cooking. Used to flavor stock, marinades, stuffings, sauces and soup; it retains its flavor well in dishes that are cooked slowly in wine. Lemon-scented thyme is added to chicken, fish, vegetables, fruit salads and jam.

Medicinal uses For bronchitis, coughs, asthma, laryngitis, indigestion, diarrhea, tonsillitis, arthritis and fungal infections. Oil is used in aromatherapy for depression, exhaustion, upper respiratory tract infections and skin complaints.

Other uses Dried leaves are used in potpourris; also used in moth-

Thyme, common or garden continued

The powerful antiseptic and preserving properties of thyme were used by ancient Egyptians for embalming. Ancient Romans bathed in thyme water to give them vigor.

repelling sachets. Leaves used in cosmetics, and in bath washes and facial steams. Essential oil used as an antiseptic in toothpastes and in mouthwashes.

Other species Creeping thyme *T. praecox* is a mat-forming creeper with tiny hair-fringed leaves; height to 2 inches (5 cm). Mauve to purple flowers in terminal clusters in summer. Not used for oil extracts. Lemon thyme *T.* x *citriodorus* is a variable hybrid with glossy leaves that are dark green, white or yellow, variegated and lemon-scented; height 10–12 inches (25–30 cm). Pale lilac flowers in summer. Not grown from seed.

Wild thyme *T. serpyllum* is a prostrate perennial with slender, creeping stems and tiny hairy leaves; height to 3 inches (7.5 cm). Clusters of purple to pink flowers appear in summer. Reputedly effective in treating alcoholism and hangovers. The oil is used to treat stress but may cause allergies. Caraway thyme *T. herba-barona* is a wiry, carpeting subshrub with tiny, dark green leaves which smell like caraway, nutmeg or lemon. Small pink to mauve flowers in summer.

Gardener's trivia In the 1600s, Scottish Highlanders would drink a tea made from wild thyme to prevent nightmares.

Trifolium pratense

CLIMATE AND SITE
Zones 6–9. Full sun
to partial shade.

IDEAL SOIL
Light, moist, sandy,
well-drained
garden soil;
pH 6.0–6.7.

GROWING HABIT
Erect to sprawling,
short-lived
perennial with
long-stalked, oval,
hairy leaves; height
1–2 feet
(30–60 cm).

PARTS USED
Flowering tops.

RED CLOVER

RED CLOVER IS ONE OF THE MEMBERS OF
THE LEGUME FAMILY AND ADDS NITROGEN
TO THE SOIL, AN IMPORTANT ELEMENT FOR
ALL PLANT GROWTH.

Growing guidelines Broadcast seed
shallowly outdoors in early spring.
Thin plants to 1 foot (30 cm) apart.
May need an inoculant or may be
hard to control.

Flowering time Summer; bright pink
to purple, sometimes cream, tubular
flowers, fragrant, in globose heads.

Pest and disease prevention Usually
free from pests and diseases. Can
be susceptible to "clover sickness"
in which toxins released by the
roots stop the plant from growing.

Harvesting and storing Collect
flowers at full bloom and dry on
paper in the shade; store in airtight
containers. Use dried for infusions,
liquid extracts and ointments.

Special tips Sow as a living mulch
or a green manure crop. The
flowers attract beneficial insects,
such as bees and butterflies, and
the nitrogen-fixing bacteria on the
roots work to enhance soil fertility.
Red clover can also be grown as
a permanent groundcover.

Medicinal uses For eczema,
psoriasis, gout and degenerative
diseases. Used to make a tea that
is said to purify the blood, relieve
coughs and be a mild sedative.

Trigonella foenum-graecum

CLIMATE AND SITE
Zones 6–10.
Full sun.

IDEAL SOIL
Rich, well-drained
garden soil;
pH 6.0–7.0.

GROWING HABIT
Annual with clover-
like stems and
leaves; height
1–2 feet
(30–60 cm).

PARTS USED
Leaves, seeds.

FENUGREEK

FENUGREEK IS A MEMBER OF THE SAME
FAMILY AS BEANS AND CLOVER. THE SEEDS
ARE USED AS A SUBSTITUTE FOR MAPLE
FLAVORING IN BAKED GOODS.

Growing guidelines Sow seed
outdoors in a thick band in spring.
Avoid growing in cold and wet
soils since seed will rot before
germinating. As a leguminous plant,
fenugreek needs no nitrogen
fertilizer; can enrich soils.

Flowering time Summer; white
flowers with distinctive pink or
purple markings that resemble
garden pea blossoms.

Pest and disease prevention Handpick snails from new growth.

Harvesting and storing Harvest pods
when ripe but before they fall;
leave seeds in the sun to dry.

Special tips For a substitute for
maple syrup, steep the seeds in
boiling water and use the strained
liquid in cooking.

Culinary uses Fresh leaves are
added to vegetable curries; roasted
seeds used in curry powder, also
sprouted as a salad vegetable. Is
important in Middle Eastern cooking.

Medicinal uses For diabetes, gastric
problems, bronchial complaints,
cellulitis and skin problems.

Other common names Bird's foot,
Greek hayseed.

Tropaeolum majus

CLIMATE AND SITE
Zones 8–10. Blooms best in full sun.

IDEAL SOIL
Average, moist, well-drained, nutrient-poor soil; pH 6.0–8.0.

GROWING HABIT
Trailing or climbing annual; height varies from 2 feet (60 cm) for dwarf bush cultivars to 10 feet (3 m) for climbers.

PARTS USED
Whole plant, seeds, leaves, flowers.

NASTURTIUM

NASTURTIUMS ARE A FAVORITE OF BOTH GARDENERS AND COOKS. THE BLOSSOMS ARE A RELIABLE SOURCE OF COLOR ALL SUMMER AND CAN BE ADDED TO SALADS.

Growing guidelines Sow seed outdoors when the soil is warm in spring; thin plants to 6–9 inches (15–22.5 cm). For bushels of blooms, hold back on the nitrogen. Also does well as a potted annual.

Flowering time Summer; red, orange or yellow funnel-shaped, sweet-smelling blossoms.

Pest and disease prevention Prone to aphids; hose off with water.

Harvesting and storing Snip young, fresh leaves and blossoms all summer as needed for salads. In autumn, pickle the unopened buds for homemade capers.

Special tips Look for dwarf, vining and variegated types of nasturtium in seed catalogs. The flowers attract beneficial insects that prey on aphids.

Culinary uses Leaves, flowers, flower buds and nectar spurs are added to salads. Chopped leaves add a peppery flavor to eggs and cream cheese. Flowers used to make vinegar.

Medicinal uses For scurvy and hair problems such as baldness.

Other common names Indian cress.

Urtica dioica

CLIMATE AND SITE
Zones 5–9. Full sun to partial shade.

IDEAL SOIL
Most garden soils; pH 5.0–8.0.

GROWING HABIT
Herbaceous perennial with leaves that have stinging hairs; height 2–6 feet (60–180 cm).

PARTS USED
Whole plants, leaves.

STINGING NETTLE

A NOXIOUS PEST TO GARDENERS, NETTLE IS HIGH IN VITAMINS A AND C AND IS USED BY PRACTITIONERS OF HOMEOPATHIC MEDICINE. THE FIBERS CAN BE USED TO MAKE CLOTH.

Growing guidelines Sow seed shallowly outdoors in early spring; self-sows readily and quickly multiplies if left unchecked.

Flowering time Early to late summer; greenish male flowers in loose sprays; female flowers more densely clustered together.

Pest and disease prevention Usually free from pests and diseases.

Harvesting and storing Harvest whole plant above the root, just before flowering; hang in bunches to dry. Collect seeds and dry on paper. Wear heavy gloves when harvesting to avoid being stung.

Precautions When touched, the hairs inject an irritating substance into the skin that will cause it to swell and sting for several hours.

Special tips If you would prefer not to grow nettle but want to use it, you can usually find it growing by the roadside in suitable climates.

Culinary uses Young leaves are cooked like spinach, puréed for soups and used to make nettle beer.

Medicinal uses For anemia, arthritis, eczema, gout, sciatica and scalp and hair problems.

Valeriana officinalis

VALERIANACEAE

CLIMATE AND SITE
Zones 4–9. Full sun to partial shade.

IDEAL SOIL
Fertile, moist garden soil; pH 5.0–8.0.

GROWING HABIT
Herbaceous perennial with divided leaves and a fetid smell like old leather; height 3–5 feet (90–150 cm).

PARTS USED
Rhizomes, roots, oil.

VALERIAN

THIS PLANT HAS POWERFUL MEDICINAL PROPERTIES AND HAS BEEN PRIZED FOR CENTURIES AS A TRANQUILIZER. DRUGS BASED UPON IT ARE STILL USED TODAY.

Growing guidelines Sow seed shallowly outdoors in spring, transplanting to the garden when plants are established. Germinates poorly. Propagate by division in spring or autumn, spacing new plants 1 foot (30 cm) apart. Dig and renew plants every 3 years.

Flowering time Summer; small, tubular, pale pink, white or lavender flowers in dense terminal clusters.

Pest and disease prevention Usually free from pests and diseases.

Harvesting and storing Dig roots in autumn or spring, before new shoots form; wash and dry until brittle. Stores well.

Special tips The roots of valerian attract earthworms. Cats and rats are attracted to the fetid smell of valerian root, so use the plant to attract or catch them.

Medicinal uses For insomnia, migraine, anxiety, indigestion, ulcers and minor injuries.

Other uses Extracts used to flavor ice cream, drinks, condiments and other food.

Other common names Garden heliotrope, cat's valerian.

Vanilla planifolia

CLIMATE AND SITE
Zone 10. Requires ample moisture, shade and humidity.

IDEAL SOIL
Vanilla is an epiphytic orchid and takes its nutrients from the air. Does not grow in soil but in a loose, friable compost mixture.

GROWING HABIT
Climbing, evergreen perennial orchid with fleshy leaves.

PARTS USED
Fruits.

VANILLA

VANILLA IS ONE OF THE WORLD'S MOST IMPORTANT FLAVORINGS AND WAS ORIGINALLY USED BY THE AZTECS. THE FLOWERS HAVE TO BE POLLINATED BY HAND.

Growing guidelines Propagate from cuttings 6 feet (1.8 m) long at any time; leave to dry for 3 weeks before placing in loose compost. Grows on walls, trees or climbing posts to which it attaches itself with wormlike aerial roots.

Flowering time Pale yellow-green flowers in spring followed by long seed capsules.

Pest and disease prevention Plants damaged by scale insects, mildew, vanilla root rot and snails.

Harvesting and storing Fruits are picked when fully ripe and scalded before undergoing various stages of fermentation and drying. This whole process can take up to 6 months. Dried, cured fruit pods, known as vanilla pods or beans, are stored whole or processed commercially for vanilla extract (essence).

Culinary uses Extract used in the flavoring of ice cream, soft drinks, confectionery, liqueurs and tobacco.

Medicinal uses Used mainly as an aid to digestion.

Other uses In cosmetics, especially perfumes and added to potpourri. Used as a pharmaceutical flavoring.

Verbascum thapsus

SCROPHULARIACEAE

CLIMATE AND SITE
Zones 4–8. Full sun to light shade.

IDEAL SOIL
Well-drained to dry soil; pH 5.0–7.5.

GROWING HABIT
Tall biennial; height 6 feet (1.8 m). Leaves are large, soft and woolly and a greenish gray in color.

PARTS USED
Whole plant, leaves, flowers.

MULLEIN

A STATELY PLANT WITH WOOLLY LEAVES AND LARGE FLOWER SPIKES, MULLEIN HAS BEEN USED FOR CENTURIES AS A MEDICINAL TREATMENT FOR RESPIRATORY DISORDERS.

Growing guidelines Propagate by seed sown in spring or by root cuttings taken in winter. Plants often self-seed in light soils. Thin to 2 feet (60 cm) apart. Stake plants in exposed sites. Tolerates a wide range of growing conditions.

Flowering time Small, five-petaled, yellow flowers packed into dense clusters on thick erect spikes appear in summer.

Pest and disease prevention Prone to attack by caterpillars.

Harvesting and storing Whole plant is harvested when flowering. Flowers are collected as soon as they open; leaves are harvested in their first season.

Precautions All parts of mullein, except the flowers, are slightly toxic. Can be an irritant. In some parts of the world, it is a noxious weed and is illegal to grow.

Medicinal uses For respiratory tract infections, coughs, insomnia, rheumatic pain, hemorrhoids, chilblains and earaches.

Other uses Flowers are used for a yellow dye. The leaves were once smoked as a substitute for tobacco.

Verbena officinalis

CLIMATE AND SITE
Zones 4–10.
Full sun.

IDEAL SOIL
Ordinary, well-drained moist garden soil; pH 6.0–7.5.

GROWING HABIT
Loosely branched perennial with deeply lobed, oblong, slightly hairy leaves; height 1–2 feet (30–60 cm).

PARTS USED
Whole plant.

VERVAIN

THIS ANCIENT PERENNIAL HAS A LONG RELIGIOUS AND MEDICINAL HISTORY. IT WAS SACRED TO MANY CULTURES AND WAS USED TO TREAT TIREDNESS, STRESS AND BRUISES.

Growing guidelines Easily grows from seed sown outdoors; thin to 1 foot (30 cm). Take stem cuttings in summer. Divide in winter to spring. Can self-sow. Mulching will encourage better flowers and foliage.

Flowering time Summer to autumn; small, tubular, pale lilac blossoms in spikes. The flowers have no scent.

Pest and disease prevention Usually free from pests and diseases.

Harvesting and storing Foliage can be picked as required. If using the whole plant, harvest it when it begins to flower.

Precautions Can be toxic. May cause nausea and vomiting.

Medicinal uses For depression, asthma, migraine, jaundice, gall bladder problems, gum disease, eczema and minor skin injuries. Gargle a tea for sore throats.

Other uses A bath prepared with vervain soothes nervous exhaustion. Can also be used as an eyewash and hair tonic.

Other species American vervain *V. hastata* has blue flowers; height 4–5 feet (1.2–1.5 m). Is also called blue vervain.

Viola odorata

CLIMATE AND SITE
Zones 6–10.
Partial shade.

IDEAL SOIL
Any well-drained
but moist, rich
garden soil.

GROWING HABIT
Tufted perennial
with kidney-
shaped, downy
leaves; height
4–6 inches
(10–15 cm).

PARTS USED
Leaves, flowers, oil.

VIOLET, SWEET

VIOLETS ARE EARLY FRAGRANT BLOOMERS
THAT GROW WELL IN SHADED LOCATIONS
DURING COOL WEATHER. THEY HAVE A
WONDERFUL PERFUME AND RICH COLOR.

Growing guidelines Sow seed
shallowly outdoors as soon as ripe,
or in autumn or spring; cover seeds,
which need darkness to germinate.
Thin to 1 foot (30 cm). Divide
mature plants in autumn, winter
or early spring.

Flowering time Late winter to
spring; fragrant purple, violet, white
or pink blossoms.

Pest and disease prevention Prone
to slugs, snails and fungal diseases.
Check for mites.

Harvesting and storing Leaves and
flowers are collected during the
flowering season. Thoroughly dry
flowers for culinary use; store in
airtight containers.

Special tips When designing a
garden for its fragrance, use sweet
violets for a thick, scented groundcover under a bench or against a
brick wall.

Culinary uses Flowers used in salads
and as a garnish. Petals candied and
used to decorate cakes and desserts.

Medicinal uses For bronchitis,
coughs, asthma and throat infections.

Other uses Oil used in perfumes.
Flowers used in breath fresheners.

Wasabia japonica

CLIMATE AND SITE
Zones 3–6. Shade.

IDEAL SOIL
Requires rich,
moist to wet soil;
pH 4.5–7.4.

GROWING HABIT
Attractive, frost-
hardy perennial;
height 8–16 inches
(20–40 cm). Has
creeping rhizomes,
upright stems and
long-stalked, glossy,
green, kidney-
shaped leaves.

PARTS USED
Roots, leaves,
leaf stalks.

WASABI

WASABI IS A CONDIMENT TRADITIONALLY
USED TO GARNISH RAW FISH AND NOODLE
DISHES IN JAPAN AND IS GENERALLY FOUND
GROWING BESIDE MOUNTAIN STREAMS.

Growing guidelines Propagate in
spring by seed kept moist or by
division of rootstock in spring and
autumn. Needs full shade; keep out
of direct sun. Can acclimatize to cool
gardens but may be difficult to grow.

Flowering time Small, white flowers
clustered along the stem are
produced in spring, followed by
twisted pods containing several
large seeds.

Pest and disease prevention Usually
free from pests and diseases.

Harvesting and storing Roots are
lifted in spring or autumn and used
fresh, dried, ground or preserved.
Roots are mature 15–24 months
after planting. Leaf stalks also used.

Special tips Wasabi belongs to the
same family as horseradish, radish
and mustard, all of which are
valued for the strong, pungent
flavor of their roots. Good, fresh
wasabi is not just spicy hot but also
sweet with a gentle fragrance.

Culinary uses In Japanese cuisine;
grated fresh roots are eaten with
raw fish; also to flavor meat dishes.

Medicinal uses Can be used as an
antidote to fish poisoning.

Zea mays

CLIMATE AND SITE
Zones 7 and
warmer. Use only
maturing cultivars
in colder areas.
Needs full sun.
Avoid windy areas.

IDEAL SOIL
Deep, well-
manured soil;
pH 6.0–6.8.

GROWING HABIT
Large annual, with
lancelike leaves;
height to 10 feet
(3 m).

PARTS USED
Cobs, silk, oil.

SWEET CORN (MAIZE)

FRESH SWEET CORN IS SUCCULENT AND
TENDER AND WELL WORTH GROWING FOR ITS
CULINARY AND MEDICINAL USES. AZTECS
USED CORN TO CLEAR HEAT FROM THE HEART.

Growing guidelines Sow after last
spring frost. Corn seed germinates
poorly in cold, wet soil and may
rot. Plant 1 inch (2.5 cm) deep and
4 inches (10 cm) apart in a block
(several short, parallel rows) to
ensure good wind pollination.
Thin seedlings to 1 foot (30 cm).
Corn grows rapidly and needs
adequate fertilizer and plenty of
water. Apply fish emulsion or
compost tea after 1 month.

Pest and disease prevention Wireworms or caterpillars (earworms)
may attack plants. Solarize soil
before planting to discourage
wireworms. Birds and animals
may damage the ears.

Harvesting and storing Harvest
when the silks have turned brown
and dry, and the kernels, if
punctured, emit a milky (not
watery) fluid. Quickly can or
freeze corn that cannot be eaten
immediately after picking, as it
begins to turn starchy within hours.

Culinary uses As a vegetable. Used
to make cornflour, cereals and
polenta. Husks used to flavor food.

Medicinal uses For cystitis, urinary
stones and urethritis.

Zingiber officinale

CLIMATE AND SITE
Zone 10 or warmer, or in a greenhouse. Full sun to partial shade.

IDEAL SOIL
Fertile, moist, well-drained garden soil; pH 6.5–7.5.

GROWING HABIT
Tender perennial; height 2–5 feet (60–150 cm); leaves strap-shaped, 6–12 inches (15–30 cm) long.

PARTS USED
Rhizomes, oil.

GINGER

FRESH GINGER HAS A ZING THAT THE POWDERED SPICE LACKS. IT HAS THE DOUBLE ADVANTAGE OF BEING BOTH SPICY AND KIND TO YOUR DIGESTIVE SYSTEM.

Growing guidelines Plant rhizomes in pots in a mix containing peat, sand and compost; keep indoors during winter, moving the pots outdoors in warm summers.

Flowering time Ginger rarely flowers in containers; in the right conditions, it produces dense conelike spikes on a stalk with yellow-green and purple flowers.

Pest and disease prevention For healthy growth, water well during the hot summer months.

Harvesting and storing Dig the plant up after 1 year and remove the leaf stems, cutting away as much root as you need; replant the remaining root. Refrigerate harvested roots wrapped in paper toweling in a plastic bag for up to 1 month. Or dry shaved bits of root and store in an airtight container.

Culinary uses Can be eaten raw, preserved in syrup or candied. Used in curries, chutneys, marinades, pickles and cakes. Can be mixed with cinnamon to make tea.

Medicinal uses For motion sickness, morning sickness, menstrual cramps, colds, coughs, lumbago and muscle pain.

PLANT HARDINESS ZONE MAPS

These maps of the United States, Canada and Europe are divided into ten zones. Each zone is based on a 10°F (5.6°C) difference in average annual minimum temperature. Some areas are considered too high in elevation for plant cultivation and so are not assigned to any zone. There are also island zones that are warmer or cooler than surrounding areas because of differences in elevation; they have been given a zone different from the surrounding areas. Many large urban areas, for example, are in a warmer zone than the surrounding land. Plants grow best within an optimum range of temperatures. The range may be wide for some species and narrow for others. Plants also differ in their ability to survive frost and in their sun or shade requirements.

PACIFIC OCEAN

AVERAGE ANNUAL MINIMUM TEMPERATURE °F (°C)

ZONE 1	Below -50°F (Below -45°C)
ZONE 2	-50° to -40°F (-45° to -40°C)
ZONE 3	-40° to -30°F (-40° to -34°C)
ZONE 4	-30° to -20°F (-34° to -29°C)
ZONE 5	-20° to -10°F (-29° to -23°C)
ZONE 6	-10° to 0°F (-23° to -18°C)
ZONE 7	0° to 10°F (-18° to -12°C)
ZONE 8	10° to 20°F (-12° to -7°C)
ZONE 9	20° to 30°F (-7° to -1°C)
ZONE 10	30° to 40°F (-1° to 4°C)

Canada

United States
of America

*ATLANTIC
OCEAN*

The zone ratings indicate conditions in which designated plants will grow well, and not merely survive. Many plants may survive in zones that are warmer or colder than their recommended zone range. Remember that other factors, including wind, soil type, soil moisture, humidity, snow, and winter sunshine, may have a great effect on growth.

Keep in mind that some nursery plants have been grown in greenhouses, so they might not survive in your garden. It's a waste of time and money, and a cause of heartache, to buy plants that aren't suitable for your climate zone.

AUSTRALIA AND NEW ZEALAND

These maps divide Australia and New Zealand into seven climate zones which, as near as possible, correspond to the USDA climate zones used in the United States, Britain and Europe and in this book. The zones are based on the minimum temperatures usually, or possibly, experienced within each zone. This book is designed mainly for cool-climate gardens, but the information in it can be adapted for those in hotter climates. In this book, the ideal zones in which to grow particular plants are indicated and when you read that a plant is suitable for any of the zones 7 through to 10, you will know that it should grow successfully in those zones in Australia and New Zealand. There are other factors that affect plant growth, but temperature is one of the most important. Plants listed as being suitable for zone 10 may also grow in hotter zones, but to be sure, consult a gardening guide specific to your area.

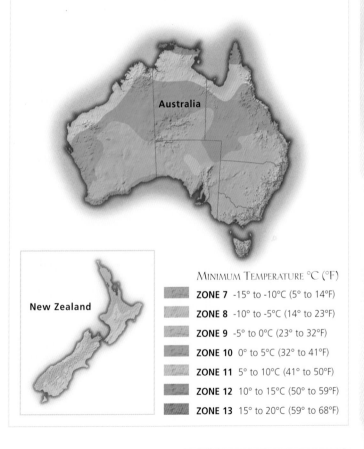

MINIMUM TEMPERATURE °C (°F)

ZONE 7 -15° to -10°C (5° to 14°F)

ZONE 8 -10° to -5°C (14° to 23°F)

ZONE 9 -5° to 0°C (23° to 32°F)

ZONE 10 0° to 5°C (32° to 41°F)

ZONE 11 5° to 10°C (41° to 50°F)

ZONE 12 10° to 15°C (50° to 59°F)

ZONE 13 15° to 20°C (59° to 68°F)

INDEX

Page references in *italics* indicate photos and illustrations.

Acknowledgments

KEY KEY l=left; r=right; c=center; t=top; b=bottom.

APL=Australian Picture Library; AZ=A–Z Botanical Collection; BCL=Bruce Coleman Ltd; CN=Clive Nichols; COR=Corel; DF=Derek Fell; DG=Denise Greig; DW=David Wallace; GB=Gillian Beckett; GDR=G. R. "Dick" Roberts; GP.com=gardenphotos.com; GPL=Garden Picture Library; HSC=Harry Smith Collection; HIS=Holt Studios International; JP=Jerry Pavia; JY=James Young; LC=Leigh Clapp; PD=PhotoDisc; PH=Photos Horticultural; SM=Stirling Macoboy; SOM=S. & O. Mathews; TE=Thomas Eltzroth; TR=Tony Rodd; WO=Weldon Owen; WR=Weldon Russell

1t AZ/Malkolm Warrington; c WO/JY; b GPL/Howard Rice **2**c JP **5**c GPL/Gary Rogers **6**tl PH; bl GPL/Rex Butcher **7**tl HSC; bl SM **10**c JP **12**tl PH; bl LC **13**tl GPL/Linda Burgess **16**tr JP **19**c GPL/Juliette Wade **21**tl GPL/Juliet Wade **23**t APL/Corbis/Michael Boys; cr GB **24**t GPL/Clay Perry **25**b GPL/Steven Wooster **26–27** GPL/Sunniva Harte **28**tl JY **29**t LC **30**tr, cr DW **31**t GPL/John Neubauer **32**bl CN **33**tl GPL/John Glover **34**br WO **34–35**tr GPL/Linda Burgess **36**br DF **37**tr GPL/David Aksham **38**tr LC; br DG **39**t APL/Gerry Whitmont **40**cl LC **41**tl LC **42**br JY **43**t APL/Corbis/Clay Perry **44**tl LC **45**br APL/Corbis/Eric Crichton **46**b DW **47**tl GPL/Jane Legate **48**l DW **49**tl GPL/Michael Howes **50**cr WO **51**tl PD **52**l DW; bc JP **53**t WO/Ad-Libitum/Stuart Bowey; b DW **54**c GPL/Christopher Gallagher **57**tl GPL/Jane Legate **58**tl LC; bl DW **59**tl GPL/Lamontagne; cr APL/Corbis/Wolfgang Kaehler **60**cr GPL/Emma Paios **61**tl PH; b GPL/Howard Rice **63**t WO **65**tr DF; cr WO **66**tl HSC; bl PH **67**bl WO **68**tr WO/Ad-Libitum/Stuart Bowey; bl GPL/Neil Holmes **69**t GPL/Lynne Brotchie; br WR **70**bl PH **71**tl Getty Images; br PH **72–73**t DF **73**br DF **74**tl WO; cl DF; bl HSC **75**tl PH; tr, cr WO; br HIS/Nigel Cattlin **76–77**tr JY **77**br GPL/Eric Crichton **78**bl WO **79**tl CN **82**bl CN **83**tr SOM **84**c LC **86**tl GPL **87**bl GPL/Gary

Rogers **88**bl LC **89**c Getty Images **91–92**tr GPL **92**tr, c, b WO/Ad-Libitum/ Stuart Bowey **93**tl APL/Corbis/Elizabeth Whiting **94**tl WO/John Callanan; bl PH **95**t, br WO/John Callanan **96**c, l WO/John Callanan **97**tr DW **98**t WO/Sharif Tarabay; b Getty Images **99**t APL/Corbis/Bob Krist; b WO/ Sharif Tarabay **100**tl PD **101**cr WO/Sharif Tarabay **102**tl WO/Ad-Libitum/ Stuart Bowey; bl APL/Corbis/Rick Gomez **103**t APL/Corbis/Michelle Garrett **104**c WO/JY **106**t COR **107**t JY **108**t GPL/JP **109**t JY **110**t JY **111**t GDR **112**t DW **113**t GPL/Juliette Wade **114**t TE **115**t DW **116**t DF **117**t TR **118**t WO **119**t JY **120**t GPL/JP **121**t JY **122**t JY **123**t JY **124**t DW **125**t SOM **126**tl GPL/Brian Carter **127**t OSF/Steven Foster **130**t GDR **131**t JY **132**t Heather Angel **133**t AZ/Malkolm Warrington **134**t JY **135**t JY **136**t DW **137**t JY **138**t WO **139**t PH **140**t GDR **141**t AZ/Alan Gould **142**t HSC **143**t TR **144**t WO/JY **145**t WO/JY **146**t GPL/Emma Peios **147**t DW **148**t TR **149**t GDR **150**t GPL/John Glover **151**t GPL/Lamontagne **152**t WO/JY **153**t DW **154**t WO/JY **155**t TR **156**t WO **157**t GB **158**t TR **159**t JY **160**t WO **161**t Ivy Hansen **162**t tl LR **163**t SM **164**t OSF/Tom Leach **165**t David Wallace **166**t WO **167**t JY **168**t PH **169**t WO/JY **170**t TR **171**t GB **172**t DW **173**t PH **174**t GPL/Mark Bolton **175**t PH **176**t PH **177**t GP.com/Judy White **178**t JY **179**t JY **180**t GPL/Brian Carter **181**t GPL/Mayer/Le Scanff **182**t GPL/Clay Perry **183**t JP **184**t JP **185**t GDR **186**t GDR **187**t TR **188**t GPL/Gary Rogers **189**t JP **190**t PH **191**t GDR **192**t GDR **193**t WO **194**t PH **195**t JY **196**t DW **197**t TR **198**t GPL/Vaughan Fleming **199**t GPL/A. Lord **200**t WO/JY **201**t GDR **202**t HSC **203**t WO **204**t BCL/Hans Reinhard **205**t TE **206**t GPL/J. Sira **207**t TE **208**t HSC **209**t GPL/David Cavagnaro **210**t TR **211**t JP **212**t GPL/Janet Sorrell **213**t BCL/Dr. Eckart Pott **214**t JY **215**t TR **216**t WO/JY **217**t WO/Kylie Mulquin **218**t WO/Kylie Mulquin **219**t JP **220**t HSC **221**t GPL/John Glover **222**t DW **223**t DW **224**t JY **225**t WO **226**t GPL/John Glover **227**t DW **228**t WO/JY **229**t WO/JY **230**t GDR **231**t JY **232**t OSF/Deni Bown **233**t GDR **234**t DW **235**t DW **236**t JY **237**t WO/JY **238**t WO/JY **239**t JP **240**t DW **241**t WO **242**t WO/JY **243**t JY **244**t GPL/ Michel Viard **245**t GPL/Steven Wooster **246**t WO/Kylie Mulquin **247**t DW **248**t PH **249**t GDR **250**t JY **250**tl GDR **251**t PH **252**t GPL **253**t JP **254**t DW **255**t JP **256**t GB **257**t PH **258**t JP **259**t PH **260**t GPL/Michael Howles **261**t GPL/Howard Rice **262**t JP **263**t JP **264**t GPL/Neil Holmes **265**t LC **266**t AZ/Pam Collins **267**t PH **268**t JY **269**t GDR **270**t GDR **271**t JY **272**t DW **273**t WO/JY **274**t AZ **275**t GDR **276**t JY **277**t TR **278**t TR **279**t Heather Angel **280**t DW **281**t OSF/Deni Bown **282**t TR **283**t DW **284**t GPL/Rex Butcher **285**t DW **286**t JY **287**t Getty Images **288**t HSC **289**t AZ/Bob Gibbons **290**t JP **291**t Heather Angel **292**t HSC **293**t DW **294**t JP **295**t CN **296**t TR **297**t AZ/Bob Gibbons **298**t JY **299**t PH **300**t DW **301**t GPL/ Howard Rice **302**t GDR **303**t HSC **304**t TE **305**t GDR **306** DW **307**t JY.

Illustrations by Tony Britt-Lewis, Janet Jones, Angela Lober, Edwina Riddell, Barbara Rodanska, Jan Smith, Kathie Smith. Maps by Stuart McVicar.

The publishers would like to thank Puddingburn Publishing Services, for compiling the index, and Bronwyn Sweeney, for proofreading.